D1531316

AS IT HAPPENED

As It Happened

BY C. R. ATTLEE

New York · 1954
THE VIKING PRESS

Contents

Contents

List of Photographs

Mr. Attlee as a freshman at Oxford

"A" Company, South Lancashire Regiment, 1914

Mr. Attlee as Mayor of Stepney, his first public office, 1919

Addressing the crowd at the great Hyde Park rally against unemployment, 1933

Alison and Martin Attlee with their father, 1940

In an air-raid shelter during the war

After the twenty-year Treaty of Alliance and Mutual Assistance between Britain and Soviet Russia, signed on May 26, 1942. On the terrace of No. 10 Downing Street: Mr. Molotov, Mr. Attlee (then Deputy Prime Minister), Mr. Lyttleton, Mr. Churchill, and Mr. Eden.

With Ernest Bevin and Herbert Morrison after the news of Labour's victory at the polls

Prime Minister Attlee with President Truman and Marshal Stalin before the final meeting at Potsdam. In the back row are Admiral Leahy, Mr. Bevin, Mr. Byrnes, and Mr. Molotov.

The Big Three in session at Berlin Conference, July 1945. President Truman is on the left, Mr. Attlee in the center, and Marshal Stalin standing on the right.

(*Above*) Mr. Attlee as a freshman at Oxford.
(*Below*) "A" Company, South Lancashire Regiment, 1914. (The author is the second from the right, front row.)

(*Above*) Mr. Attlee as Mayor of Stepney, his first public office, 1919.
(*Below*) Addressing the crowd at the great Hyde Park rally against unemployment, 1933.

(*Above*) Alison and Martin Attlee with their father, 1940.
(*Below*) In an air-raid shelter during the war.

(*Above*) After the twenty-year Treaty of Alliance and Mutual Assistance between Britain and Soviet Russia, signed on May 26, 1942. On the terrace of No. 10 Downing Street: Mr. Molotov, Mr. Attlee (then Deputy Prime Minister), Mr. Lyttleton, Mr. Churchill, and Mr. Eden. (*British Information Services*) (*Below*) With Ernest Bevin and Herbert Morrison after the news of Labour's victory at the polls.

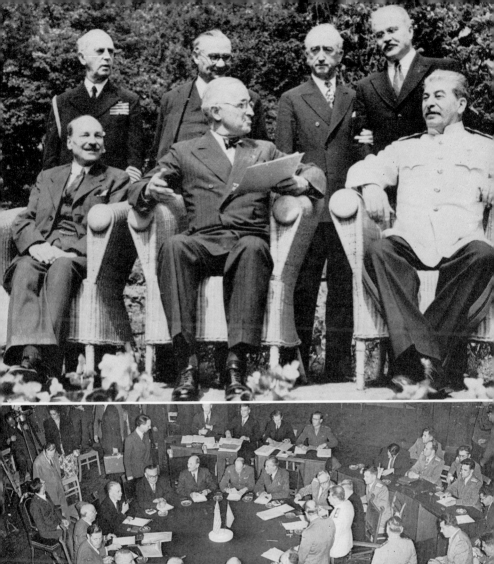

(*Above*) Prime Minister Attlee with President Truman and Marshal Stalin before the final meeting at Potsdam. In the back row are Admiral Leahy, Mr. Bevin, Mr. Byrnes, and Mr. Molotov. (*British Information Services*)
(*Below*) The Big Three in session at Berlin Conference, July 1945. President Truman is on the left, Mr. Attlee in the center, and Marshal Stalin standing on the right. (*British Information Services*)

Mr. and Mrs. Clement Attlee.

Mr. and Mrs. Attlee returning the waves of voters after successful campaign.
(*British Information Services*)

The Right Honourable C. R. Attlee.

AS IT HAPPENED

Early Years

I WAS born on January 3, 1883, the seventh child and fourth son in a family of eight. My father was a solicitor of high standing in the City of London. For many centuries the Attlee family have lived in Surrey. The county historians say that the family lived at Effingham, where there is a Great Lee Wood from which our name is derived. For many generations they had lived at Dorking, carrying on business as millers, corn merchants, and farmers. The old mill existed until recently, and the family business still continues. My grandfather, who was born in 1795, had a family of ten children. Two sons succeeded to the family business, two were brewers, and one a clergyman. My father, the ninth child, was articled to solicitors in London when he was sixteen and eventually became head of the firm and president of the Incorporated Law Society. I had many cousins on my father's side; two were well-known doctors, several girls became missionaries.

My mother was the eldest of six girls—daughters of T. S. Watson, secretary of the Art Union of London. My grandmother died young, and T. S. Watson was the only

3

grandparent still living when I was born. Among my
mother's ancestors were a number of doctors, one of
whom was a fashionable practitioner in the eighteenth
century in Soho.

My grandfather went to Westminster School and Caius
College, Cambridge. He left a diary of his early life in
which this incident is recorded. When he went to Cambridge his father made him promise not to join the Boat
Club. Apparently, in the 1830s, these clubs were considered to be dissipated. However, at the instance of a fellow old-Westminster boy, he compromised by not joining
the club but rowed regularly in the College Eight.

My grandfather lived with four daughters and one son,
who were all unmarried, in an old house on Wandsworth
Common—The Gables—which formed an important part
of the background of my childhood, for my aunts and my
uncle were always very kind to all of us. The Gables was
an old Queen Anne house of very distinctive character.
One part of the house had been made semi-detached and
was inhabited by three old ladies, the Misses Bellamy. The
family lived mainly in the drawing room, which was furnished with an old gilt tapestried suite which sold very
well a few years ago. There were many glass "lustres" on
the mantelpiece. The dining room was very dark. We
were intrigued by its window, which was placed over the
fireplace. The other rooms on the ground floor were
rather full of furniture and books and were more in the
nature of passage rooms, though one was more or less ap-
propriated to Aunt Edith. Upstairs there were great four-
poster beds. Aunt Janet's room was very jolly—it had a
hob grate with Dutch tiles, deep window seats, and a

shining mahogany wardrobe; I see it most clearly in the firelight of a Christmas evening when we used to dress up to act a play. There were little closets giving off it, used for washing and pervaded by a general smell of Pears' soap. I just remember the smoking room in my grandfather's time. There were no curtains and, I think, no carpet, and there were swords and daggers on the wall. There was a big room upstairs, belonging to Aunts Emma and Edith, which had a very wavy floor and fascinating cupboards that we always thought ran a very long way down into the house. I spent four weeks when recuperating from some ailment in this room—perhaps I was merely in quarantine—but I got to know it well.

There was a large smoky garden with a big cedar tree surrounded by a great circle of ivy, a tennis court cut off by an old brown brick wall, and a fascinating greenhouse and sheds. Uncle Alick did a good deal of pottering in the garden. He was, from our point of view, an ideal uncle, as he had a pleasant habit of sending us out to buy his "baccy" with the injunction to spend the change on sweets.

Our family lived in Putney, which was then quite an outer suburb of London. Market gardens stretched between Putney and Wandsworth. There were big houses with fields and farms near at hand. We were close to Wimbledon Common and Richmond Park, while the fields began quite close to Wandsworth High Street. This street had still the aspect of a country town with numerous queer little "pubs."

We had a roomy house with a good-sized garden in quiet, leafy Portinscale Road. We were, I think, a typical family of the professional class brought up in the atmosphere of Victorian England. There were eight children in our family, separated conveniently, from the point of view of remembering ages, by a uniform two-year interval. Two boys came first, then three girls, and then three boys.

All the boys were educated at Haileybury College, a school of which my father became a governor, and at different colleges at Oxford. The girls, however, were taught at home by a succession of governesses. There was, I think, some prejudice against girls' schools. Dorothy and Margaret went to Karlsruhe in Germany for a year for a finishing course.

We younger boys were brought into contact with our sisters' governesses. One of them was French, and from her I learned to recite fables of la Fontaine with an admirable French accent, but this, with other nonsense, was speedily knocked out of me when I went to school. Another, Miss Hutchinson, who taught my sisters for many years, had previously been employed by Lord Randolph Churchill to teach his little son, Winston, whom she described as a very determined little boy. She could never have thought that the two little boys were destined in turn to be Prime Minister. A story was current in our family that one day a maid came into the room and asked Miss Hutchinson if she had rung the bell, whereupon young Winston said, "I rang. Take away Miss Hutchinson, she is very cross."

We were a happy and united family. As one of "the little boys," I was brought up with a great reverence for my seniors, who, it seemed to us, had attained a standard of virtue which we could never hope to approach.

Early days remain fresh in the memory, and I can still recall very clearly the atmosphere of those times. Standing in our garden, one could hear the roar of London traffic as the horse hoofs beat on the paved streets. I recall the dust in summer and the mud in winter, the occasional ride in a hansom cab and the more frequent one in the dusty, musty four-wheeler with straw on the floor. I recall our annual visits to the seaside. The first, I remember clearly, was a visit to Lowestoft when I was two years old. Later on we went often to Seaton in South Devon. I remember many features of those days which have long since disappeared—crossing sweepers, German bands, Frenchmen with tame bears.

The first public event I recall was the Jubilee of Queen Victoria in 1887, which I celebrated by putting out a flag on the porch of our house.

An annual event of great importance to us was the University Boat Race, for the Cambridge crew used to stay in the house next door to us. We fervently supported Oxford and always hoped that one day the two crews would meet in the street, when, if they followed our example, there would be a fight. Any visitor to our house was at once asked, "Are you Oxford or Cambridge?" Our general view was that the Universities existed solely for the purpose of this race.

Our family were strong supporters of the Church of England and Sunday was strictly observed. There was much church-going, special reading, and no games. Walks were the only relaxation on Sundays, though this puritanism was later relaxed.

Until I was nine I was taught by my mother, who was very well read. My brothers Tom and Laurence went to day schools in Putney, but for some reason I was taught at home. I learned to read early and was a voracious reader. Our house was well stocked with books, and I roamed widely among them, being especially fond of poetry.

My father was a Gladstonian Liberal, but the rest of the family was Conservative, with the exception of a great-uncle, who was a Chartist, and my uncle Simmonds, who, it was said, was the only parson in the diocese of Hereford who shared the Liberal views of his bishop, Dr. Percival. When I was young the Irish Home Rule controversy divided families, and a tactful mother generally tried to change the subject when political affairs threatened to come up in conversation.

At the beginning of the summer term of 1892 I joined my brother Tom at a preparatory school at Northaw Place, Potters Bar, Hertfordshire, kept by an old friend of the family, the Reverend F. J. Hall. I was rather small for my age, having indeed been overtaken in height, much to my chagrin, by my younger brother Laurence. The school was accommodated in a fine old house standing in extensive and beautiful grounds and contained between thirty and forty boys.

Hall himself was a mathematician, while his assistant, the Reverend F. Poland, was no scholar, and the other assistants who came from time to time, B. M. Humble and Alan Clover, had not been trained to teach and were not qualified to give other than fairly elementary instruction.

There was one large schoolroom and a classroom. The various "sets" worked at forms or tables in the large hall and were called out to stand in a line when the "set" was taken in Latin "construe," those not called out continuing their work through the noise. A great deal of time was devoted to the Bible, particularly the Old Testament, and one left with a meticulous knowledge of the Kings of Israel and Judah. The history of the Jews was taken straight through from Joshua and Judges to Ezra and Nehemiah. It is incredible the amount of time wasted in acquiring this useless knowledge, for there was no critical exegesis at this time. It was all holy writ.

Geography and history were taught in the usual manner of the time, mainly a list of facts. The teaching of the classics was thoroughly bad, so that those who went from Northaw found themselves handicapped as against the boys who had been to schools where the masters understood how to teach and knew their subjects. On the other hand, the care taken of the boys was immense and the amenities of the place delightful. Mrs. Hall, who managed the commissariat and looked after the health and comforts of the boys, was an extremely competent person. An old Scotswoman, Mrs. Ross, was a kindly matron. The food was excellent, the grounds open to the boys extensive and beautiful, and I certainly had a very happy time there.

The real "religion" of Hall and Poland was cricket. The ideal in life was to become a first-class county cricketer; the holy of holies, the pavilion at Lord's. Throughout the summer we played cricket every afternoon. In the breaks and at odd times during the day we practised with cut-down bats and rope balls, in the paved stable yard and in the gravel yard. In the evenings in the schoolroom we played "paper cricket," dabbing with a pencil on a paper marked with runs and cricket happenings, and scoring the results against the names of members of rival teams —not infrequently the Kings of Israel and Judah, the former being always captained by Jehu on account of his driving prowess. We knew the names and scores and the likenesses of all the principal cricketers of that epoch, headed, of course, by W. G. Grace, then at the height of his renown. I never was much use at the game. A good field, nothing of a bowler, and a most uncertain bat, I hovered on the edge of the team but never got my colours. If the school at Northaw sent out few scholars, it sent out plenty of good cricketers, for Hall and Poland were both skilful performers and painstaking instructors. As a nursery for producing gentlemanly professional cricketers the school could hardly have been bettered.

In the winter we played rugger, which had not then taken its final form. The number of halves and three-quarters was still experimental. Except for matches against other schools, the whole school played, the surplus over the fifteen on each team being added to the scrum, while Poland and Humble, both very big men, also played in the scrum. Though very light and small, I got my colours fairly early as a forward, but later developed into a halfback. Hall, despite his age, played rugger regularly with the boys until he was well over fifty, for he had been nearly first-class and had always kept in training. I remember a match against Bengeo School when our opponents, an exceptionally large-sized lot, scored ninety-two points.

During the breaks in the winter and Easter terms we played "blackthorn," a form of prisoners' base, either in the yard or round the garden. For a time this was superseded by "bushrangers," when certain boys would be the robber band and lie in wait in what was called "the jungle" (a narrow path that ran round the field) for the approach of "the coach" made up of other boys.

Nostalgic memories, mostly happy, flood my mind as I think back: the noisy, crowded, gas-lit schoolroom on a winter's evening with the dust hanging in clouds; a slide made with two forms placed against the top of the four-decker lockers down which small boys are glissading; one or two of the quieter boys making messes with ink at the tables, others nib-fighting or playing "paper cricket," whilst all over the schoolroom continual scuffles are taking place; Sunday evenings in the beautiful drawing room scented with rose petals where boys are singing hymns and carols while Mrs. Hall plays the piano; the hard winter of 1895 with snowballing and when we were able to skate on the pond almost until April; warmer days, when round the same pond we fished for dace and perch, sailing boats or adventuring with Humble in a very leaky punt made in the carpenter's shop; basking in the sunshine on the lawn between the house and the old gates with one of the boys reading *Uncle Remus* aloud; long, lazy afternoons during cricket matches, meticulously keeping scores and bowling analyses while we lay stretched on the grass drinking ginger beer, which was always provided on these occasions; the freshness of

the dewy garden and the smell of the potting shed from
which Dodson, the gardener, might, under great pressure, produce an apple; interminable futile idlings of
the small boy trying to tightrope-walk along the iron
railings that separated the park from the yard; walking
round the Hertfordshire lanes, including, on Sundays,
visits to an opulent neighbour, Mrs. Kidston, who provided an orange or an apple for each boy; pillow fights
in the early morning in the big dormitory with its six
beds, one (known as the "Iron Pirate") with an iron super-
structure designed for curtains and originally intended
for the use of the Young family, but upon it we performed gymnastics—often in a quite literal sense, for it
was the age of nightgowns. These and many other memories remain young in my mind.

I well remember being ill and confined to a spare
room in the Master's part of the house and being a long
time in the dark, too shy to get someone to bring a light.
There was, too, the misery of mumps. Laurence and I
both suffered in this respect and were proudly the most
swelled of anyone, largely through being sent out for a
walk while an east wind was blowing.

Two of my contemporaries at Northaw have had distinguished political careers. Hilton Young, later Lord
Kennet and Minister of Health in Ramsay MacDonald's
last administration, was head boy when I entered the
school. I always remember an act of kindness by him. I
had some slight illness and was sitting alone with a dull
tea of only bread and butter. He came by and, seeing my
position, fetched me his own private pot of jam. Years
later, when I was in the government, I was able to do

him some slight service, whereupon he wrote, "It seems that if you cast your jam upon the water it will, like bread, come back to you after many days."

William Jowitt, later to become a distinguished lawyer and Lord Chancellor in the Labour government, was put in my care when he came to Northaw as a new boy. We had no presentiment that years later we should be colleagues in government or that he would marry one of three pretty little girls who lived next door to us at Putney.

In the Easter term of 1896 I went to sit for my entrance examination at Haileybury College. I remember very well that Hall bought me a newspaper to read during the train journey across Hertfordshire; in it was a vivid account of King Menelik's defeat of the Italians at the Battle of Adowa. I little thought then how much that distant country of Abyssinia would occupy my mind in the days when I was to lead the Opposition in the House of Commons. I passed my entrance examination and was placed in the top form of the Lower School.

Education

HAILEYBURY COLLEGE was then under the head-mastership of Edward Lyttelton. There I stayed for five years, going up the school slowly and eventually becoming, in my last year, a prefect and a member of the Lower Sixth. In those days all boys who reached the Sixth, unless under sixteen, automatically became pre-fects. It was no doubt a good training for a young boy to have to keep order in a dormitory of forty-two boys.

Conditions were a good deal more primitive than they are today. For instance, there were only two baths for eighty boys; the rest used zinc "toepans." Our sanitary needs were taken care of by three rows of earth closets illuminated in the evenings by one feeble gas-jet in each row. Many of the form rooms opened straight onto the quadrangle. In winter one either froze or roasted accord-ing to one's geographical position between the fire and the door. Forks and spoons were washed by being thrown in a large tub of hot water and stirred with a brush; hence the well-justified warning, "Never smell a college spoon."

I was on the classical side but never became a classical scholar, though I knew enough to pass "Smalls" at Oxford. I was, however, above the average in English subjects, largely due to home influence, especially history, for which I have always had a great liking. I also scored in general knowledge exams. Mathematics and French were not greatly considered on the classical side, and the hours devoted to them were regarded rather as a relaxation from the hard grind of Latin and Greek. If I could have anticipated the future, I should have worked hard at French, which I now often have to employ. My housemaster, F. W. Headley, was a considerable scientist, but for some reason the subject failed to attract me, and I recognize here a great deficiency in my knowledge.

We had a first-rate history lecturer in the Reverend W. D. Fenning. His lectures were really stimulating, setting one's mind on inquiry. Another master, the Reverend L. S. Milford, was keen on English literature and ran a Shakespeare Reading Society to which I belonged for three years. These two men probably influenced me most.

Another outstanding master was "Pongo" Vaughan of the Upper Fifth. He was a great student of military history. When we suffered a series of defeats in the opening stages of the Boer War we in his form had to watch our steps, for he felt these disasters acutely. One peculiarity he displayed was a frequent lapse into spoonerisms. For instance, he was telling a war story and related, "The poor soldier was lying on the ground when the Afghan came up and discharged the contents of his body into his rifle." On another occasion he said, "Yes, my young friend, I know all about you; I've got your father's drawers in my letter upstairs." His parting words to me when I told him that I was going to the Bar and that my father, being a solicitor, would be helpful, were, "Yes, my friend, but in these days a man must stand on his own feet and sit on his own bottom." He was a great character.

I saw little of the headmaster as I never rose above the Lower Sixth.

There was one feature of our life at Haileybury which differed from that at most public schools. There was not a great segregation into Houses. The whole school, except for the boys of one House, took their meals together, and thus one met at table boys from other Houses. Similarly, in my day it was possible, and indeed usual, to share a four-roomed study with boys from another House. I have often found that I had a wider acquaintance among my schoolfellows than is usual in public schools.

We were not well fed and we supplemented the diet from our own resources. Bread and butter for breakfast and tea needed the reinforcement of jam and marmalade from home. Later the food was more generous. The hiatus between dinner at one-thirty and tea at six-forty-five was filled by afternoon tea in the study. On Saturdays and Sundays there was "the study grub," when quantities of porridge, muffins, sausages, and bacon were cooked on the study fire and consumed by us. This early introduction to the art of cookery proved useful in later life.

I played games keenly but without distinction. Proficiency in games was almost essential if one desired to be prominent in the school, and our heroes were those who excelled at cricket and football. The school rifle corps

had a high reputation. Indeed, when Lord Wantage offered a bugle in a competition of all the Public School
Corps, Haileybury won it three times in succession. In
the summer term younger boys not big enough for the
corps were enrolled in the juniors and drilled with an-
cient Snider rifles. I belonged to the junior, and subsequently to the senior, corps throughout my schooldays,
going to camp at Aldershot in my later years.

There used to be a good many lectures and entertain-
ments. I recall a lecture on William Morris just after his
death with the title, "Morris the Poet, Morris the Uphol-
sterer, Morris the Socialist." I already knew of Morris the
Poet, but Morris the Socialist was news to me. It made
little impression at the time. Another lecture was on the
break-up of the Austrian Empire. I remember too an
early demonstration of wireless telegraphy, and a meeting
in which the founding of a boys' club in East London was
explained to us by Lionel Curtis (whom I was years later
to recommend for the Companionship of Honour for his
distinguished services in the field of political science)
and Cecil Nussey, of whom I shall write later.

I remember very well as an outstanding event the Dia-
mond Jubilee of Queen Victoria in 1897. My brother and
I went up to London and saw the procession, which was
an expression of the British Empire at the height of its
power and prosperity.

In my last two years at Haileybury the Boer War was in
progress, and the school as a whole was imperialist. The
influence of Rudyard Kipling was very strong, especially
as the school had a great tradition of service in the Army
and the Indian Civil Service.

The only time that I was caned was when—on the refusal of Lyttelton, the headmaster, to give us a holiday to celebrate the relief of Ladysmith—the majority of the school marched down to the neighbouring town of Hertford and indulged in a patriotic demonstration. I was one of the seventy-two who were caned that evening by Lyttelton, who was suspected of having Boer sympathies. Prefects were too old, and the Lower and Middle Schools too young and perhaps too numerous, to be punished, so we of the Upper School expiated the sins of the rest.

I belonged to the school Antiquarian Society and, through its meetings, got some acquaintance with architecture and archæology. In my last year I was a member of the Literary and Debating Society. I spoke occasionally in the debates but was then, and for many years later, afflicted with a most painful shyness, so that to do anything in public was a torture to me. I was always a rapid and voracious reader and used to read about four books a week at school.

My brother Laurence came to Haileybury in 1898 and my brother Tom departed for Corpus Christi College, Oxford, in 1899. My elder brothers had been at Oriel and Merton, and it was decided that I should go to University College. Two other Haileyburians, Charles Bailey, now Canon Bailey, and George Day, were also to go there, while another close friend, Owen de Wesselow, subsequently a distinguished medical professor, was to go to Corpus. There were no school certificates in those days, and we enjoyed the experience of going to Oxford and staying in College for the matriculation examination known as "Smalls." Looking back on my schooldays, there were lights and shadows, but the lights predominated, and I have always had a devotion to my old school.

As I have recounted, the family used to go away every August for a holiday, generally to the seaside, but once on the River Thames at South Stoke, where we indulged in much boating under the guidance of my elder brothers just down from Oxford. However, in 1896 my father bought a country house with a good deal of land attached, in the village of Thorpe-le-Soken in Essex, and henceforward we took our holidays there. The old redbrick house had been built by a Huguenot refugee, Captain Comarques, and was called after him. It was subsequently owned by Arnold Bennett, the famous writer, and is now the property of Lord Fairfax. I can recall many pleasant days there, with country occupations, rabbit shooting and ferreting, cricket with the village team, and much bicycling, for the days of the motorcar were still to come. My father enjoyed the country very much, for, despite his long years in the City, he was in his heart a countryman. On Sunday mornings at Putney the same countryman's interest led him to take us for walks before church round the market gardens which then lay between Putney and Wandsworth.

We entertained a good many visitors at Comarques, including an old family friend, Joseph Sturge, of the famous Birmingham Quaker family. My first visit abroad, in January 1899, was due to him. He took me to Switzerland for a fortnight, and we stayed near Montreux. He was the son of the famous anti-slavery man and free-trader, and was a most interesting companion, opening one's mind to new ideas.

The coming of the motorcar has, of course, made great changes in country life, and I am glad that I had the opportunity of seeing it in the days when villages were still fairly isolated and when horse transport or the bicycle reigned supreme on the dusty roads. It was part of Victorian England soon to pass away, an England we took for granted, something as fixed and immutable as Queen Victoria. Her death in 1901 was a tremendous shock. She had reigned so long and had become a symbol of her age.

In the autumn term of 1901 I went up to University College, Oxford, lodging in "the High" with Bailey and Day, as, owing to rebuilding, there was not room for all the Freshers in College.

Oxford at the turn of the century was still a quiet place. In William Morris's words, "a long winding street and the sound of many bells." The other William Morris, who was to become a leader in the motorcar industry, was still working in his bicycle shop in Long Wall. Cowley was a small suburb, and Headington a mere village on a lonely road. The old horse-trams plied down "the High" and up the Woodstock and Banbury roads. We were driven to and from the station by the lordly Oxford hanson, sometimes in the care of the famous "Trinity cabby" whose resounding "Just another little one, Oxford" used to be heard across the rugger ground. The Victorian Age had only just ended, and there was little apprehension of the troubles that lay ahead when civilization enshrined in Oxford was to be assailed by the barbarians—Hitler and Stalin.

Oxford has been described by so many more competent writers that I shall not attempt to emulate them, but it is difficult to overestimate the abiding influence that it has had upon me. Usually in life one is either looking forward to the future or backward to the past, so that it is seldom that one says to oneself, "What a glorious time I am having." But I can recall that very often this thought came to me as I walked past the old grey buildings. In later years I often sought to recapture the magic of those days and of that city.

University College had some hundred and forty undergraduates—in my view just about the right size. It was at this time a leading college. We were "head of the river," provided the captains of both rugger and soccer teams, and were, in fact, well represented in every form of sport. We had two presidents of the Union in my first year and several distinguished scholars. There was no division between athletes and scholars. Several of my contemporaries were both "blues" and first-class honours men. I very soon made a number of close friends and had, besides, a wide circle of less intimate acquaintances, for we were a very sociable college. And through my brother Tom and my friend Owen de Wesselow I had a great many friends in Corpus.

I spent three exceedingly happy years at Oxford. I was, I think, rather young for my age and was quite prepared to take life easily and as it came. I played all games but without distinction, amused myself on the river, especially on the upper river, sailing boats, and savoured to the full all the joys of Oxford. On Sundays Tom and I would go for long walks, lunching in country inns and often ending up at Wolvercote, where my brother Bernard was vicar.

My bent at that time was wholly romantic. I delighted
in poetry and in history, which was "the school" I had
chosen for my degree. I did not read for "schools" with
any great assiduity, being beguiled into all kinds of mis-
cellaneous reading not strictly germane to the course I
was studying. My special period was the Renaissance, and
I took the Italian "special" and steeped myself in these
fascinating subjects.

I attended some debates at the Union but was much
too shy to try to speak there. In fact, my only essay in
speaking was at the College Debating Society, where I
championed protection against the late Sir Basil Blackett,
who stood for free trade. The tariff controversy had just
broken out and was hotly debated; my history tutor,
Arthur Johnson, often animadverted on Joseph Chamberlain's heresy. He was not a very inspiring teacher. Indeed,
the teachers of history at Oxford at that time—Sir
Charles Oman, J. A. R. Marriott, C. R. L. Fletcher, and
E. Armstrong—were rather dull. In later years I was to
cross swords in the House of Commons with the two first
named. The exception was Ernest Barker, then a young
don, to whom I went in my last year. He was indeed the
only don who made much impression on me.

Oxford was at that time predominantly Conservative,
though there was a strong Liberal group, notably at Bal-
liol, which counted among its undergraduates such men
as R. H. Tawney and William Temple, the future arch-
bishop, whose influence on socialist thought was in later
years to be so great. Socialism was hardly spoken of, although Sidney Ball at St. John's and A. J. Carlyle at my

own College kept the light burning. I cannot recall any great discussion on the subject among my friends, although there was a great deal of interest in social reform. At that time the Labour Representation Committee, which was to develop into the Labour party, had only just been formed. Keir Hardie was the only Labour Member of Parliament. The Liberals were still engaged in internecine warfare as the result of the Boer War controversy. Conservatism reigned supreme, with Joseph Chamberlain as the dynamic leader.

I was at this time a Conservative but I did not take any active part in politics. I never belonged to any political club. There were also a number of societies seeking support from undergraduates, especially in the religious field, but I was not attracted, though a number of my closest friends belonged to them. Several of them became parsons and two of them bishops.

Some of my friends were interested in the University Settlements—Oxford House and Toynbee Hall and, especially, the Oxford and Bermondsey Mission. In particular, Alec Paterson, the future prison reformer, was a very strong influence among the younger men. I attended some meetings but remained uninterested. I think I had adopted a rather common pose of cynicism. I certainly gave no real thought to social problems, and I had no political ambitions. My general idea was to find some way of earning my living that would enable me to follow the kind of literary and historical subjects that interested me.

I had begun to "eat dinners" at the Inner Temple with a view to being called to the Bar. It seemed a fairly obvi-

ous course to take. My father was a solicitor, and therefore I might look to some help at the start. No doubt at
times I dreamed of a successful career in the Law.

I have said that my father was a Liberal in politics, but
he was also a Liberal in the wider sense. He never sought
to impose his views on his children, nor did he show the
least resentment that I was opposed to him politically,
whether as a Tory or a Socialist. In the same spirit he
brought no pressure to bear on his children in the choice
of a profession. Everyone had to choose for himself. He
would give us any help, but the choice must be ours. He
was, I think, a very able man and also an extremely generous one. Although he had a large family to maintain,
he assisted a great number of his relatives, some of whom
had only a remote claim on him.

My tutor thought that I might get a First in "schools,"
but in the event I got a Second with which I was quite
content. I left Oxford with an abiding love of the city
and the University and especially for my own College,
which has, through the years, shown me much kindness,
including making me an Honorary Fellow. I was deeply
appreciative of the honour conferred upon me in 1943
when a portion of one of my speeches was set for trans-
lation into Latin prose in a scholarship paper for a group
of the Oxford Colleges. The speech was one I made in
the House of Commons in 1938 on a motion for the erec-
tion within the precincts of the Palace of Westminster
of a bust of Asquith.

During my time at Oxford I made three visits to the
Continent. The first was to the South of France where my
maternal uncle and three aunts were staying at St. Jean

de Luz. I stayed with them there and also at Pau and Argelès. I recall visiting Lourdes, which struck me as very tawdry with an atmosphere of an Earls Court exhibition. I also crossed the border into Spain and saw the old castle at Fuenterrabia.

The following year I had a holiday with my parents and Laurence in Belgium. Our house in Essex was within driving distance of the embarkation port of Harwich, which made continental journeys easy. We stayed at Antwerp, Brussels, and Ghent and then went to Dinant in the Ardennes. The next year, with my father and Bernard, I went to Holland, staying at Nijmegen and Utrecht and The Hague. I also visited Germany, staying at Cleve and Cologne—my only visit to that country on a holiday. Twice in those years I visited the English Lake District with de Wesselow and enjoyed rock-climbing on Scawfell. I also went to Cornwall on a walking tour down the north coast with Laurence.

In 1904 this pleasant time came to an end, and I started work in London, reading in chambers with Sir Philip Gregory, one of the leading conveyancing counsels of that day. He was quite a hard taskmaster, and his pupils were expected to know the documents very thoroughly. My father thought that I ought also to get some experience of common law work, and after a year in Lincoln's Inn I went as a pupil to Theobald Mathew, who was an old family friend. Lord Robert Cecil, with whom I was later to collaborate in support of world peace, was the K.C. (King's Counsel) in the chambers, and I did some work for him. I recall getting my first fee by drafting a bill for the Licensed Victuallers' Association. I also worked for Lord Cecil on the celebrated Norfolk Peerage case, and on the strength of it reviewed a book on peerage law with all the assurance of youth. The third occupant of the chambers was Malcolm Macnaghten, later a fellow member of the House of Commons and a High Court Judge. Theobald Mathew was a great character, full of humour—as all who have read his *Forensic Fables* will agree—and I had an enjoyable time working with him.

I had passed my Bar examinations without difficulty while in Gregory's chambers and was called in 1905.

While I was with Mathew a vacancy occurred in the office of either the Charity or the Ecclesiastical Commissioners for a conveyancer. Gregory was asked to recommend someone and proposed me for the job. I should probably have got it had it not been found that I lacked some months of standing at the Bar. So near was I to settling down to a respectable permanent job.

When I finished my time as a pupil I went into chambers in which Sir H. F. Dickens, son of the novelist, was the K.C. I joined the "home" circuit and went round assizes and sessions, but only once got a brief. In London, also, I had only two or three briefs. I became tired of doing nothing and my interest in the Law was, to put it mildly, very tepid.

I was at this time living at home in Putney. I learned to ride, an acquisition that proved useful when I joined the Army in the First World War. I also shared a shoot in Sussex with some of my father's friends, but I was never very keen on field sports. I used to spend a good deal of time practising billiards, the only game in which I have shown any proficiency.

The first year after I came down from Oxford passed pleasantly enough. I belonged to a literary club formed by my brother Tom and some of his friends at which papers were read and discussed. Its membership was largely made up of young civil servants but also included E. G. V. Knox, the future editor of *Punch,* and Professor Baynes, the authority on the Byzantine Empire.

This, then, was the pattern of my days when in October 1905 an event occurred that was destined to alter the whole course of my life.

East London

THERE was in our family a strong tradition of social service. My mother was a district visitor for the Church. My elder brothers had helped at boys' clubs and an aunt had left home in order to live in a poor street in Wandsworth, over a club for factory girls which she managed. It was in accordance with family practice that I should consider doing something of the sort.

Haileybury College supported a boys' club in Stepney in the East End of London. It had been started by Lionel Curtis, now the distinguished Fellow of All Souls. I thought it would be a good idea to have a look at the club, and so one October evening in 1905 my brother Laurence and I took a local train from Fenchurch Street Station to Stepney. The club was essentially planned to cater to the needs of boys in a very poor and rough district. Stepney was the home of underemployment and sweated labour. The boys mostly followed blind-alley occupations. Many were van boys. They earned little money, but that little was needed to help keep the family going. By the time they reached eighteen years of age and wanted an adult wage, they were generally thrown out of work, with no training for anything. The club was also a Company of the 1st Cadet Battalion, The Queen's Regiment, and its membership was drawn from a fairly wide radius.

Few members of the club wore collars and ties and not many had any other than their working clothes. It was one of the advantages of the Cadet Corps that when in uniform these boys could feel smart and take pride in their appearance.

In the residence attached to the club lived three or four men who were engaged in earning their living in professions during the day and worked in the club in the evenings. There were also several men who came to help for one night a week. The club manager was a very fine man—Cecil Nussey, a solicitor—who did great work for the boys'-club movement over many years. He had a perfect sense of justice—a great asset to a club manager.

I became interested in the work and began making the journey from Putney to the club one evening a week. Soon my visits became more frequent, and I took a commission in the Cadets. In 1907 the club manager resigned and Nussey asked me if I would take over the job. I agreed, went to live at Haileybury House, and thus began a fourteen years' residence in East London.

I had always been painfully shy, and it took me some time to settle down, but East London boys are very friendly. There is no better way to get to know what social conditions are like than in a boys' club. One learns much more of how people in poor circumstances live through ordinary conversation with them than from studying volumes of statistics.

The practical experience I got in those days of how poor people live was a great help to me in after-years. For example, when I was Prime Minister a senior civil servant was outlining a fuel-rationing scheme and emphasizing the importance of householders storing fuel. I told him that many people had nowhere to store it, adding, "When I lived in East London I kept the coal under the bed. At first I bought too big a sack."

I soon began to learn many things which had hitherto been unrevealed. I found there was a different social code. Thrift, so dear to the middle classes, was not esteemed so highly as generosity. The Christian virtue of charity was practised, not merely preached. I recall a boy who lived in two rooms with his widowed mother. He earned seven shillings and sixpence a week. A neighbouring family, where there was no income coming in, were thrown out on the street by the landlord. The boy and his mother took them all into their own little home.

I remember taking the club's football team by local train to play an "away" match. Young Ben had come straight from work with his week's money—a half-sovereign—and somehow he had lost the gold coin. There was no hesitation amongst the boys. Jack said, "Look, a tanner each all round will make 'alf of it." They readily agreed, yet probably that tanner was all that most of them would have retained for themselves from their wages.

I found abundant instances of kindness and much quiet heroism in these mean streets. These people were not poor through their lack of fine qualities. The slums were not filled with the dregs of society. Not only did I have countless lessons in practical economics, but there was kindled in me a warmth and affection for these people that has remained with me all my life.

From this it was only a step to examining the whole basis of our social and economic system. I soon began to realize the curse of casual labour. I got to know what slum landlordism and sweating meant. I understood why the Poor Law was so hated. I learned also why there were rebels.

My brother Tom was an architect and a great reader of Ruskin and Morris. I too admired these great men and began to understand their social gospel. Tom was helping at the Maurice Hostel in the nearby Hoxton district of London. Our reading became more extensive. After looking into many social-reform ideas—such as copartnership —we both came to the conclusion that the economic and ethical basis of society was wrong. We became Socialists. I recall how in October 1907 we went to Clements Inn to try to join the Fabian Society. Edward Pease, the secretary, regarded us as if we were two beetles who had crept under the door, and when we said we wanted to join the society he asked coldly, "Why?" We said humbly that we were Socialists and persuaded him that we were genuine.

I remember very well the first Fabian Society meeting we attended at Essex Hall. The platform seemed to be full of bearded men—Aylmer Maude, William Sanders, Sidney Webb, and Bernard Shaw. I said to my brother, "Have we got to grow a beard to join this show?" A fiery young man with red hair was attacking the Webbs from the Left-Wing point of view. He is now Lord Haden Guest. H. G. Wells was on the platform, speaking in

a little piping voice; he was very unimpressive. Other
speakers were Chiozza Money, full of statistics; Shaw,
confident and deadly in argument; Webb, lucidly ex-
planatory; and Hubert Bland with his eyeglass. They all
seemed pretty formidable to a neophyte.

A few weeks later an East End wharf-keeper—a fiery
little Welshman, Tommy Williams—came to Haileybury
House burning with indignation occasioned by a particularly harsh action by the Charity Organisation Society.
During his denunciation, Williams proclaimed his socialist faith, and I, after listening, said, "I am a Socialist too."
He invited me to come on the following Wednesday to
join the local branch of the Independent Labour party.
This was my first step into political life. The branch I
joined was only about a dozen strong, and some of these
dared not openly declare their membership for fear of
losing their jobs. But we were full of enthusiasm and ran
three or four open-air meetings each week at the street
corners.

For some years my normal round was four evenings a
week in the club and one evening at the I.L.P. branch,
while the weekends were partly filled with refereeing for
the boys' football matches and open-air speaking on Sundays. The rest of the weekend I spent at home at Putney.

The club work was interesting. It was astonishing how
wide were the interests of the boys in all kinds of subjects. Sometimes they produced very good aphorisms. For
instance, we were discussing friendship one evening. One
boy summed it up by saying, "A pal is a bloke wot knows
all about yer and yet loves yer." Another time we were
discussing the qualities of a gentleman. One said, "A

bloke wot does no work." Another said, "A rich bloke."
Young Dicky, a bright lad, said, "I reckon a gentleman
is a bloke wot's the same to everybody." It was Dicky, too,
who said that women ought to have the vote because
"only a working woman knows what a working woman
has to go through." Sometimes views were a bit confused.
One boy asked my colleague, "Is God a Jew?"; to which
he replied, "Not exactly." Said another, "Well, his son
was anyway"; to which a third retorted, "Garn, his
mother was a Roman Catholic." I have many memories
of those days and of the boys whom I knew so well.

Our club was secular though there was a voluntary
religious class taken by an old lady—a person of very
wide sympathy. There was a good deal of feeling against
some of the religious clubs. As one boy said, "They say,
'Come to our service and we'll give you a ticket for an
entertainment'—garn." Yet there was a very distinct atmosphere in the club, which expressed itself one day.
The boys asked for the use of the club for a meeting
among themselves. They formed a league, taking its title
from the Haileybury School motto—the Sursum Corda
League. Its principles were these:

> To endeavour to live a clean and manly life.
> To abstain from all bad language.
> To help all fellow cadets when in trouble in rightful
>   circumstances.
> To endeavour to get the club a good name.
> To endeavour to do everything with a good heart.
> Sursum Corda.

One boy said that there was really no need for this because everyone knew this was what the club stood for.

We had developed a system whereby the senior boys, who were N.C.O.s, took responsibility. I found that in the next street there was a gang of small barefoot boys of school age who had nowhere to go, and they asked me if I could do something for them. I arranged to open the club from seven to eight o'clock each evening before the senior club opened. Several of the senior boys volunteered to help keep order and instruct in boxing and gymnastics. This meant that senior boys snatched a very hasty meal after a long day's work before hurrying to the club. They had no easy task either, handling these rough little boys, most of whom were quite handy at throwing stones. But they stuck to their jobs, and it showed, I thought, a good conception of service.

I recall that many years later, after I entered Parliament, I went to speak in a town and stayed with one of my old club boys. He had taken an active share in starting a boys' club there and wanted others to have the opportunities he had enjoyed.

Haileybury House was a good school of citizenship. Most of the managers of the club of those days are dead —several were killed in the First World War—but I recall them with gratitude for their kindness to me.

The club and Cadet Company still go on. I visited them not very long ago. I noticed one striking change—an immense improvement in physique. Many of our club boys did not get enough food, especially when unemployed, for, as one said to me, "You can't take the food when you haven't brought anything in."

Our Cadet Battalion consisted of companies in various

parts of London. The headquarters were in Southwark; another company was at Hackney Wick, run by the Eton Mission. Another was in Westminster. My youngest brother Laurence later took over a company in Islington and went to live there. We had cheery times at Kingston Barracks at Easter and at camps in various seaside places.

Our officers were a delightful lot of men. There was Charles Phillimore, a banker, who used to call me "Keir 'Ardie." There were Freddie Elliott, Gerard Hillyard (later a K.C.), Claude Hay, who acted as quartermaster, and Harold Bond of our own company. Our colonel was an old regular—Colonel Beresford—who had taken part in Lord Roberts' march to Kandahar, while Major Bennett was one of the original officers from the start in 1885 and continued to serve until a few years ago. When Prime Minister, I had the pleasure of recommending him for a decoration for his lifelong social service.

I attended an Officers' School in Bermondsey, where I stayed with Alec Paterson and other friends at the Oxford and Bermondsey Mission. I recall discussing with him his well-known book *Across the Bridges*.

During these years I continued to attend chambers. I shared a room with a Corpus friend, Bertrand Devas, who was killed in the First World War, but I made little progress, and indeed my heart was not in the job. I applied for various positions but without success. Socialist activities in those days were not looked upon with favour.

In September 1907 I paid my first visit to America. A cousin was married to a parson who was working in a small town in Saskatchewan, and my sister Mary had gone

out to help them when the arrival of their first child was
expected. I was sent out to escort her home from Montreal. I sailed from Liverpool on an Allan liner. Among
the passengers was old General William Booth of the Sal-
vation Army. I distinctly remember his going ashore at
Rimouski, crying, "Save your souls, save your souls." Mar-
coni was on board, and also one of the Allan family with
whom, in 1915, I was in hospital at Malta. At that time
one of the members of the shipping firm was the representative of Scotland on the National Administrative
Council of the Independent Labour party. After an enjoyable trip up the St. Lawrence, I went ashore at Quebec, saw the Plains of Abraham, and eventually landed
in Montreal. Finding that my sister would not arrive
there for three days, I decided to spend a weekend in the
United States, where I visited Boston, saw Harvard
University, had a look at New York City, and sailed up
the Hudson, meeting my sister at Niagara Falls. This
proved to be my last visit to America until the Second
World War, when I crossed the Atlantic as a member of
the war cabinet.

On my way home I made friends with a Canadian businessman who had big interests in railways and lumber.
Twice in later years I was somewhat embarrassed by his
referring to me on business matters, stating that he would
be prepared to go in for a big deal if I would be willing
to vouch for the bona fides of those with whom he was
in contact. It showed a remarkable trust in a casual acquaintance.

My father's health had been failing for the past year

and in the autumn of 1908 he died. I had enough money
to continue to live at Haileybury House, but I was tired
of waiting for work at the Bar and was constantly looking
out for some other occupation that would at once be more
congenial and bring in some income.

❊   I V   ❊

Social Work and Politics

IN 1909 the famous Report of the Royal Commission on the Poor Law was published. The commission, which took over four years to issue its report, could not agree either on principles or remedies. The minority report, to which George Lansbury, Bishop Wakefield, and Francis Chandler were cosignatories with Mrs. Sidney Webb, was a remarkable document challenging the whole conception of public relief of distress, which was still, theoretically at least, based on the principles of the 1834 Poor Law. It expressed a socialist philosophy. The majority report, on the other hand, was inspired by the Charity Organisation Society, the coordinating body of a number of voluntary societies, and one to which I was soon to be violently opposed locally.

The Webbs decided to open a campaign for popularizing the proposals of the minority report and gathered round them a number of young Fabians, notably the late C. M. Lloyd and A. Colegate, now the Conservative Member of Parliament for Burton. I ceased to practise at the Bar and became the campaign's lecture secretary.

My task was to offer lectures to various societies and then to find suitable lecturers to meet these engagements. We had a fine list of speakers, mainly drawn from the Labour movement, but we had support from adherents of both the Liberal and Conservative parties. Robert Harcourt and Sir Gilbert Parker were active in the House of Commons for their respective parties, and an amusing incident arose out of this. It occurred while I was speaking at Gravesend for the Independent Labour party, where our speakers were usually given a rough time by the local Conservative supporters. Anticipating this, I spoke at length on the minority report amid much interruption and booing. When at the end of my speech I said, "I gather that you Conservatives object strongly to these proposals," there was a great shout of "Yes." "Then," I said, "you had better take it up with your local Member, Sir Gilbert Parker, who is a strong supporter of them." The vociferous Conservatives retired to their club in some embarrassment.

A difficulty in my work was that almost all societies wanted our "star" lecturers. Sometimes these broke their engagements, and I often had to act as substitute at short notice. I recall addressing a very large gathering of Liberal women in Bolton, attracted by the name of Bishop Wakefield, on "Problems of Birth and Infancy," with which, as a bachelor, my acquaintance was purely theoretical. The rough and tumble of street-corner speaking had taken away the shyness with which I had been afflicted.

The campaign was great fun and had a big effect in the country, but the Liberal government refused to do anything. John Burns, a Liberal M.P. and president of the Local Government Board, was completely in the hands of his reactionary colleagues on the board; while Lloyd George was engaged in developing his insurance plans. We were all sanguine that in a few years the old Poor Law would pass away, but the struggle took longer than we imagined and it was not until nearly forty years had elapsed that the last vestiges of it were removed from the statute book by the Labour government of which I was Prime Minister.

In 1910 I was offered and accepted the secretaryship of Toynbee Hall, Whitechapel, one of the first social and educational settlements in East London, and went into residence there. My new work brought me into contact with a great variety of social-reform activities, but, although kept very busy, I still attended the Haileybury House Club whenever possible and worked for the I.L.P.

I had been made a school manager some time before and I was a very active member of a School Care Committee. I had also done some investigation work in preparation for the Trade Boards Act in association with J. J. Mallon, whose work in drawing attention to the dreadful conditions in sweated industries—particularly by arranging an exhibition in London—had been instrumental in getting the act passed in 1909. As a result of this act, boards were established covering a number of industries and consisting of representatives of workers and employers and nominated members. They investigated industrial conditions, and amongst their powers was that of fixing minimum rates of wages. Tailoring was one of the industries covered by the act, and I visited "outworkers" in the tailoring trade, of whom a great number lived in Stepney. The conditions of these people who toiled for long hours in their own homes were appalling. I remember seeing two women who worked at trouser finishing. They were paid a penny-farthing a pair, out of which they had to buy their own thread. Their weekly wage amounted to about five shillings.

After the act had been passed, elections were held for the workers' representatives on the board for the tailoring trade. There were in East London four rival Jewish organizations, and I was asked to take the chair at a joint meeting. After I had opened the meeting the proceedings were conducted almost entirely in Yiddish, a language quite unknown to me, though old Lewis Lyons, a veteran trade unionist, tried to translate at intervals. Frequently several people were speaking at once amid great uproar. One man in a top hat and a long black coat and a beard leaped onto the platform, shouting and waving an umbrella. I shoved him off and carried on. Eventually, when the clamour was at its height, I closed the meeting and found, somewhat to my surprise, that it had been a complete success and that the representatives had been nominated satisfactorily.

I made many good friends at Toynbee Hall—notably Frank Wise, who was then a clerk in the House of Commons—but my affections were not in Whitechapel; they were in Stepney and Limehouse, and I was not sorry to leave Toynbee Hall at the end of the year and return to what I had come to look upon as my own district.

My next work was as an official explainer of the Lloyd George National Insurance Act of 1911. This act, which provided for free medical attendance and treatment and sick benefits to a large number of workers, involved the cooperation of the Friendly Societies, mutual-aid associations which were to become "Approved Societies" for the administration of the act. The government, wisely, I think, enrolled a number of people to tour the country to explain the provisions and how the act would work in practice. Lloyd George had got together an exceptionally able team of civil servants, notably Sir Robert Morant, Lord Schuster, and Sir John Anderson, together with a number of younger men, two of whom, Sir John Brooke and Frank Wise, were personal friends of mine. After instruction, we "temporaries" gave lectures on approval and were then despatched around the country. Among other assignments, I toured the counties of Somerset and Essex, of which I acquired considerable knowledge.

I admired the public spirit of the county notables, mostly Tories, who had been bitterly opposed to the act but were most cooperative once it had become law in helping the work of information. I recall speaking to an assemblage in a country vicarage to which I had bicycled over the hills on a hot day. I heard the local vicar say, "I suspect that young man is a Socialist. He wears a soft collar."

On another occasion when I was staying with a local magnate, his daughter said, "I suppose you are a keen supporter of Lloyd George and the Liberals," to which I replied, "Good Lord, no." She said, "Then you are a Conservative." I said, "Oh no." "Then what are you?" she asked. When I said, "A Socialist," there was a distinct sensation.

I remember speaking at Woodford in what is now Churchill's constituency. A number of young Conservatives sat in front and booed loudly whilst I talked. I told them that I was only an "official explainer," but they continued to boo. I then said, "You don't like Lloyd George?" "No," they yelled. "You don't like Churchill?" "No," again. "Then when next you see a sailor you'd better hit him, because Churchill is First Lord of the Admiralty." That quieted them.

Several of my colleagues in this campaign became regular members of the Civil Service. I daresay I might have done the same, and some of my family, I think, hoped that I might now get a settled job, but I was not prepared to sacrifice my freedom and to give up propaganda work for socialism. In the last stage of the campaign I was posted in the London office to answer inquiries. Shortly afterwards I was out of work again.

Meanwhile my brother Tom, who helped at the Maurice Hostel in Hoxton and was active in the Wandsworth Independent Labour party, was still living in Putney. He had become interested in the work of the Wandsworth Labour Exchange and its service to young people. He also became interested in the secretary, Miss Kathleen Medley, who was a Labour member of the Poplar Borough Council and an equally enthusiastic social worker.

My brother proposed that he and I should live together in Limehouse. We took a London County Council flat in Brightlingsea Buildings, Narrow Street. We did our own cooking and so on, though neighbours were always helpful over such matters as washing and mending socks. During this year I was—to use the admirable phrase coined by Sir William Beveridge— "a man of discontinuous employment." I did a large amount of unpaid work and a lot of speaking for the Independent Labour party and in the Poor Law campaign. I gave a course of lectures on trade unionism once a week at Ruskin College, Oxford, which had been founded some years earlier to provide a liberal education for workers in a residential college. Except for a few lectures for which I received payment, I had little remunerative employment.

One day my brother came into our flat and announced his engagement to Miss Medley. This broke up our establishment, and I returned to Haileybury House. There was a great wedding in Poplar Parish Church. A rather Conservative relative found herself in a carriage with Will Crooks, then an East End Labour Member of Parliament and tireless agitator for improved social conditions.

In 1912, largely through the influence of Sidney Webb, I was appointed a lecturer and tutor at the London School of Economics in the Department of Social Science and Public Administration. I was not appointed on the score of academic qualification but because I was considered to have a good practical knowledge of social conditions. The school was then comparatively small but had many distinguished teachers, such as Professor Edwin Cannan, Graham Wallas, and Lionel Hobhouse. My immediate chief was Professor Urwick, a very delightful man, and my work, apart from giving lectures on local government and other social subjects, was tutoring students—mostly women—who were about to engage in some branch of social work. The salary was small but sufficient for my wants, while the hours left me plenty of

time for social work and also for socialist propaganda, for
it was a fundamental rule of the school that no one could
be restricted in venting his political opinions.

At this time I became a very active member of a
School Care Committee for Trafalgar Square School, a
very large school in a poor district. There was much detailed investigation of cases, involving house-to-house visiting in connection with school meals. Public opinion had
forced the Conservative London County Council to provide meals, but they did the work very grudgingly. As a
result, the supervising of meals was left to voluntary workers, and I frequently supervised the meals of over four
hundred children of various ages. To do this, I organized
a kind of prefect system, which worked well. Naturally I
had many friends among the children. I recall walking
along the street one day when a little barefoot girl came
and joined me. She said, "Where are you going, Mr.
Attlee?" I said, "I'm going home for tea." "Oh," she said,
"I'm going home to see if there is any tea." This seemed
to me to put very neatly the difference between the comfortable and the insecure classes.

In the local association of Care Committees we used to
have great fights against the adherents of the Charity
Organisation Society, who believed in the Poor Law
principle of deterrence. I recall a parson who advocated
giving children only burned porridge served at the most
inconvenient place and time. However, Christians of a
different mind and Jews combined to defeat the reaction-
aries.

I recall many incidents of those years. There was the
famous siege of the anarchists in Sidney Street in the East

End of London in 1911 when Winston Churchill, who
was then Home Secretary, took command of the situation
and guardsmen opened fire on the murderers, who had
barricaded themselves in a house. I had the headmaster
of Haileybury, Dr. Wynne Willson (afterwards Bishop of
Bath and Wells), staying with me. I was taking him for
a walk to show him something of the district when I met
one of our club boys who said, "I can't get to work—
they're shooting like anything down the street." I said,
"Let's go and see," and we went and viewed the scene.
I certainly showed Dr. Willson more of East London life
than he had expected.

I remember two great strikes—that of the dockers in
London in 1911 and that of the Irish transport and general workers led by Jim Larkin in Dublin two years later.
In the former, our branch of the I.L.P. was active in serving meals to dockers' children, and I remember cutting
up many loaves of bread. During the strike in Ireland
I recall long hours spent collecting funds at the bottom of
Petticoat Lane and admiring the generosity of the passers-by, particularly of a heavyweight boxer who emptied
his pockets to the tune of several half-crowns.

All this time I was active in the Socialist movement, doing a great deal of weekend speaking in all parts of the
country besides the regular work in our own branch. I
was twice runner-up for the representation of London
on the National Administrative Committee of the Independent Labour party. At this time we had an accession
of strength in the adherence of Dr. Harry Roberts, a well-
known doctor in Mile End Road. He started the Stepney
Labour League, which was in its way an anticipation of

the present local Labour party. He was a bit of an individualist and not easy to work with, but his influence in the district was considerable.

I also did some work for my own union—the National Union of Clerks—and for the London Carmen's Trade Union. Together with Sam March and Will Godfrey, officials of the Carmen's Union, I spoke from the back of a cart in Mile End Road. There were many May Day demonstrations in which I joined, and I know what it is to carry a banner from Mile End Waste across Central London to Hyde Park.

I recall many international meetings. I remember hearing Jean Jaurès, the French Socialist leader, speak, and seeing Anatole France kiss Bernard Shaw at a meeting in London. My work had become known to some of our leaders and, in consequence, I was invited to a number of dinners and receptions—among them, one to the South African deportees and another to Andrew Fisher, the Australian Labour Prime Minister.

On several occasions I visited the Continent, walking in Normandy and visiting other parts of France and Belgium. There was a memorable tour of Italy with Tom, Margaret, and a brother and sister of my future wife, when we visited Tuscany, Milan, and the Italian lakes. One year my brother, together with his wife and myself, ran a cooperative holiday for the Poplar Labour League at Wimereux in France, during which I officiated as assistant cook.

Looking back on those days, one is inclined to think of them as quiet and peaceful compared to the present time, but they were, in fact, filled with controversy. There was the struggle with the House of Lords and the Home

Rule for Ireland controversy. There were serious industrial disputes and times of international tension. There
was the suffragette agitation, and I assisted the constitutional side of the movement of votes for women. Many of
the suffrage agitators were drawn from the ranks of the
Independent Labour party and were old friends of mine,
such as Mrs. Despard and Mrs. Cobden Sanderson. I served
on a local committee with Miss Scott, the head of the Rat-
cliff Settlement, the finest social worker that I have ever
known. It will be seen that during these years from 1907
to 1914 I served my apprenticeship in the Labour and
Socialist movement and in social work; I was a rank-and-
file member with no special ambitions.

It is no part of my purpose in this book to relate the
story of the Labour movement, but it is, I think, desirable
to say something of what was the situation of the Socialist
movement when I joined. The Labour party had shared
in the great victory of the 1906 General Election, when
the Liberals for the last time achieved power. For the first
time there was a Labour party—not merely a Labour
group of Members—in the House of Commons. It was
only twenty-nine strong, but there was also a group of
trade unionists—scarcely less numerous—which was an
integral part of the Liberal party. The Labour Members of
Parliament were by no means all Socialists. Socialist propaganda had had a big share in leading to the creation of
the Labour party, but probably the Taff Vale judgment
had had as much effect in causing trade unionists to vote
Labour in that election. By this House of Lords judgment
a railway union had to pay heavy damages to the Taff Vale
Railway Company as damages for loss sustained during a

strike. The effect of this was to make big strikes nearly impossible, and the Labour party stood for complete reversal of the judgment.

But the fighting core of the party was the I.L.P., whose leader, Keir Hardie, was now reinforced in the House of Commons by Ramsay MacDonald, Philip Snowden, J. R. Clynes, and others. Without the I.L.P. this attempt to form a new party might have failed, as had happened before. The I.L.P. was a remarkable organization that enlisted the devotion of thousands of men and women. It was not rigidly dogmatic. It was inclusive rather than exclusive, and it preached a socialism that owed far more to the Bible than to Karl Marx. It was indeed a characteristically British interpretation of socialism, a way of life rather than an economic dogma. The I.L.P. had set itself to convert the trade unions to socialism. The Labour Representation Committee, which was formed in 1900 as a federation of trade unions and Socialist societies, of which the most important was the I.L.P., and from which the Labour party grew, had the simple object of getting Labour representatives into Parliament. As Keir Hardie foresaw, a party formed on this basis was bound in time to become socialist.

As a contrast, the Social Democratic Federation was completely Marxist and preached the class war. Its outlook was more materialist than the I.L.P.'s. Although the S.D.F. took part in the inaugural meeting of the Labour Representation Committee, it subsequently withdrew and maintained an uncompromisingly independent attitude. It was led by the veteran Hyndman, who was a good deal of an egoist. In its membership were two separate strands, which time and events were to disentangle. At the end of the First World War the S.D.F. split into sections, one of which joined the Labour party, while the other, the ultra-Marxists, became the nucleus of the Communist party.

The Fabian Society was open to all Socialists and included members of the Social Democratic Federation, the Independent Labour party, and Liberals. Indeed, at this time the Fabians were by no means committed to the Labour party. As I have said, there were still many trade unionists in the Liberal party. Most of the miners' M.P.s were still Liberal-Labour.

These divisions in the ranks of Labour were very real in London. John Burns and Will Steadman were Liberals. Will Crooks was a Fabian, George Lansbury belonged to the Independent Labour party, while Will Thorne was a member of the Social Democratic Federation. The Independent Labour party and the Social Democratic Federation were fairly equally matched in London, but there was an unholy alliance on the London Trades Council between the S.D.F. and Liberal-Labour against the I.L.P. At that time the Labour and Socialist movement was weak in London. There were only two Labour Members of Parliament in the county—Charles Bowerman of Deptford and Will Crooks of Woolwich, while Will Thorne held Southwest Ham. Outside Woolwich and Poplar there were few Labour councillors. Indeed, in those days they were very important people, and we knew most of them by name.

In the Socialist movement one soon got to know all the more active spirits in the London area. This position of being a small fighting minority gave one a certain sense of exaltation. The capitalist fortress looked very strong and formidable, and our forces were weak. We were crusaders in enemy-occupied territory. It followed also that we had a fellow feeling for other minorities; holders of unpopular opinions tended to stand together.

Our Stepney branch of the I.L.P. met weekly in a small dingy church hall, but we ran at least two and sometimes three or four open-air meetings a week. I was early pressed to speak and made my first attempt under a flickering gas-light at the bottom of Barnes Street, speaking in a loud voice to call the crowd. It is not easy to speak to an empty street in order to try to attract the passers-by, but I did a lot of it in those days. The people I admired were those who did the tedious jobs, collecting our exiguous subscriptions, trying to sell literature, and carrying the improvised platform from one street corner to another. They got no glamour. They did not expect to live to see victory but, uncomplainingly, they worked to try to help on the cause.

As time went on I began to take speaking engagements for other London branches; indeed, there were few recognized street corners that I did not attend. There was a wonderful comradeship in those days. We were mostly wage-earners. Middle-class people were not many in the East London movement. The late C. M. Lloyd in Bethnal Green and R. C. K. Ensor in Poplar were the most prominent. Both were distinguished scholars from Oxford and had much influence in our East London movement. A year or two later we had two notable recruits—Susan Lawrence from the Conservatives and Dr. Salter from the Liberals. It was uphill work and our branch grew slowly.

Another comrade and I used to visit the various trade-union branches to try to interest them in the political movements. These met mostly in public houses, and I got to know the members quite well, but the response to our appeals was not great. In 1908 I became secretary of our I.L.P. branch and was a delegate to the Annual Conference at Edinburgh. This was the conference at which Hardie, Snowden, MacDonald, and Glasier resigned from the Administrative Council, owing to an adverse vote on the question of the treatment of Victor Grayson. This was the only time I saw this curious character. He won a sensational by-election in Colne Valley as an unofficial candidate and made a rather theatrical display in Parliament. After his defeat he faded out and disappeared from public view, though rumours of his having been seen used to circulate from time to time. He was a fine mob orator but a man of unstable character.

In East London our great leaders were Lansbury and Crooks. Crooks's great fight on the Poplar Board of Guardians[1] was a striking episode in the battle against the Poor Law. He was a fine character, a real East Londoner, a master of humour and pathos. His Sunday speeches at the dock gates were a notable feature of East End life. Of Lansbury I shall have much to say later. I was to meet many of the propagandists of those days later on in the House of Commons. Some were to serve under me in government, half a dozen were to go to the House of Lords on my recommendation, but little did we anticipate such a future in those days. Other good friends, like Harry Orbell and

[1] Each borough had its Board of Guardians to administer the Poor Law under the supervision of the Central government. The Law as such was superseded by the National Assistance Act of 1948.—*Ed.*

Bill Devenay of the Dockers, and Jack Scurr of the Social Democratic Federation, have passed on.

The various strains in the movement found their echo in our branch meetings, and we used to discuss vehemently such topics as the advantages of revolutionary or reformist tactics and the question of industrial, as opposed to political, action. I am sure that a substantial apprenticeship in the ordinary work of a local branch is of great value to anyone destined to play any part in political life, especially if he is to become prominent in a national sphere. Not that I had any anticipation of future prominence in those days. I had no idea of anything more than working as a member of the rank and file and perhaps getting onto a local council.

Twice in those days I was a candidate for the Stepney Borough Council and twice for the Limehouse Board of Guardians, but without success. It will be realized that the franchise then was far more restricted than it is today. These were propaganda fights, and to get a hundred votes in a local contest was regarded as a moral victory. We made various efforts to increase our effectiveness. In conjunction with the local S.D.F. we started a weekly paper called *The Stepney Worker,* but after three numbers the Whitechapel S.D.F., who were dyed-in-the-wool Marxists, found some deviation, withdrew their support, and the venture failed.

We tried to run rather ambitious premises and a club, but our money soon gave out. We attempted several times to form a Trades Council, but the more skilled trade-union branches were located outside our borough and the others were apathetic. Apathy—how the word recalls one of the best of our comrades, George Cressall. How often he deplored the apathy of the workers! In 1951 his widow, our first lady member in the movement, made a speech at the Annual Conference of the Labour party that roused the delegates to great enthusiasm. As I listened to Mrs. Nellie Cressall I felt very proud of my old friend and comrade of Stepney days. There are not many of the old lot left now.

Many interesting characters were members of our branch from time to time. I have already mentioned Tommy Williams, the wharf-keeper. He was a vehement temperance reformer, and no wonder, for he had been brought up by a drunken father. Once Tommy was launched in a speech he took a lot of stopping, despite the fact that a visiting speaker might be waiting his turn. There was Joe Pert, a sardonic riverside worker, with his invariable formula, "As fur as that there goes," often followed by, "There ain't no manner of sense in it absolutely." There was a most devoted worker, Kinchin, who for years was responsible for carrying the platform from corner to corner. Quite a character was Jack Edwards, a Corporation dustman. He was a great lover of words. He would select one from the dictionary and use it for several weeks. Once it was "adamant"; he pronounced it "adamnant," which made it more impressive. While he was "adamnant" he opposed practically everything. Finally he "took umbrage" for several weeks, a phrase that suited his personality, and we had a gloomy time. Bill Painter was another character, a woodworker, always on the Left Wing. We used to have great theological discussions at his house. Yes, the old Stepney branch of the I.L.P. was indeed a good comradeship.

So the years passed until August 1914, when fortune once more changed the current of my life. I was on holiday in Seaton in Devon with Tom and his wife when the First World War broke out.

War Service

THE First World War marked the close of an epoch. The Victorian certainty in progress passed away and the secure position of Britain in the world was gravely shaken, as was the social system, which had been steadily undermined by the propaganda of Socialists and by the writings of Shaw and Wells. Years of uncertainty lay ahead.

Looking back, one can see now that the German and Austrian ruling classes, by their ill-considered action in making war, destroyed the class society that gave them their privileged position. The outbreak of the war caused great heart-searchings in the ranks of the Labour and Socialist movement, especially in the membership of the Independent Labour party, which had always been strongly pacifist. It had always been held that war would be prevented by the international solidarity of the workers. There had been a great underestimate of the strength of national and patriotic feelings; also a failure to realize that the issues presented by a war are seldom as clear-cut as the theorists imagine.

The difference of view in the party was well illustrated in our family. My brother Tom was a convinced conscientious objector and went to prison. I thought it my duty to fight. We ended the war as near neighbours in Wandsworth—I in hospital and he in jail—but with no breach of our mutual affection.

I do not suppose that my war experiences were very different from those of most men of my generation, but four years in an entirely different milieu had their effect on my outlook.

I was told when I first tried to join the Army that I was too old at thirty-one. I tried to enlist but could not do so, as I still held a volunteer commission in the Cadets. However, I joined the Inns of Court Regiment and for a fortnight or so drilled recruits in the square of Lincoln's Inn. At the same time a relative of one of my pupils, who was commanding a battalion of Kitchener's Army, had applied for me, and one Sunday morning, on returning from doing a guard at Lincoln's Inn, I found a letter telling me to report as a lieutenant to the 6th South Lancashire Regiment at Tidworth. There I found plenty to do, having had more experience than most of the subalterns, and I soon found myself in temporary command of a company of seven officers and two hundred and fifty men. Most of them were still in "civvies," and I remember going home one weekend and collecting spare trousers from neighbours in Putney in order to make good deficiencies. Our lads were mostly from Wigan, Warrington, and Liverpool and were excellent material. We had six regular officers in the battalion and a limited number of regular or reserve N.C.O.s.

The task of creating a new unit was one of very great interest. I enjoyed our period of training at Tidworth, Winchester, and Chobham, and I found most of my fellow officers very congenial.

We had a fine adjutant, Captain Marsh of the Indian Army, but early in 1915 he was sent to France to serve with an Indian unit that had a shortage of experienced officers. I was appointed in his place. Towards the end of our training we were on operations most days and did the office work in the evening.

We expected to be sent to France, but in the late spring we got orders to equip with tropical kit. I realized that our destination was either Gallipoli or Mesopotamia. At the end of May, Marsh returned to us, and I took over command of B Company; I was the only amateur company commander. In June 1915 we sailed from Avonmouth for the East and had an uneventful voyage through the Mediterranean to Alexandria. Thence we had a more interesting time, passing up through the Greek islands with their little white villages in the hills. Moudros harbour, crammed with shipping, was a wonderful sight. After bivouacking for two nights in a vineyard we went up on destroyers by night to the Gallipoli Peninsula, landed, and proceeded to the Gully Ravine. Here I met Hunter-Weston, the Corps commander, subsequently to be a fellow member of the House of Commons. We stayed our first night in the trenches with the Lancashire Fusiliers of the 29th Division. Their battalion strength was about the same as that of my company. Our lads found many old friends and settled in very well. I had three or four weeks at Helles, experiencing the heat and smells and flies. Like

many others, I got dysentery, a complaint for which our
diet of bully beef, biscuit, and tea without milk was not
very suitable. Eventually I fainted and was carried down
to the beach and embarked for Malta. I thus missed the
big attack at Anzac, where our division had six or
seven thousand casualties, including many of my friends
of the South Lancashires.

I had a fairly severe attack of dysentery, but was well
looked after in a small hospital at Hamrun in Malta. Later
I had a restful time at an officers' convalescent centre in
the Scicluna Palace, where my chief companion was a
young gunner, F. N. H. Davidson, whom I was to know
later in the Second World War as a major general.

In late September I sailed for Egypt. I had heard that
my brother Bernard had joined up as a chaplain in the
Navy. On arriving at an hotel in Alexandria some instinct
urged me to ask if there was a Chaplain Attlee there. The
reply was, "Just arrived half an hour ago." He had come
to join the Royal Naval Division. We had a pleasant time
together before he went to Helles and I ultimately to
Suvla, but we were destined to meet again in Port Said.
Incidentally, I had another curious meeting later in the
war. When returning from France I got into a carriage of
a London Underground train and found myself next to my
brother Laurence who was also returning to England from
overseas.

After a few days in Alexandria I went to Moudros,
where Lord Kitchener, who had come out to consider the
question of evacuation, reviewed the details of our division. There were tiresome delays in the base camp as the
weather was stormy. Eventually I got off in a small Clyde

River steamer. We had a very rough time for forty-eight hours; the wind blew strongly and the boat rolled violently. However, I was O.C. Troops, and by dint of devotion to duty and bridge I was not sick, a circumstance that gave me great confidence in later voyages. I rejoined my battalion, which was at Suvla holding part of the front line in front of Chocolate Hill. It was a great relief to be back again, although so many of the old lot had gone. We held the same trenches until the evacuation, never leaving the line. The most notable incident was the blizzard; heavy rain turned our trenches into moats, and frost and snow followed. Numbers of men had to be evacuated with frozen feet, and a good many died.

At the Suvla evacuation I was in command of the rearguard holding a perimeter round the evacuation beach. The various parties passed through peacefully. I left with the last party just before General Maude.

The Gallipoli campaign will always remain a very vivid memory. I have always held that the strategic conception was sound. The trouble was that it was never adequately supported. Often I have thought how near we came to victory, and I have tried to work out what the consequences would have been in that event. Unfortunately the military authorities were Western-Front-minded. Reinforcements were always sent too late. For an enterprise such as this the right leaders were not chosen. Elderly and hidebound generals were not the men to push through an adventure of this kind. Had we had at Suvla generals like Maude, who came out later, we should, I think, have pushed through to victory. Even as it was we came near to success. But for General Baldwin's column losing its way, it would have joined the Gurkhas and the South Lancashires on Sari Bair. But for Mustafa Kemal Pasha being in command of a Turkish division at the crucial point, we might have held that height. It was a tragic failure. I always feel a sympathy with all old Gallipolitans; as James Thomson the poet says, I "feel the stir of fellowship in all disastrous fight."

I recall the heat and the flies and later the frost and the snow. I remember many talks with men on the night watches. One night in the front line I had a lively discussion with two of my sergeants—a railwayman and a car-man—on craft and industrial trade unionism, while Johnny Turk kept up a brisk fire. I remember the discussions we used to have at battalion headquarters. Colonel Charlton, commanding the battalion, and Captain Withers —two of the best—would say, "Let's have a good 'strafe' tonight—have Attlee to dinner," and we would discuss socialism or some similar controversial topic. I recall discussing what would happen after the war. The commanding officer said that there were so many people who had served in the war that justice would be done to the ex-servicemen. I said that I feared not. Unfortunately I was right.

After a period at Moudros and some weeks at Port Said, training and refitting, we were ordered to Mesopotamia. We were under the impression that we were going to a "well-run show," but we were to be disillusioned. I was ship's adjutant on the voyage under a very cheery old gunner colonel. He was one of the world's worst bridge players, but I was luckily drawn against him for the last two days. He summed me up once to my commanding of-

ficer as "A charmin' feller, just going to play bridge with
him, but a damned democratic, socialistic, tub-thumping
rascal."

At Basra we embarked on paddleboats to go up the Ti-
gris. I had half the battalion and a collection of Indian
details, without officers. Fortunately one of my N.C.O.s
could speak a bit of Hindustani, as it had not occurred to
anyone to provide an interpreter. After a week's voyage
we arrived at Sheikh Saad and disembarked. We had had a
couple of barges, full of mules, tied onto each side of our
steamer. They were rather lively on landing, and I told
our somewhat bewildered transport officer that he was putting on the best circus I had seen in years. We had a pretty
heavy tonnage of stores, which we had to manhandle. I
was not very pleased when a staff officer made us shift them
twice to other locations. I complained to a senior officer,
and he said, "Was it that bloody fool with an eyeglass?" I
said, "Yes, sir. Thank you very much."

We were to go into an attack before long and practised
it diligently. Our divisional commander, General Maude,
was a first-rate leader and explained everything to us
fully. We attacked on April 5, 1916, at El Hanna, but
found, as I had anticipated, that the Turks had for the
most part withdrawn. However, a shell—fired, I found
out years later, by one of our own batteries—caught me
with a bullet through the thigh and a piece of nose-cap in
the buttocks, and I had to be carried off the field. In two
subsequent attacks our division suffered very heavy losses,
so perhaps I was fortunate. I went down to Basra on a river
steamer crowded with wounded soldiers, and then to Bombay. Thence I went to Alexandria, and so home to Eng-

land, which we reached in June. By this time I could walk about a little. I remember that as we neared England we heard of the loss of Kitchener, the War Minister, who had been drowned on his way to Russia.

After convalescing for a month or two I went to a training battalion at Prees Heath in Shropshire. It was not very lively. In December, however, Colonel Woods, who had commanded our battalion until the Anzac show, applied for me to join him at Wool, in Dorset, where he was commanding one of the new tank battalions. I had an interesting year with the Tanks, going to France twice on instructional tours. The last trip also took me to Passchendaele in Belgium, where I assisted in the preparations for the attack on Poelcapelle. I was promoted to the rank of major and became supernumerary to our battalion, with the result that I was left at Wool to start a new battalion. After some weeks a colonel took over, and, not unnaturally, wanted to fill up with senior officers of his own choice. I did not want to go to the Depot and so returned to the Infantry.

After a spell in a training camp at Barrow, where I conducted a successful class in trade-union history for a number of invalids who could not go on parade, I was eventually successful in getting sent to France to our 5th Territorial Battalion, which had just taken part in the brilliant defence of the Givenchy-Festubert sector as part of the 55th Division under General Jeudwine.

It was interesting to contrast the backgrounds of the officers of 1918 with those of 1914. In the 6th Battalion they were all from the public schools and many from Oxford or Cambridge. In the 5th there was far greater variety.

I had a Lancashire miner who had been in Gallipoli with me and a lad who had been an errand boy, but they were very good material. The latter was quite a rough lad. He was sent on an officers' course and, when asked to write a tactical appreciation, said to the instructor, "Dost think Ah'm Douggy 'aig, lad?" He was reported as being unfit to be an officer, and this infuriated General Jeudwine. He asked me for a report. I said that he was an excellent officer, a good disciplinarian, and that the men would follow him anywhere. The general was delighted and gave the school commandant "a raspberry" for suggesting that one of his officers was unworthy of his rank.

I recall one day when a soldier was brought up to me in handcuffs. He had accumulated sentences of twelve years' imprisonment, which would await him at the end of the war. I told him that he must now set to work to get remission and that we would help him. Our lads, too, were all determined to help. As one lad of nineteen said, "I reckon that poor lad has never had a chance. He's been dragged up." I think myself that he was not entirely sane. However, we all set out to help him. He volunteered for every patrol. He lay out between the lines sniping and in a few weeks I got about six years of his sentence remitted. A little later I recommended the remission of the rest. Next evening I found him and his sergeant outside my dugout. The sergeant said that he refused to go back to the line. On my questioning him, he talked wildly about being fed up and so on. I was much annoyed that all our trouble should go for nothing, so I adopted a method I had found useful with disobedient boys. I took out my watch and said, "You've got one minute to return to

duty," and then counted slowly. At forty-five seconds he
sloped arms and returned to the trench. I suppose it was
irregular but I did not put him on a charge, and when I
left the unit he was still doing well.

Our old club boys had, of course, joined up, and most
of them speedily got promoted to N.C.O. rank. I met only
one of them in the war. He had become a flying officer. In
later years he used to come to the House of Commons in
striped trousers and a tail coat, "lobbying" for a trade
association of which he was secretary. He was a bright
lad and the only club boy who had joined the Independent Labour party before the war.

I served in France for some weeks and saw the approach-
ing end of the war, evidenced by a reluctance of the Germans to attack. We were advancing towards Lille when I
fell sick and had to have a minor operation. Evacuated to
England in October, I celebrated the armistice in hospital. I was suffering from some painful boils, which seemed
to get no better. A Canadian brought in some champagne
to cheer us up.

Having decided to try to get away for Christmas, I
dressed and made out a pass in the presence of a surgeon
who, knowing nothing of my case, signed it. My brother
Rob was waiting with a taxi, and I got away to Salisbury
to stay with my sister. A civilian doctor cured me in three
days. On my return I was demobbed and received a useful
little wound gratuity.

Local Government Work

A S SOON as I got my discharge from the Army I went to Stepney to see how things were moving in East London. Haileybury House was closed. The younger men who had been running the club had been killed in the war, and there was no one immediately available to replace them. As I wanted to live and work in Stepney, I once more took up residence at Toynbee Hall (then being run by Eldred Hitchcock) as a temporary measure, while I looked round for somewhere to live. I also returned to the London School of Economics, where Professor Urwick welcomed me again on his staff.

Like everything else, the war had changed the school, which was rapidly expanding. There was a large enrollment in the Social Science Department. Among my students was an interesting group of young ex-soldiers, ex-physical training instructors who were training to be welfare workers in industry. I took charge of them, and they brought a pleasant variety into my tutorial work, which was otherwise mainly directed to girls training for the social science certificate.

Politically I found great activity in East London. For the first time the Labour movement was organized. Arthur Henderson's reorganization of the party on the basis of individual membership and local Labour parties was bearing fruit. There were active Labour parties in Mile End and Limehouse, while in Whitechapel and St. George's there were two rival organizations which were soon to be amalgamated. All three seats had been contested at the December 1918 General Election, and although our candidates had been heavily defeated, yet the fact that Parliamentary seats had actually been fought by Labour made a new situation. Besides this, the extension of the franchise had given votes to the women and to many of the workers for the first time.

The breaking up of the Liberal party and the course of events in Ireland had set free the Irish voters from their old-time allegiance and they now formed a most valuable element in the movement.

There was now a Trades Council and Borough Labour party in Stepney, to which a high proportion of the trade-union branches in the borough were affiliated. The moving spirit in the Stepney movement was a chemist in Mile End, Oscar Tobin, who had shown considerable organizing ability. I had a long talk with him and learned that it was proposed to contest the London County Council elections. I was invited to offer myself as a candidate either for Mile End or Limehouse, and I chose the latter. In the party there, my old comrades of the Independent Labour party were prominent, along with a strong contingent of Irish formerly aloof from Labour only because of the Home Rule issue. I was speedily adopted as candidate, together with Con Bryan, an official of the Watermen and Lightermen's Union.

We fought a vigorous campaign for the London County Council[1] and were successful in returning my colleague, Con Bryan, but I was beaten by some eighty votes by an excellent man, a Liberal baker with a strong local following. My defeat was largely due to the intervention of a parson who stood as an ex-serviceman candidate and took away some of the votes I might have had. Later, when I was in the first Labour government, he sought my aid to be made a dean. Apart from his unsuitability, I did not think his previous interposition gave him a valid claim on me.

Close on the London County Council elections came those for the Boards of Guardians, and we decided to contest all the seats on the Limehouse Board.

In the course of the London County Council elections a demand had arisen that I should contest Limehouse at the next Parliamentary contest, which was then considered as quite likely to occur before long, as the Coalition government might easily break up. I was duly adopted, and it was therefore decided that I should not put up for the Guardians. At this election we won twelve of the sixteen seats. At the first meeting of the board it was decided to co-opt me as a member, and I thus gained my first experience of public administration. I served on the board for some years and was chairman of the Children's Home

---

[1] The London County Council is responsible for the administrative county of London, an area of 117 square miles, and deals with questions affecting the county as a whole. There are 124 councillors elected by popular vote every three years, four by the City of London proper, and two each by the sixty electoral divisions. The councillors elect 20 additional members, called aldermen, and a chairman.—*Ed.*

in Essex. I was also chosen as the board's representative on the Metropolitan Asylums Board, which was an indirectly elected body controlling a large number of hospitals and other institutions. Among them was a training ship on the Thames for boys. I served on the committee that administered this. We changed the policy of the Limehouse Board, which had tended to be conducted on the principles of the Act of 1834. We did much to humanize the institutions, and sought to preserve, instead of breaking up, the families that sought the assistance of the Poor Law.

Meanwhile I had found a place to live in. There was an old house, formerly the home of some well-to-do merchant in a cul-de-sac off the Commercial Road behind Limehouse Free Library. It had fallen on evil days and had until recently been occupied by the local Conservatives. The house contained some good rooms with Adam mantelpieces, but was in a dilapidated condition. I took it on lease and made some repairs. Part of it was used as a club for the local Labour party. I had a flat on the first floor, and two other flats were let to members of the party. A coalman occupied part of the yard.

Just at this time a former batman of mine wrote to ask if he could come to me as a personal servant, not realizing that I did not employ a valet. However, he came and looked after me for some time, but then returned to Lancashire, where he married a widow whose pursuit of him he had sought to avoid by coming south. After an old club boy had looked after me for a month or two, I was fortunate to secure a local ex-service lad, Charlie Griffiths, who has remained a close friend of my family and myself ever since. He is a great character with a genius for making friends.

Elections followed thick and fast in 1919. In the autumn came the Borough Council[1] elections. Previously the council had always met in the afternoon, a time very convenient to the publicans who formed a considerable part of it, but, of course, prohibitive for the attendance of workingmen. It was therefore essential for us to capture the council. A minority party could not have functioned.

In London boroughs all councillors retire every three years. In Stepney there were sixty seats to contest, and we decided to fight them all. There were two Liberal members of the council who had come over to us; otherwise, our candidates were without municipal experience. I wrote the election address, in which was set forth faithfully the sins of commission and omission of the old council, every paragraph being followed by the slogan "Sack the Lot," a phrase which at that time Admiral Lord Fisher had been using freely. The result was a great shock to our opponents, for we won forty-three seats, including all fifteen in Limehouse.

The question of the mayoralty at once arose, a difficult matter where three local Labour parties were concerned. There were veterans who had claims for consideration, but the councillors decided to co-opt me as mayor. I thus began my municipal career from the top, as the youngest mayor the borough had ever had. I had an extensive knowledge of local government, but it was only theoretical.

[1] The London County Council area is divided into twenty-eight metropolitan boroughs, each with its mayor and borough council, which deals with purely local matters. Each borough is subdivided into wards.—*Ed.*

The year that followed was one of very hard work and gave me a great deal of useful experience. I made a careful selection of chairmen of committees, giving due weight to each of the parties, and my recommendations were accepted. I used to have frequent meetings with the chairmen in order to concert policy. We were fortunate to have as leader of the council and chairman of the Finance Committee a very able barrister, Hubert Hull, who lived in a Catholic Settlement in Wapping. Our party had a considerable contingent of Irish Catholics and a number of Jews, and some diplomacy was needed to get harmonious working, but this was successfully achieved.

Our powers to deal with the housing situation were limited and there was not much space for building, but we did what we could. It was, however, possible for us to get existing houses repaired. We appointed a number of extra sanitary inspectors, made a complete survey of the borough, served over forty thousand legal notices on house-owners to repair their property, and saw that these were enforced.

In another field great progress was made. Infant mortality had long been high. We instituted health visitors, prenatal clinics, and soon brought the death rate down to one of the lowest in London. I recall in this regard an incident at the end of my mayoralty when votes of thanks were moved to the chairmen of committees. A somewhat untutored member was charged with moving the vote of thanks to the chairman of the Public Health Committee. He came to me and asked what he should say. I said, "Well, you know what we've done in reducing the infant-mortality rate." He, however, when the time came, said,

"Mr. Mayor, I move a very hearty vote of thanks to the chairman of the Public Health Committee. During the year there has been a great increase in the birth rate, mainly due, as we all know, to the personal efforts of the chairman."

There were in the borough a large number of unemployed, many of them ex-servicemen, and, in default of government action, the councils had to do what they could to find work for them. This put a great burden on the local rates.[1]

The year 1920 brought the quinquennial valuation of the property in the borough. I was chairman of the Valuation Committee. We found that many properties, especially the licensed premises, had never been properly valued. We employed professional valuers, with the result that without increasing the assessment of residential property we added over £200,000 to the rateable value of the borough. Despite this, owing largely to expenses incurred in trying to relieve unemployment, our rates went up to over twenty shillings in the pound. This was due to the division of London into rich and poor boroughs, causing a disparity in financial resources that was not remedied until after the Poplar councillors had gone to prison as a protest.

We also set up advice bureaus to advise tenants on their rights under the Rent Restriction Acts, and thus got many thousands of pounds out of the clutches of the slum landlords. Altogether, it was a fruitful year of office. I ended my mayoral year with a reception that was graced by the

[1] Rates are local taxes on the occupiers of real property.—*Ed.*

presence of Lord Milner, then Secretary of State for the Colonies, the only time I met him.

Fifteen other London boroughs had Labour mayors, and we formed an association, which still exists, for the purpose of meeting together and coordinating policy. I was made chairman.

There were three memorable events in my year of office. There was the death in Brixton prison of the Lord Mayor of Cork, who had been on a hunger strike. An impressive service was conducted by Cardinal Mannix, and a funeral procession through London was organized in which my fellow mayors and I marched.

There was a Conference on Unemployment which I called on behalf of the London mayors and which was held in Shoreditch Town Hall. It was well attended by mayors and provosts from all over the country, and resolutions introduced by George Lansbury, then mayor of Poplar, and other Labour mayors were discussed and carried. We were constantly pressing the problem of the unemployed. I recall a meeting at the Mansion House where the Lord Mayor was proposing some mild measures. I asked to be allowed to speak, which was contrary to precedent at these meetings, where the proceedings are generally cut and dried. I made a forcible appeal for more vigorous measures, and my fellow mayors followed on the same lines, rather to the consternation of the City Fathers.

The government did little or nothing, and eventually we decided on a deputation to the Prime Minister. The unemployed—largely ex-servicemen—assembled at various points and were marched by their mayors to the Embankment. I led the Stepney contingent, a big one, from Mile End Waste. At the Embankment a halt was called while we mayors went to Downing Street. We were received by Lloyd George, who had very little to offer, and strong speeches were made. When we came out we found Whitehall filled with a mass of men, with mounted police trying to control the crowd. There were some rough elements that had determined to provoke a riot, and George Lansbury tried in vain to address the crowd. I then went round by George Street and found the Stepney contingent marching down Bridge Street in perfect order with a police sergeant at its head, about to be led into the scrimmage. I ordered the column to halt and turn about and led them back to Stepney, thus saving some broken heads. The demonstration did, I think, have some effect on the government.

One other activity of my term of office as mayor may be mentioned. I happened to meet Miss Lena Ashwell, who had done great work with her theatrical company entertaining the troops during the war. She wanted to continue her work of bringing good drama to the people. I suggested that, in cooperation with the mayors of the Labour boroughs, good plays at popular prices might be staged in the various town halls. This was done with considerable success in some boroughs, though, unfortunately, in Stepney we had no suitable hall.

My tutorial and lecture work allowed me to do some municipal work in the daytime. There were in London a great many organizations formed of representatives from the borough councils, such as the Standing Joint

Committee and various Whitley Councils.[1] I was the Stepney Borough Council's representative on all of them and thus gained a wide knowledge of London problems. The one, in particular, which was to engage my attention for several years was that of the Municipal Electricity Authorities of Greater London. I was elected vice-president of this body and collaborated closely with the chairman, Sir Duncan Watson. For many years thereafter he and I worked in perfect harmony. We met in the Council Chamber of the Westminster City Council.

I summed up the position in the following verse:

> Oh, East is East and West is West
> And never the two shall meet
> Till Watson and I sit side by side
> On the Westminster mayoral seat.

I was somewhat handicapped in my work as mayor by being unmarried. My sister Margaret was kind enough to act as mayoress on several occasions, but, living in Putney, she could not get down to Stepney very often, as she had to be with my mother a good deal. During the year my mother died and the old home at Putney was broken up. My sister Dorothy also died the same year.

In the course of my term of office I was chosen to fill a vacancy on the Aldermanic Bench caused by the death of a Labour veteran, and I continued to serve in that office until 1927.

---

[1] The Whitley Councils were formed at the end of the First World War as a means of bringing representatives of labour and management together to discuss wages, conditions of work, and so on.—*Ed.*

Marriage and Parliament

IN THE summer of 1921 I began to feel the need of a
holiday and readily accepted the invitation of a college friend of my brother Tom—Edric Millar—to accompany him to Italy. I had visited Italy with him and a
party of relatives of both families in 1912 and looked forward to seeing more of that country, for, as I have stated,
I had in my Oxford days made a fairly close study of the
Renaissance and later read much of the Risorgimento.

A few weeks before we were to leave, Edric asked me if
I would mind if his mother and youngest sister accompanied us. I readily agreed, little knowing what effect on
my life this was to have. We had a very delightful visit,
mainly in Tuscany and Umbria, but extending to San Ma-
rino, Rimini, and Cadenabbia. As our tour proceeded it
seemed that I was more often the companion of Miss Vio-
let Millar than of the other members of the party. A week
or two after our return I asked Miss Millar to go to a football match with me. When the day came the ground was
too hard for football and we went to Richmond Park instead. During the afternoon I proposed and had the

good fortune to be accepted. Our families were well acquainted, but it will be realized that Socialists were not so generally accepted in those days as they are now, and I was just a street-corner agitator. I had thought it only fair that she should see me orating from a platform before I proposed, so that she might know the worst.

We arranged to be married in January, but the housing situation was very acute. My brother Laurence had recently married and settled at Woodford Green in Essex, and they found a semi-detached house near them which they thought would suit. We lost no time and secured it within three days. There was here a curious coincidence. When I joined the South Lancashire Regiment I shared a room with one Tom Naylor. Henceforward, wherever I went he seemed to precede me and be there to welcome me—at Suvla Bay, Prees Heath, and in France. Walking along the street to buy the wedding ring, whom should I meet but Tom. I told him we were going to live in Monkhams Avenue, Woodford, and I was hardly surprised when he said, "That's where I live." So, in January 1922, my fourteen years' residence in East London came to an end. Charlie Griffiths referred to my wife as "her what done me out of my job," but extended to her the same devoted friendship he had always shown to me.

Woodford Green was handy to East London, and I continued my activities in Limehouse though with somewhat less intensity. I also remained active in the Independent Labour party and in other Labour activities, and I worked a good deal with G. D. H. Cole and others on proposals for local government reform.

I was also one of a small "ginger group" in the Independent Labour party, the membership of which reads rather curiously today, for, in addition to myself, there were Fenner Brockway, who, after a long period in the political wilderness, rejoined the Labour party; Clifford Allen, who supported MacDonald's "National" Government in 1931; and John Beckett, who adhered to Sir Oswald Mosley, who founded the new party that later developed into the British Union of Fascists. We were a good deal influenced by the propaganda of G. D. H. Cole on Guild Socialism and were generally desirous of seeing a better and more Left-Wing programme adopted by the party. I recall negotiating at the Independent Labour Party Conference for the acceptance of some of our resolutions with a member of the Administrative Council, Emanuel Shinwell, whom I then met for the first time.

The autumn of 1922 saw the fall of the Lloyd George coalition and a General Election. In Limehouse the incumbent Member was Sir William Pearce, who had held the seat as a Liberal since 1906 and now stood with Conservative support. My campaign manager was John Beckett, whose later defection I have already referred to, then a keen young Socialist.

We conducted a vigorous campaign, holding meetings in every street, and I had not much doubt of the result. My wife acted as one of the tellers at the count, a duty she has performed at every General Election since then. In the result the figures were:

C. R. Attlee (Lab.)	9,688
Sir W. Pearce (Con. Lib.)	7,789
Majority	1,899

The Labour party was returned with 142 Members in the House of Commons. The first business was the selection of a sessional chairman. A meeting was called of the Independent Labour party at a hotel, where it was decided to do everything possible to secure the election of Ramsay MacDonald. In the result, on the proposal of Shinwell—who subsequently defeated him in the 1935 General Election—MacDonald was elected in preference to J. R. Clynes, who had been the Leader during the election campaign. Like others, I lived to regret that vote. This, however, was for the future.

MacDonald chose me to be one of his Parliamentary Private Secretaries. The other was Jack Lawson (now Lord Lawson), with whom I then began a friendship which has increased steadily throughout the years.

I made my maiden speech rather unexpectedly, in the debate on the Address on the King's Speech. I came into the Chamber after dinner and found that there had been a succession of speeches from the Clydesiders. The Speaker said that he must have a change. Charlie Ammon, our London Whip, asked me whether I would speak. I agreed and was told that I would be called next. My speech was mainly devoted to the problem of unemployment. The following passage sets out what I considered to be the socialist approach to the economic problem.

> Why was it that in the war we were able to find employment for everyone? It was simply that the government controlled the purchasing power of the nation. They said what things should be produced; they said, "We must have munitions of war. We must have

rifles; we must have machine-guns; we must have shells; we must have ammunition; we must have uniforms; we must have saddles." They took, by means of taxation and by methods of loan, control of the purchasing power of this nation, and directed that purchasing power into making those things that are necessary for winning the war. Today the distribution of purchasing power in the nation is enormously unequal. I recall a speech by the present Prime Minister in which he said that one of the greatest reforms in our national life would be a better distribution of wealth among the individuals composing this nation. I entirely agree with him. While the purchasing power of this nation is concentrated in the hands of a few, there will be production of luxuries and not of necessaries. It was found necessary during the war for the government to take hold of the purchasing power—which, after all, determines what goods shall be made—and deliberately to say that certain things were essential because we were at war, and that those things and no others should be made. They said to those who were running industry that their factories must be turned away from producing luxuries and must produce those sheer necessities. That is what we are demanding shall be done in time of peace. It is possible for the government, by methods of taxation and by other methods, to take hold of that purchasing power, and to say that, exactly as they told manufacturers and workers that they must turn out shells and munitions of all sorts to support the fighting men, so they must turn out houses and necessities for those who are making the country a country of peace.

It may not be without interest to recall that twenty-

seven years afterwards, in my General Election broadcast, I struck the same note when I said:

> . . . The Labour party believes that if you want
> certain results you must plan to secure them; that in
> peace as in war the public interest must come first,
> and that if in war, despite the diversion of most of
> our energies to making instruments of destruction,
> and despite the shortage of supply imposed by war
> conditions, we were able to provide food, clothing
> and employment for all our people, it is not impos-
> sible to do the same in peace, provided the govern-
> ment has the will and the power to act. . . .

I did not speak often in this session as the competition
from our Benches was intense and a Parliamentary Private Secretary is not expected to speak often. However,
I learned the ways of the House and made many friends
in all parties. I also got some experience working for
MacDonald.

Arising out of my work at the London School of Economics, I was asked by Messrs. George Bell & Sons to edit
a series of books to be entitled *The Social Service
Library*. This I did, and contributed an introductory volume on social service that was used as a textbook for some
time in our Social Science Department.

In February 1923 our first child, Janet, was born.

During this period I continued to devote a great deal
of attention to the problem of electricity supply, serving
as a member of the Stepney Borough Council Electricity
Committee and for some years as its chairman. In 1922, in
company with my wife, I attended the Conference of the

Institute of Municipal Electrical Authorities at Wolver-
hampton, which enabled me to make the acquaintance of
many people in the field of municipal electricity. In Stepney we had a very progressive and prosperous undertaking with a first-class engineer, W. C. P. Tapper, and I
took much interest in the developments. The undertaking was one of the most efficient in the country and supplied light and power at very low rates. It was the policy
to stimulate industrial use by offering exceptionally good
terms. As Stepney was a borough of small industries,
there had been built up a very big power load, and our
load factor was exceptionally good. We did not use the
profits of the undertaking to relieve the rates, but to
lower charges and to develop our plant. In particular,
we provided a system of free wiring and a generous system of hiring apparatus. It will be realized that in those
days there was no shortage of generating plant. The principal concern was to attract more custom.

Electricity undertakings at that time were owned either
by municipalities or by companies. In London the position was about equal between the two. It was, however,
recognized that the areas of supply, which had been de-
limited when the industry was in its infancy, were frequently too small and that there was a strong case for
larger authorities. The clash came over the question as to
whether electricity should progressively become a public
service or a private monopoly.

In the Greater London area the municipalities had got
together and formed the London and Home Counties organization of authorities owning electricity undertakings
in order to defend their interests against the companies.

The borough councils, irrespective of whether they were controlled by Labour or Conservative majorities, were united in upholding public ownership. In fact, they were good municipal socialists. Thus it was possible for Sir Duncan Watson, the Conservative representative of St. Marylebone, and I, the Socialist from Stepney, to work in complete harmony for many years.

The companies were very strong. One of their leaders, George Balfour, was in Parliament, while men like Sir Harry Renwick and Sir James Devonshire were able and redoubtable opponents. It is true that there were rivalries among them, but this was also true of the municipalities. Everyone hated the thought of amalgamation even though the technical reasons for it were overwhelming.

In the course of time, although I had very little technical knowledge, I acquired a good understanding of the problem, which stood me in good stead in the House of Commons. In the 1924 Parliament the Conservative government introduced a bill, the purpose of which was to coordinate main-line transmission and generation and to make possible joint action by smaller authorities. In fact, though not in strict terms, generation and main transmission were to be nationalized. I was put on the committee of the House to examine the bill. There were three Front Bench Labour men senior to me, but they did not know the subject and speedily dropped out, so that I became the leader of the Labour Opposition.

The position in committee was interesting. The Minister of Transport, Sir Wilfrid Ashley (afterwards Lord Ashley), was president of the Anti-Socialist Union, but found himself in charge of the socialistic measure. Actually, the

Attorney General, Sir Douglas Hogg (later Lord Hailsham), was the principal spokesman, while the Under Secretary, J. T. Moore-Brabazon (now Lord Brabazon), was far abler and more knowledgeable than his chief. There was a phalanx of Members, led by George Balfour, who were interested in companies, with a fringe of less intimately connected Members. Supporting the government were a number of Conservatives, some of whom subsequently attained ministerial rank, whose job was to give silent support to the government. We called these two groups the "undertakers" and the "mutes." The Labour Members formed about a quarter of the committee, and in the committee held the balance of power. We gave general support to the government but naturally used our influence to give increasing emphasis to the public interest. In course of time, the Ministers tended to wait for my approval or disapproval before accepting amendments. This was so marked that when we came to the report stage a Conservative objected to the undue deference shown to my views.

During that Parliament I had the pleasure of defeating two bills promoted by electricity companies with a view to acquiring territory at the expense of local authorities. This was due to the quite irrelevant fact that these companies were not employing a proper quota of ex-servicemen, and this brought a number of Conservatives to our side when voting took place. I also exerted myself successfully to get a Municipal Electricity Bill through. All this was in one week, and I had my first *Punch* picture, entitled "Major Ajax Attlee defies the Electricity Bills," wherein I am depicted in the guise of a Greek hero.

When the Electricity Bill had become law it was necessary to set up a Joint Electricity Authority for London and the Home Counties. The proportion of company, municipal, and other representatives was laid down in the statute, but it was for us to frame a plan for municipal representation. I drafted a scheme which was on the principle of representation on the basis of units sent out. My scheme, which involved getting neighbouring authorities to agree on a representative—no easy matter—was accepted and elections duly took place. I had expected the representation between Labour and Conservatives to be slightly in favour of the Conservatives, but actually Labour had a majority, since the Borough of Croydon and the Surrey County Council—both Conservative bodies—sent Labour men to represent them. During its period of life this Joint Authority did very good work in bringing together the smaller authorities in the London area.

In 1927, when I was appointed to the Indian Statutory Commission and had to go to India, I resigned from the Stepney Borough Council and ceased my connection with the electricity problem. It was not until nearly twenty years later that I took it up again, when Prime Minister. I then had the pleasure of seeing the whole industry brought under public ownership and control.

In the course of these years I served on the Joint Industrial Council of the electrical industry as a representative of the employers, and also had to deal, of course, with our own employees. The relations were sometimes strained and strike action was occasionally threatened. Invariably the first step taken by the men's leaders was to ask for the use of a room in the Labour Club on my premises for a strike meeting. The only really serious incident was that which arose out of the General Strike. Our employees threatened to cut off the supply if we continued to supply power to firms where the men were on strike. Rightly or wrongly, we decided to supply light and essential services only. The situation was very tense in East London at the time. It is easy to be wise after the event, but this was the action decided by the committee on which Labour was in a majority. Our Conservative colleagues acquiesced. The sequel was an action for damages brought against the Labour members of the council. This was heard in the courts a long time after the incident. We had thought that we were covered by the Public Authorities Protection Act. However, the jury, under Mr. Justice Avory, found against us on the ground of malice. This was an action by one firm, but, if successful, other actions would have been brought, with the result that I should have gone bankrupt and my political career would have been interrupted, if not terminated. However, we decided to appeal, and the case was heard while I was in India. The commission was just sitting down to dinner in our train outside Lahore when a telegram arrived telling me that our appeal had been unanimously allowed by the court.

Labour in Office

WHEN the House resumed in the autumn of 1923, Baldwin, rather unexpectedly, announced that he could not carry on unless he could introduce "protection," and he decided to appeal to the country on that issue. My opponent at this General Election was a Conservative, a local manufacturer called Miller Jones. He was a pleasant man but had not much platform ability. I recall a joint meeting of the unemployed addressed by both of us. He started by saying, "I know nothing of politics or economics." General uproar followed, and at last one man was heard to say, "Look 'ere now, guvnor, if a bloke came to you for a job and said he knew nothing abart it, what would you do?" His subsequent attempt to show that the hothouse flower he was wearing was a means of finding work for miners and bricklayers was equally unsuccessful. In the result the voting was:

C. R. Attlee (Lab.)	11,473
Miller Jones (Con.)	5,288
Majority	6,185

87

The new House contained 191 Labour Members, 155 Liberals, and 259 Conservatives. Baldwin decided to carry on until the New Year as there was uncertainty as to what line the Liberals would take. However, Asquith led the Liberals into the Opposition lobby in support of a Labour amendment to the Address. The government was beaten, and the King called upon MacDonald to form a government.

I do not think MacDonald had envisaged having to take office, and the party programme, except on foreign affairs, was very much a minority document. It gave no clear lead on priorities. The position of a minority government is always difficult. There were those in our ranks who thought we should have declined the responsibility. I am quite sure they were wrong. The electors at that time needed to see a Labour government in being, if they were to appreciate that Labour was now the alternative to a Conservative administration. Refusal on our part to accept responsibility might have given a new lease on life to the Liberal party.

One must recognize that MacDonald, who was without ministerial experience, was faced with a very difficult task. The prewar members of the party were, for the most part, old, while the new members were inexperienced. He might, I think, have been bolder in trying out some of the younger Members in positions of responsibility. As it was, with the exception of Sidney Webb, the only cabinet minister from among the new recruits was John Wheatley, who amply justified his selection, but a number of them were made under secretaries.

I became Under Secretary of State for War under Stephen Walsh, who, though he had no experience of military matters, was an excellent chief and very popular with the Army. Jack Lawson became Financial Secretary. I found that my particular sphere of work was the Territorial Army. When I attended at the War Office, the Permanent Secretary said, "I will introduce you to the director," and in came General Jeudwine, whom I had last met in France as the Commander of the 55th Division in which I had been a regimental officer. He was a first-class soldier and we got on very well. Indeed, Jack Lawson and I got on excellently with all the soldiers, and they frankly told us that it was pleasant to work with men who were keen on their jobs in contrast to our Conservative predecessors, who were, they said, idle fellows.

There was another amusing reversal of roles when we lunched one day at the Gunners' Mess at Woolwich. Jack Lawson had last entered it when doing duty as a mess waiter.

It was obvious that a government with no independent majority could not do anything very drastic in home affairs, though some useful measures were passed. Mac-Donald, who was Foreign Secretary as well as Prime Minister, made a considerable success at Geneva where the League of Nations had hitherto been rather neglected. The Geneva Protocol, in 1924, which strengthened the League for the prevention of aggression, was a real step forward, and it was, in my view, a misfortune that the Conservative government later refused to ratify it.

The precarious position of the Labour government was a source of some amusement to us. I used to ask, "Who is keeping us in this evening?" for at any moment a combination of Liberals and Tories could have thrown us out. The Labour government made earnest attempts to arrive at an agreement with the U.S.S.R., Lord Ponsonby, the Under Secretary of State for Foreign Affairs, showing great patience. The position was not made more easy by the activities of the British Communist party.

A breach with the Liberals came over the Campbell case, in which an ill-judged prosecution of J. R. Campbell, the editor of a Communist weekly, on a charge of attempting to seduce soldiers and sailors from their loyalty to the King, was withdrawn by the government. It was alleged that the prosecution was stopped for political reasons, and Asquith's motion for an inquiry was carried against the government. MacDonald sought, and obtained from the King, a dissolution.

In the General Election (1924) that followed, although the Labour party vote increased by over a million, we lost fifty seats, while the Liberals were reduced to a handful. During the election the *Daily Mail* produced a letter alleged to have been written by Zinoviev, the secretary of the Communist International, the implication of which was that the Labour party was much the same as the Communist party. The matter was badly handled by MacDonald, and the rights and wrongs of it have never been fully revealed. The effect was undoubtedly damaging to the Labour party, and the incident was passed down to history as the "Red Letter" case.

The electors of Limehouse, however, were not influenced by it. This time, I had, in addition to my old opponent Miller Jones, a Liberal in the person of Harry Marks, the local baker who had defeated me for the Lon-

don County Council in 1919, but I increased my vote.
The figures were:

C. R. Attlee (Lab.)	11,713
Miller Jones (Con.)	5,692
H. Marks (Lib.)	2,869
Majority	6,021

I now had to settle down to four and a half years of
Opposition. Three General Elections in successive years
had been rather a strain on my finances. I had given up
my position at the London School of Economics in 1922,
and had now to depend on my Parliamentary salary of
£400 a year, some casual earnings from writings, and
some private means.

In August 1925 a second daughter, Felicity, arrived.

I took my place on the Front Opposition Bench and was
also at this time appointed one of the temporary chairmen
of committees in the whole House and occupied the chair
from time to time.

The position of an ex-junior minister does not give one
much opportunity of speaking in the House, except when
the estimates of one's previous department are under consideration. I spoke regularly on the Army Estimates, but
had it not been that the government introduced two
measures on which I could speak with some authority, I
should have been rather a silent Member.

The first of these was Neville Chamberlain's Rating and
Valuation Bill. In committee upstairs, I assisted Josiah
Wedgwood in leading our side. I recall an amusing incident on the report stage. Josiah Wedgwood had, a few
weeks before, denounced the leaders of the Parliamentary

Labour party for being too ready to come to agreement with the government and had retired to the Back Benches to lead, as he said, the guerrilla forces. As a devout single-taxer, he had taken a great interest in this bill, especially in the derating of industrial hereditaments; hence he had agreed to come on the Front Bench again and lead the party. One evening I came back from dinner, went on the Front Bench, and said, "How goes it, Jos?" He said, "It's all right; there'll be no more votes. I have fixed everything up with the government." The other bill was Wilfrid Ashley's Electricity Bill, of which I have already written.

Meanwhile, the policy of the Baldwin government, especially the unwise return to the Gold Standard, created unemployment and industrial unrest, which culminated in the General Strike of 1926. The idea of the General Strike as a political weapon had been current in the Labour movement for many years, especially just before the First World War. To resort to extra-Parliamentary action was not an innovation by the Labour party. The Liberal passive resistance to the Balfour Education Act, and Conservative obstruction to the Lloyd George National Insurance Act, blazed a trail followed more dangerously by the suffragettes and by the Tories in the Home Rule controversy. The "holy horror" at the action of the trade unions was hypocritical. In my view, the attempt to use the industrial weapon in this way was bound to come. That it passed off with so little disturbance reflected immense credit on the British people. In the Labour movement there was a swing back to political action, which showed itself in the next General Election.

In the summer of 1927 MacDonald sent for me and told me that the government had decided to send out a commission to review the position in India and to make recommendations for constitutional developments, and asked me to be one of the two Labour members. The other was to have been Stephen Walsh, but owing to reasons of health he decided not to go, and my colleague was to be Vernon Hartshorn, the ablest of the South Wales miners in the House. I agreed to serve and set myself to learn all I could about India. Hitherto I had not taken any special interest in the problem, and my knowledge was only that of the ordinary educated man. Sir John Simon was appointed chairman, and the other members were Lord Burnham, Lord Strathcona, George Lane-Fox, and the Hon. Edward Cadogan. We had two able Secretaries in Sir Findlater Stewart and Sir Archibald Carter, and in India they were reinforced by Sir Joseph Bhore and Edward Perry of the Indian Civil Service. I also had the opportunity of talks with the Secretary of State for India, Lord Birkenhead, who showed me every kindness.

We paid a preliminary visit to India in the autumn of 1927. In Bombay, where we landed, no untoward incident occurred, though a bomb had been prepared for us. Its custodian, however, dropped it from the rack of a railway carriage with unfortunate results for himself. From Bombay we went to Delhi, but our principal purpose was to make a rather detailed study of district administration in two provinces—Madras and the Punjab.

It was unfortunate that the Congress party decided to boycott the Simon Commission. I think that it was a mistake not to have appointed simultaneously a committee

from the Indian legislature. We endeavoured to correct
this error by getting the Baldwin government to invite
the Indian legislature to appoint a committee to collaborate with us. This was done, but the Congress party would
not cooperate, with the result that we tended to hear
a great deal more of communal differences than might
otherwise have been the case.

In the autumn of 1928 the Simon Commission went out
to India again. Several of the members were to be accompanied by their wives, and my wife and I were keen that
she should share in this great experience. My son Martin
had been born in 1927, so that there were now three
young children to be looked after. However, we found
some friends who were ready to take on the task, and they
came to live in our house while we were away.

Our first visit had lasted three months. The second was
to be more extensive, for we were to visit every province,
including Burma, and sit to hear oral evidence. We did,
in fact, visit every province, though, owing to illness, I
was not able to go to the Central Provinces. We heard evidence in all the provincial capitals and visited areas
inhabited by backward people, such as the remoter parts
of Assam. No doubt our knowledge of this great sub-
continent was superficial, for we were only cold-weather
visitors, but it was extensive. Very few Europeans and,
for that matter, only a few Indians had studied conditions
in all parts of India. Very many people were authorities
only on their own provinces.

The commission worked hard, and were a very harmonious body. I made many friends among people of all

communities. I received much kindness and consideration from all the members of the commission, and especially from the chairman. My wife returned home in January 1929. As it turned out, this was fortunate, for, on arrival, she found our boy suffering from pneumonia. We had a most interesting visit to Burma and speedily arrived at the conclusion that its inclusion in the Indian Empire was a mistake.

On our return to England we found that Baldwin had decided to go to the country and that a General Election was in full swing. This time I had three opponents—the Hon. Evan Morgan (later Lord Tredegar); J. J. Addis, a young Liberal solicitor; and W. Tapsell, a Communist. The result, declared at the end of May 1929, was:

C. R. Attlee (Lab.)	13,872
Evan Morgan (Con.)	6,584
J. J. Addis (Lib.)	4,116
W. Tapsell (Com.)	245
Majority	7,288

This was the biggest vote that I had ever had, but my absolute majority was only 2,927.

The General Election gave Labour 287 seats, while the Conservatives had 260, the Liberals 59, and the Independents 9. Baldwin resigned and MacDonald again took office in a minority. MacDonald had assured Hartshorn and myself that membership of the Indian Statutory Commission would not in any way militate against our inclusion in the next Labour government should the next General Election result in Labour's taking office. However, neither of us was included, and it was characteristic of MacDonald that he did not take the trouble to inform us of his decision.

The Indian Commission had not yet reported, but it might be supposed that its members had acquired some useful information. MacDonald proposed to deal with the Indian question himself, but neither then nor subsequently did he give even five minutes to ascertain the views of his two emissaries.

The writing of the report took many months. The first volume, describing India and her problems, was mainly drafted by Sir John Simon and was a masterly survey. I contributed drafts for a number of chapters in the second volume, which gave the commission's conclusions, but both volumes were edited in detail by the whole commission. Our recommendations, although they represented a very great advance in constitutional progress, were condemned in India by the Congress party and did not satisfy Labour opinion. Actually they were realistic recommendations. A very great advance in self-government in the provinces was recommended, but it was pointed out that progress at the centre was difficult because of three outstanding difficulties.

First, there was the communal tension, particularly between the two major communities, the Moslems and the Hindus. It was customary at that time to suggest that communal differences were deliberately fomented by the British on the principle of *divide et impera*. This was quite untrue, as the sequel showed, for when this problem was handed over to the Indians in 1947 to settle for themselves they had to resort to partition.

Next, there was the position of the Indian states. India was an intricate mosaic of British provinces and Indian states to the rulers of which the British government was bound by treaties and sunnuds. The British had no right to hand the states over against their will to another power even if that power was Indian. They had the right to be maintained, and the British government had to have troops available in case of need. Our report envisaged getting over this difficulty on a federal basis, but until this was done it was not possible to concede dominion status to British India alone. Here again, the problem was ultimately settled by an Indian government.

Third, there was the position of the Armed Forces. At that time, the Armed Forces of India were composed of British troops and Indian units led for the most part by British officers, for the process of Indianizing the officer cadre was still at an early stage. There were few, if any, Indian officers who had even reached field rank. The Armed Forces had the double role of external defence and the maintenance of internal security. It was not possible to separate the forces for these two duties, and it would have been quite wrong and contrary to all precedent to place British troops at the disposal of a government not responsible to the House of Commons. The position was very different in 1947, when there were well-trained Indian senior officers available.

These dominant considerations were often ignored by those who thought our report insufficiently advanced. In fact, India was governed on the Simon Commission plan from 1935 onwards, and it was on our recommendation that Burma gained its freedom from India.

The writing of the report absorbed all my time, and during this period my activities in the House were confined to voting.

In 1929 the Labour government was caught in the economic blizzard that started in the United States. Admittedly, it was not easy for a minority government to take very drastic action. If MacDonald had been prepared to work with Lloyd George and the more progressive section of the Liberals, something might have been accomplished, but the two men did not get on together at all. MacDonald had appointed four Ministers—Thomas, Lansbury, Johnston, and Mosley—to be a special body to deal with unemployment, but whatever constructive proposals they may have made had no chance of acceptance against Snowden's pedantry (he was Chancellor of the Exchequer) and MacDonald's inability to take decisions.

In 1930 Mosley resigned his office of Chancellor of the Duchy of Lancaster and I was appointed in his place. At the same time, Hartshorn became Lord Privy Seal. The duties of the Chancellor in respect of his office are very light, though there is interesting work in administering the estates, which are scattered over England. I recall an effort made by the South Wales coal owners to get a reduction of their royalties in their own interests. I brought in Hartshorn, who, having a very complete knowledge of the subject, discomfited them. I was also interested in some of the antiquarian aspects of this old survival.

However, the Chancellor of the Duchy is used as a kind of maid-of-all-work, and my first task was to assist the Prime Minister in dealing with the Imperial Conference of 1930. This brought me into contact with Commonwealth problems. It was interesting to see how the Dominions, such as Canada and Australia, who gave no trouble on political matters were very difficult over economic questions, whereas South Africa and Eire were all sweetness in the latter field but very awkward on Commonwealth political relations. The principal result of the conference was the passing of the Statute of Westminster, which really gave statutory effect to what was already accepted in practice; namely, the equality of all the Dominions in the Commonwealth.

I had been fortunate to secure as my Parliamentary Private Secretary Mary Agnes Hamilton, the distinguished historian, novelist, and biographer, who had been returned as Member for Blackburn. During her all too brief career in the House she made a very marked impression and I benefited very much from her help.

I was directed to prepare a paper on some aspects of the economic situation, especially in connection with the re-equipment and redeployment of industry. With the help of my Private Secretary—the very distinguished statistician and economist, Colin Clark—I prepared and submitted what was, I think, within the terms of reference, a useful and constructive paper. It was circulated to the cabinet, but, as was not uncommon in the MacDonald government, never reached the stage of being discussed.

I also sat on the Prime Minister's Economic Advisory Committee, where I was brought into contact with J. M. Keynes and Ernest Bevin. There were interesting discussions but nothing constructive ever emerged.

Hartshorn and I, like many others in the party, were disturbed at the failure of the government to take any drastic steps to deal with unemployment. Several times the cabinet asked us to wind up debates on unemployment, but we both replied that until we saw signs of a more vigorous policy we would not speak.

However, my next employment proved more fruitful. Dr. Addison (he had not yet been given a peerage despite his having held high office in the government of Lloyd George both during and after the First World War) had accepted the minor post of Under Secretary in the Board of Agriculture, and in 1930 he succeeded Lord Noel-Buxton as Minister. He proceeded to act with great energy and skill. Brought up on a farm, he had a good practical knowledge of agriculture, and had for some years been helping in the preparation of Labour's agricultural policy. He took up at once the marketing problem. As the Under Secretary, Lord De La Warr, was in the House of Lords, he needed a helper in the Commons, and I was detailed for the job.

Addison was a remarkable administrator and a most skilful pilot of bills through the House. He managed to get the whole of his department enthusiastically behind him. Among the officials, Sir Arthur Street was outstanding, and it was in connection with Addison's agricultural policy that he first became prominent. I helped in the preparation of the marketing and other bills and served on the Parliamentary committees that considered them. Here again, Addison showed his skill. Not only did he make the Labour members into an effective team, but actually converted the Opposition. As one of them said to me one day, "How can we oppose this man? He's so decent." In his fight for getting through his policy, not

least of the obstacles to be overcome was the inertia of
MacDonald and the negative attitude of Snowden. A
great success was achieved, for the Agricultural Marketing Act proved to be the real foundation of the recovery
of the countryside, which was later to be effected by R. S.
Hudson and Tom Williams.

In 1931 the carrying of an amendment in the House of
Commons to an Education Bill led to the retirement of
Sir Charles Trevelyan as president of the Board of Education. H. B. Lees-Smith took his place, and I in turn replaced Lees-Smith as Postmaster General. I found the
work of the department, which is really a collection of
varied business enterprises, fascinating. The Secretary
of the Post Office was Sir Evelyn Murray, a very able man
who had held his position since 1914 and had become
something of an autocrat. I remember that Baldwin con-
gratulated me on my appointment, saying, "You'll find
your real difficulty will be Murray." I did indeed have
some trouble at first, but after some plain speaking we
got on very well.

At this time I was fortunate in being offered the services, as a voluntary Secretary, of a young Oxford man,
John Dugdale—now a Member of Parliament and a Privy
Councillor. For the next nine years he gave me most un-
selfish and devoted service. With his help I inaugurated a
number of reforms.

Public relations had hitherto been rather neglected,
but it seemed to me essential to gain the utmost goodwill
of the users of the service and to get proper publicity. To
this end I formed a Publicity Committee. On their advice
I set up a Public Relations Service and was fortunate in

obtaining the services of Sir Stephen Tallents, who had done fine work at the Empire Marketing Board.

I sought the advice of some able businessmen, notably Sir F. W. Goodenough, who was very prominent in the gas industry, and Sir William Crawford, a leading advertising expert. I was sure that there were useful things to be learned from businessmen which could be applied to the Post Office. I found them most ready to help me.

I started advertising the Post Office in the newspapers, and have never forgotten the frank assurance given to me in public by a newspaper magnate to the effect that there was a very close link between the advertising and editorial management of his newspapers and that anything given to the first had an immediate effect on the second. I found that he was quite right: a small expenditure yielding good results.

In connection with the government's efforts to provide work, I was asked to do everything possible to develop the use of the telephone, not a very easy task considering the industrial depression. The methods in vogue for getting business were very old-fashioned. I called in a very able business expert, Harold Whitehead, who submitted to me an admirable report on the day before I left office. His recommendations, like other reforms initiated in my time, were adopted and fully implemented by Sir Kingsley Wood, who generously acknowledged his predecessor's work.

I also examined the constitution of the Post Office with a view to correcting the overcentralization that resulted from Murray's autocratic rule. My plan was the formation of a functional council of officials under the chairmanship of the Postmaster General to deal with policy matters. It was adopted in substance by the Bridgeman Committee, before whom I gave evidence, and proved a desirable reform. The report by the committee on its inquiry into the Post Office was issued in 1932.

There is a great amount of detailed work at the Post Office in connection with staff matters and personal claims. I had an admirable Under Secretary in Sam Viant, who had long trade-union experience. Every new Postmaster General receives old claims that have been turned down by his predecessors but are hopefully put forward again. I recall one pension claim in which I had to reply that I could not dissent from the decision given by my predecessor, the Duke of Norfolk, who ruled at the Post Office in Queen Victoria's reign.

Opposition

WE NOW had four children and required more room, so we moved from Woodford to Stanmore in Middlesex. We were also nearer to my wife's family there. This proved to be a fortunate move, for at the end of 1931 my wife was seriously ill with sleeping sickness, which caused her to lose control of her movements. Anyone of less determination might well have become a permanent invalid, but she set herself to regain control, and this she achieved after a year or two. She was able to start by playing tennis on our court at Stanmore, and this was a big factor in her recovery.

Throughout the year 1931 the economic crisis continued to grow in intensity, and the figures of unemployment continued to mount. It was, of course, easy for the Opposition to put it all down to the Labour government. MacDonald had no constructive ideas, while, at the Treasury, Philip Snowden had fallen completely under the spell of orthodox finance and the influence of Montagu Norman, Governor of the Bank of England. He

clung obstinately to the Gold Standard while retaining a
fanatical devotion to free trade.

The Parliamentary Labour party was increasingly res-
tive. The I.L.P. had become more and more irresponsible
under the leadership of Jimmy Maxton. With many
others, I found it necessary to part company with this
organization. This was a matter of very great regret, for
I had spent my political life in its ranks. It was, I think,
a great loss to the Labour movement when the I.L.P.
broke away, The I.L.P. became more and more a narrow
sect rather than a broadly based political party, and its
influence steadily declined. It may be that the super-
session of the I.L.P. branch by the local Labour party was
inevitable, but much fine enthusiasm ran to waste.

Yet another group in the Labour party was forming
round the personality of Sir Oswald Mosley. This was at
first not much more than a "ginger group" that attracted
such young men as Aneurin Bevan, John Strachey, and
John Beckett, but the fact that it depended mainly on the
personality of its leader, who had considerable dynamic
force, brought it into line with the fascist ideas prevalent
on the Continent. Genuine Socialists left him, while he
and the residue became the British Union of Fascists.

But discontent in the party was not confined to these
two sections. Many members of the government, of whom
I was one, were seriously disturbed at the lack of constructive policy displayed by the leaders of the government. We were also conscious of a growing estrangement
between MacDonald and the rest of the party. He was
increasingly mixing only with people who did not share

the Labour outlook. This opposition, however, did not crystallize because the one man who could have taken MacDonald's place, Arthur Henderson, was too loyal to lend himself to any action against his leader. Instead of deciding on a policy and standing or falling by it, MacDonald and Snowden persuaded the cabinet to agree to the appointment of an Economy Committee, under the chairmanship of Sir George May of the Prudential Insurance Company, with a majority of opponents of Labour on it. The result might have been anticipated. The proposals were directed to cutting the social services, particularly the unemployment benefit. Their remedy for an economic crisis, one of the chief features of which was excess of commodities over effective demand, was to cut down the purchasing power of the masses. The majority of the government refused to accept the cuts, and it was on this issue that the government broke up. Instead of resigning, MacDonald accepted a commission from the King to form a so-called "National" government.

Matters came to a head in August while I was on holiday with my wife and family at the seaside. I was summoned to Downing Street, where were assembled all the members of the government outside the cabinet. MacDonald informed us that the Labour government was at an end and that he, with Philip Snowden, J. H. Thomas, and Lord Sankey,[1] were going into a coalition government of which he was to be the head. He said that this was only a temporary measure, that he did not wish any of us to join, and that there would certainly not be a

---

[1] Snowden was Chancellor of the Exchequer; Thomas, Secretary of State for Dominion Affairs; Sankey, Lord Chancellor.—*Ed.*

"coupon" General Election. He would soon be back with us, he said. These remarks were received with scepticism by those who knew him best. Having already distributed the offices in the new government, he would have been embarrassed if any Labour ministers had wished to join, though this did not prevent him in the future from denouncing them for deserting him. Probably he had counted on more Members following his lead than the handful who did so. No local Labour party supported him.

It is appropriate here to say a word about MacDonald. In the old days I had looked up to him as a great leader. He had a fine presence and great oratorical power. The unpopular line he took during the First World War seemed to mark him as a man of character. Despite his mishandling of the Red Letter episode, I did not appreciate his defects until he took office a second time. I then realized his reluctance to take positive action and noted with dismay his increasing vanity and snobbery, while his habit of telling me, a junior minister, the poor opinion he had of all his cabinet colleagues, made an unpleasant impression. I did not, however, expect that he would perpetrate the greatest betrayal in British political history. I realized that Snowden had become a docile disciple of orthodox finance, but I did not think him capable of such virulent hatred of those who had served him loyally. The shock to the party was very great, especially to the loyal workers of the rank and file who had made great sacrifices for these men.

When the House met again the Gold Standard, to preserve which such great sacrifices had been demanded, had been abandoned, and MacDonald announced his intention of holding a General Election. The Labour party met at Scarborough for its Annual Conference, but I remained in London to make the final speech of that Parliament.

In the General Election of 1931 the Labour party sustained the most crushing defeat in its history. Instead of the 287 Members returned in 1929, the Labour party was reduced to 46, while five members of the Independent Labour party were returned. Arthur Henderson and all the ex-cabinet Ministers, except George Lansbury, were defeated. I had not anticipated that our defeat would be so severe, as, in Limehouse, my supporters stood solidly behind me. This was surprising in view of the fact that Catholic electors were being asked to vote against all Labour Members who had opposed an amendment to the Education Bill, moved by John Scurr of Mile End, which was strongly supported by the Catholics. I remember returning on polling day and seeing some early returns showing that the Labour candidate had been defeated in the stronghold of St. Helens, so that on going to the count in my own constituency next day I was very doubtful as to the result. I was, however, one of the fortunate few to survive. The figures were:

C. R. Attlee (Lab.)	11,354
R. Girouard (Con.)	10,803
H. L. Hodge (Mosleyite)	307
Majority	551

The campaign of the Coalition government in the 1931 General Election was the most unscrupulous in my recol-

lection: our erstwhile leaders vied with Liberals and
Tories in misrepresentation. MacDonald distinguished
himself by flourishing worthless German notes and suggesting that Britain would experience what had happened in Germany; while Snowden, who knew the truth,
supported the lying story that the Labour government had
improperly used the money in the Post Office Savings Bank
to maintain the unemployment fund. Numbers of people
were taken in, particularly those who had in the past
looked to MacDonald and Snowden as the foremost leaders
of socialism.

On going to the first Parliamentary Labour party meeting after the election I had a message from Arthur Henderson that George Lansbury would be proposed as
Leader and myself as Deputy. These nominations went
through without opposition. At this time we faced a very
heavy task. Three of our most experienced leaders had
deserted to the enemy. Almost all our other leaders had
fallen in the disastrous landslide, and there remained
only forty-six men to carry the full burden of opposition.
Naturally, among the survivors were the older members
—holders of safe seats in the mining areas—who were not
accustomed to speak frequently in the House and could
not contribute much beyond their votes. The whole work
of debate in the House and in committee had to be sustained by scarcely more than thirty men. There was no
one left who had had the responsibility of planning and
arranging the fight in opposition, for George Lansbury
had always tended toward individual action and was
somewhat of a free-lance. Stafford Cripps had been less
than a year in the House, while the rest of the Front

Bench was composed of members who had held only junior positions in government and had not been prominent in the counsels of the party.

The Labour movement, therefore, owes an immense debt of gratitude to Lansbury for the way in which he tackled a task that was not particularly congenial. He was by nature an evangelist rather than a Parliamentary tactician. Yet during those years in which he led the small party in the House he showed great skill and powers of everyday leadership. A leading Conservative once replied to a Labour Member who said that he thought George Lansbury was one of the best men he had ever known—"The best! Is that all? He's the ablest Opposition Leader that I have ever known." It was, of course, a great source of strength to him that he commanded the personal affection of his followers. He had also a wise tolerance—an attribute that is not so common in the enthusiast.

Stafford Cripps had entered the House as Solicitor General and had displayed immediately his great Parliamentary gifts in helping to pilot through the House the land clauses of Snowden's Budget. Many great lawyers have failed to adapt themselves to the House of Commons, but from the start Cripps showed that he was the exception. He brought to our ranks wide knowledge, fine debating powers, and a first-class mind. His only weakness was a lack of practical acquaintance with the movement. He was not always a good judge of men, nor had he very much experience with which to temper his enthusiasm. For a time, however, he was very content to follow Lansbury's lead. It was not until the Second World War that he arrived at a balanced political judgment.

The other members of the Front Bench put in a great deal of hard work. Most of them previously had contented themselves with dealing with subjects on which they had special knowledge, but now they had to extend their range to less familiar ground, for the Labour point of view had to be stated on all matters coming before the House. Among others, Tom Williams, who had not previously held office, devoted himself to the subject of agriculture with such good effect that he was recognized on all sides as speaking with real authority. The hard work of those years bore fruit when later he was an outstanding success as Minister of Agriculture and Fisheries in the 1945 Labour government.

Lansbury invited Cripps and me to share with him the Leader of the Opposition's Room at the House, and the three of us worked together in great harmony. One of us was always present on the Front Bench throughout the sittings.

The work of Opposition fell heavily on the Back Benchers as well as on the leaders. Men like Joe Batey, Joe Tinker, and Gordon MacDonald could always be relied upon to take their share in any debate that was going forward. Aneurin Bevan made a series of brilliant speeches on the problem of the depressed areas and on the unemployment regulations. The I.L.P. members, under the leadership of Jim Maxton, were often helpful in sustaining the fight.

Arthur Greenwood, both before and after his return to the House, was in charge of the Labour Party Research Department. It was sometimes thought that there was an elaborate organization for supplying us with briefs, but, in fact, we mostly depended on our own resources. It is not much use speaking on a subject merely from a brief; it is necessary to have the background information.

The years from 1931 to 1935 were very busy ones for me. I usually left home at nine o'clock in the morning and seldom got back until after midnight. I had to deal with many subjects that formerly I had not studied with any close attention—for instance, foreign affairs and finance. I often had to speak three or four times a week. In 1932 I filled more columns of *Hansard* than any other Member, and, as I am generally considered to be rather a laconic speaker, it can be judged that my interventions in debate were numerous. These years were a very useful training. I acquired a complete knowledge of House of Commons procedure and a fairly good acquaintance with many subjects. Compared with my previous nine years in the House, they were like the Western Front in the First World War contrasted with the South African War.

I recall an amusing incident when a careless Minister left his brief, containing many Tory amendments to a bill, lying about. It was brought to Cripps. On every point, before the Minister spoke, Cripps gave the government reply. The Minister could only get up and agree with this extraordinary man who knew all the answers.

Another amusing incident of those days comes to my mind. I and some of my colleagues were the guests at dinner of American Ambassador Robert W. Bingham. He was a keen sportsman and asked whether any of us had ever done any big-game shooting, not a likely recreation for Labour Members. I said, "Yes," and when he asked, "What were you shooting?" I said, "Germans."

During this Parliament we were joined by some of our former colleagues who had been returned at by-elections, notably Arthur Greenwood and Arthur Henderson, but Henderson was in bad health and devoted the short remainder of his life to the Disarmament Conference, of which he was chairman. There had been several occasions when he might have become Leader of the party, but until 1931 he had loyally supported MacDonald. Seldom has such loyalty been so ill requited.

In 1934 Lansbury had an accident and was in hospital for many months, during which time I led the party. I had my first experience of making one of those formal speeches on the death of some distinguished person which I always rather dread. The occasion was the death of the King of the Belgians. I remember that Austen Chamberlain, with typical generosity, sent me a note of congratulation after the ordeal.

The party in the House put up a strong fight against the reactionary measures of the MacDonald government, but without success. Labour opposition to the proposed regulations for unemployment assistance, however, forced their withdrawal and the transfer of the Minister to another post.

I took part in the proceedings of the Joint Select Committee on the Indian Constitution and, with my Labour colleagues, presented a minority report. I also took part in the debates on the Government of India Bill, when we frequently had to support the government against Churchill and the "diehards." In 1935, on the occasion of King George V's Jubilee, I was made a Privy Councillor. I was surprised and gratified by the large number of letters of congratulation that I received from Members of all parties.

Meanwhile, the Labour party had to face the growing international tension caused by the emergence of aggression—first in the Far East and then in Abyssinia. There was also the growing strength of Hitler in Germany. The party, under the guidance of Henderson, had adopted the policy of strong support for the League of Nations, but there was in our ranks a strong pacifist section led by George Lansbury. When the government embarked on rearmament, this division in our ranks became more apparent. The party was prepared to rearm provided that it was in support of a genuine League policy.

With Sir John (later Lord) Simon at the Foreign Office, we had every reason to distrust the government. His attitude on the Japanese action in China showed his readiness to acquiesce in aggression and his lack of support for the principles of the League of Nations. Furthermore, we knew that many Conservatives looked upon fascism as a useful offset to communism. The party had no illusion as to the nature of communism and had resisted every attempt made by its adherents to infiltrate. At this time Cripps was inclined to believe it was possible for the Labour party to work with the Communists in a "united front" against reaction, but the trade unions were resolute in resisting any such alliance. I believed in the party policy and therefore disagreed with both my closest Parliamentary colleagues.

The crisis came over the question of the application of sanctions against Mussolini for invading Abyssinia. After a very full discussion at the Annual Party Conference at Brighton in October 1935, the pacifists were overwhelmingly defeated. A few days later Lansbury resigned the leadership. This was a grief to all of us, for we had a great admiration and affection for him, but he was right in thinking that his position had become impossible. .

I was elected Leader in his place. Cripps took a course of his own. He had conceived a very unrealistic idea that fascism and the drift to war could be countered by industrial action. This was due partly to a well-merited distrust of the government's professions of loyalty to the League of Nations and partly to his inexperience of the Labour movement, but also to reliance on the advice of irresponsible people.

The government saw in Labour's disunity a good opportunity for an appeal to the country. There was also a desire, I think, to cash in on the sentiment aroused by the Jubilee, which was thought to favour the Conservative party. Baldwin, who had for the last few years enjoyed power without the responsibility of being Prime Minister, now displaced MacDonald, whose powers had been failing for some time. His eyesight, too, had been affected. We were caught at a disadvantage, not only because of the disunity in our ranks, but also because the government went to the country on a programme of full support for the League of Nations. Our distrust of the government proved to be well founded, but the majority of the electors were deceived. The loss of two such outstanding personalities as Lansbury and Cripps was serious. The result was that though we increased our vote by two million and nearly got back to the 1929 figure, we won only 154 seats. We did, indeed, get back to the House many of our prominent leaders.

During the campaign I spent most of my time touring the country, but, despite this, my vote at Limehouse was the highest I had ever had. I had only a Conservative opponent and the result was:

C. R. Attlee (Lab.)	14,600
J. Busby (Con.)	7,355
Majority	7,245

When I was elected to lead the party in the House after George Lansbury's resignation a writer in the *Daily Mail* said, "I don't think he will hold it long." This was not an unreasonable supposition, for the General Election brought back to the House a number of Labour Members who had held cabinet office—among them, the veteran J. R. Clynes, Herbert Morrison, A. V. Alexander (now Lord Alexander), and Tom Johnston. Clynes decided not to stand for the leadership. I did not take any steps in the matter but found that I had been nominated, together with Morrison and Greenwood. The first ballot was indecisive. I had 58 votes to 44 for Morrison and 32 for Greenwood. On the second ballot I was elected by 88 votes to 44. I have been re-elected ever since without a contest.

During the previous Parliament, Labour had won a great victory on the London County Council. Morrison was leading it with great ability and thought it wiser to continue to devote himself to his work there rather than stand for Deputy Leader. Arthur Greenwood was therefore elected unanimously to that position, and he gave me loyal support and good counsel in the years to come. Lord Snell, who had succeeded Lord Ponsonby as the Leader of the Labour group in the House of Lords, led his little band with great distinction.

I appointed a Lancashire miner, Guy Rowson, as my Parliamentary Private Secretary, but his early death cut short a promising career. His successor, a Welsh miner, Arthur Jenkins, served me ably and devotedly until in the closing stages of the war government he became Under Secretary of State at the Ministry of Town and Country Planning. The work of a Leader of the Opposition is extremely heavy. In those days there was a party meeting at least once a week, while the executive committee met for an hour every day before Question Time to settle plans for the day. We had a very able Secretary in Scott Lindsay, who had been with the party since 1906. His long experience and skill in drafting amendments and motions were of great help.

Family expenses were increasing, and it was a relief to me when, in 1937, the Ministers of the Crown Act, which remedied many anomalies in the remuneration of Ministers, provided for a salary of £2,000 a year for the Leader of the Opposition. This provision often surprises foreigners, who think it strange that money should be paid to someone in order that he may effectively oppose the government of the day, but it is actually a recognition of the fact that Parliamentary government depends on having an effective Opposition and that the choice of Leader should not be restricted owing to financial considerations. Provision was also made for a pension for ex-prime ministers. This was, I think, a desirable step, for in these days

a prime minister may have little or no private means, and
it is not easy for anyone who has held the post of First Minister of the Crown to take up other work. There was also
established a fund for the payment of small pensions to
former Members of Parliament and their widows who are
in need. The provision is inadequate but has done something to remedy a very deplorable state of affairs. I have
known Members of long standing in the House who were
clearly nearing the end of their lives and unable to do
their work but could not retire for lack of means.

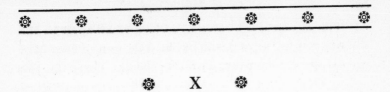

Eventful Years

IN JANUARY 1936 King George V died. I had met him only on a few occasions, when I was a minister and when I was appointed to the Simon Commission, but I had a high regard for him. I admired his steadfast devotion to duty and the example he had set to the nation. I endeavoured to express this in the speech I made on behalf of the Opposition in the House of Commons. After pointing out the great change that had come about during his reign, I said:

> Even without a world war, those years, I think, must have been years of stress. The advance of science, the spread of education, the progress of ideas of self-government at home and overseas, the pressure of economic forces must have called for difficult readjustments. The world war came and accelerated all these developments. It was a forcing house of change. The old world passed away and a new one was born.
>
> Two things, I think, were required of the Sovereign of a great state in those conditions. The first was sympathy with new ideas and readiness to accept change and to adapt himself to altered conditions.

The second was to give to society, bewildered by the rapid progress of events, a rallying point of stability. These things were found in King George in full measure. They are not common. History affords many examples of rulers who failed, of thrones which were overturned because their occupants stubbornly set themselves against the march of events. King George succeeded where others failed because he was a democrat. He was a supreme exponent of the difficult art of constitutional kingship. He knew and understood his people and the age in which they lived, and progressed with them. Let me note some outstanding examples. The right to vote has been given to practically every man and woman of full age. The franchise now depends on citizenship and not on the ownership of property. The power of the Upper House has been diminished. Such a change elsewhere and at other times has been resisted by monarchs. King George accepted it as a necessary and just consequence of modern conditions. In the same spirit he accepted the achievement of office by a new party, the members of which were predominantly drawn from the manual workers, an event almost unthinkable a few decades ago. He agreed to a series of acts whereby the Dominions attained equality with the mother country. The Irish Free State was created and India was set on the road to self-government. He relinquished his nominal sovereignty, or rather he allowed his nominal sovereignty to be apparently diminished, but by doing so he established his real sovereignty in the hearts of the peoples of the Empire. It is the glory of our Constitution that, under it, great changes effected elsewhere by violence are brought about peaceably owing to its adaptability. All this requires that this same quality should be displayed by the King, and this King George did.

Equally important, I think, has been the power of the King to offer a point of stability in a distracted world. The movements of mass hysteria which have been witnessed elsewhere have passed his country by. One reason has been the presence of a king who commanded the respect and affection of his people and who was beyond the spirit of faction. There was no need to elevate some individual party leader into a national hero, because the King was there to express the views of his people.

King George throughout the long years of the war took his full part in the national effort. His example inspired his people in the struggle. But he was no glorifier of war. He stood always for peace. He sought as soon as the war ended to do his utmost to heal its wounds and re-create good relations between nations. No less in the difficult postwar years he shared in the work of reconstruction. He was a real social reformer and took the keenest personal interest in the problems of the day. He recognized the claims of social justice and felt equally the tragedy of unemployment. He shared to the full the life of his people.

What were the qualities which enabled the late King to succeed where others failed? It seems to me they were his selflessness and devotion to duty, his kindliness and humanity, his practical wisdom and his courage at all times. The ceremonies which we have witnessed during the last few days carry us back to a time when the functions of a king were very different. The duties of kingship have had to be reinterpreted with the passing years. King George showed an incomparable understanding of what is required of a king in the modern world. It has been a great piece of good fortune, I think, for our geneation that, just when scientific invention has enabled, for the first time, so many citizens of the British Commonwealth to hear for themselves the voice of their King, we should have had on the throne a man who so well understood how to speak to his people, a man who set before the nation ideals of peace, justice and service. We have seen the end of a noble life, a life devoted to the welfare of humanity. In the long roll of British Sovereigns none will, I think, take a higher place than King George.

I always feel anxious when making speeches of this kind. It is so easy to sound a false note, but on this occasion the speech was well received. My wife and I attended the funeral in St. George's Chapel, Windsor. We little thought that only sixteen years later we should be there again to pay our last respects to King George VI.

As a Privy Councillor, I attended the meeting of the Accession Council in St. James's Palace. There was a characteristically British incident on that occasion. Notice was given to us suggesting—but only suggesting—that the royal dukes should sign the roll first. I thought that King Edward looked very nervous and ill at ease. I remember that Baldwin expressed to me his anxiety for the future and his doubts as to whether the new King would stay the course. I had met him on several occasions when he had been most charming, and I was struck by his genuine solicitude for the unemployed. I do not think I saw him more than once or twice during his short reign. I was not a reader of the American press, nor was I much interested in society gossip, so that it was not until a late stage that I became aware of the position that had arisen with regard to Mrs. Simpson. I went to Baldwin and asked him for information. Later, as the crisis developed, he invited me to tell him what I thought would be the Labour attitude to the various proposals that were being made, in particular that of a morganatic marriage.

The talk was confidential, so that I could not consult the party or even my intimate colleagues. I had to give him what, in my judgment, would be the reactions of the party. I said that while Labour people had no objection at all to an American's becoming queen, I was certain that they would not approve of Mrs. Simpson for that position and would object to a morganatic marriage. I told him that it was important not to think that London was typical of the country as a whole and that opinion in the Commonwealth was likely to coincide with that of the provinces rather than of the metropolis. I found that I had correctly gauged the party attitude. Despite the sympathy felt for King Edward and the affection his visits to the depressed areas had created, the party—with the exception of a few of the intelligentsia who can be trusted to take the wrong view on any subject—were in agreement with the views I had expressed.

I suppose that few prime ministers had a more difficult task than that which faced Baldwin, and, in my view, Britain owed him a debt of gratitude for the way in which he handled it. In the country there was much criticism of the way of life which had obtained in the royal circle, and this found expression during the discussions in the Civil List Committee on which I served. The Labour members suggested that there was room for simplification at Court and for changes in accordance with modern conceptions. I explained the views of the party in a debate on the committee's report. It happened that I was dining the next evening at Buckingham Palace. This might have been embarrassing, but I found not only that what I had said met with no resentment, but a complete understanding of the point of view expressed.

The whole business of the abdication was very unfortunate and undoubtedly affected for the time the prestige of the monarchy, but in the event it was fortunate, for it enabled King George VI and Queen Elizabeth to raise it to a greater height than ever before and gave the country, in the testing time to come, the leadership it needed.

During this period I did a good deal of writing. Besides occasional articles in the *Daily Herald* I wrote fairly regularly for *Paris-Soir* and also for an agency run by a friend, Paul Reves, which supplied syndicated articles to a number of foreign newspapers.

In 1937 I undertook a more considerable task. The very enterprising publisher Victor Gollancz had established the Left Book Club, with a very considerable membership. Most of the publications supplied to subscribers were what we should now call "fellow travelling" in outlook, and I welcomed the opportunity, at his suggestion, of writing a book that would try to set out the general position of the Labour party. I therefore wrote *The Labour Party in Perspective*. My intention was, as I stated in the Introduction, "to show the Labour party in its historical setting as an expression in place and time of the urge for socialism, to show it as a characteristic example of British methods and as an outcome of British political instincts, and to consider its future in the light of present-day conditions." The book had a considerable sale and has been translated into French, Spanish, Dutch, Japanese, and some other languages. In considering the future, I set out the programme I thought a Labour government in power should carry out. In 1945 I had the pleasure of seeing that programme implemented. I recall an occasion when we were in office. A Lobby journalist was asked how he always seemed to be able to anticipate the next move of the government. He replied, "I read *The Labour Party in Perspective.*" A new edition, with a foreword by Francis Williams dealing with the history of the party since 1937, was published in 1949.

I also had published a volume of my speeches, edited by John Dugdale.

I recall many interesting and dramatic scenes in the period leading up to the Second World War. There was the resignation of J. H. Thomas after the inquiry into the Budget leakage. We of the Labour party had never forgiven him for the part he played with Ramsay Mac-Donald in 1931, but we admired the dignity with which he met this disaster and could not withhold our pity for such an end to his career.

There was the gradual decline of MacDonald. His speeches became increasingly incoherent, and for the last years of his life he was only a melancholy passenger in the Conservative ship.

One of the most exciting debates was that on the new Prayer Book, which divided parties and revealed a great deal of latent Protestantism in unexpected places. Two dull speakers, Sir William Joynson-Hicks and Sir Thomas Inskip (later Lord Caldecote), rose to unaccustomed heights, while the brilliant Lord Hugh Cecil was for once a failure.

Foreign Visits

BEFORE the 1930s I had had little or no contact with foreign Socialists except for hearing prominent leaders speak at meetings and conferences, but I now began to take part in international gatherings. In May 1932 I attended a conference in Zurich in company with Joseph Compton and George Lathan. I met and talked with Renaudel and other French leaders, and for the last time saw the German Social Democratic party in its full strength. We did not realize then how soon it was to be destroyed by Hitler. I found Breitscheid and Tony Sandler very interesting and pleasant, but I felt, as always with the German Socialists, that they were strong on theory but weak in action.

Thenceforward I visited the Continent once or twice every year. In 1933 I was a delegate to an International Conference of League of Nations Socialists at Montreux. The leader of the British delegation was Lord Cecil. The Germans were represented by some very tough-looking Nazis, the first of the breed I had seen. They looked, and probably felt, out of place, but Germany was still in the League of Nations at that time.

In June 1934 I went with Walter Smith and William Gillies to a Workers' International sports gathering at Prague. I travelled by air in a small and somewhat unstable plane, and for the first and only time was very sick in the air. I came down at Leipzig and had to wait some hours before proceeding by train. It was not a pleasant time to be there. It was only a few days after the big purge in which Röhm and Schleicher were killed, and the whole town was very nervous.

We had a very good time with the Czechs. I admired their free democratic spirit and made many lasting friendships. Members of our team did quite well in the bicycle races and at table tennis, but undoubtedly the highlight of the meeting was the display of physical drill in the great stadium by the Socialist Gymnastic Societies. The women, many of them quite middle-aged, were very impressive. Dressed in white with red berets, they performed in perfect time. The whole parade was in charge of a stocky little man who had been a corporal in the Buffs in the war. In the evening there was a great torchlight procession through the streets of Prague. While we marched we frequently shouted in chorus, *"Ha ha Rudhe Praha Nasdar,"* which meant, "Greetings to Red Prague."

I went up to the castle, noting the windows that had been the scene of the famous Defenestration that had started the Thirty Years' War, and had a talk with President Beneš. Talks with him were apt to become monologues in which he expounded with great fluency his policy and his view on events. He always seemed to me to be too optimistic and too ready to think that his diplomatic skill would get his country through all the dangers that faced it, but he was a good democrat and a good European. I never quite understood the position of his small party. The Social Democrats had a number of fine men, and he would, I think, have been wiser to have put more trust in them. Alas, most of them were subsequently murdered by the Nazis.

In the same year, 1934, I was invited by K. Zilliacus, who was doing very good work as an official of the League of Nations, to give a lecture at the Geneva Institute of International Relations in a series called "Problems of Peace." I spoke on the socialist view of peace and set out the policy of the Labour party, especially the need for giving power and authority to the League by the establishment of an international police force. I was a strong supporter of this idea, which was advocated especially by Lord Davies, who gave much time and money to the cause. I had a very pleasant stay and recall especially the beauty of Lake Annecy. The lectures were subsequently issued in a volume entitled *Pacifism Is Not Enough,* published by George Allen & Unwin.

In the spring of 1935, with David Grenfell and Joseph Compton, I was a delegate to the International Socialist Conference at Brussels. Vandervelde was then leading the Belgian party, de Brouckère was in the chair, and Léon Blum was the leading personality. In 1952, at the conference in Milan, I noted that all the leading personalities of that earlier day were gone. Indeed, I was, I think, the only delegate who had been present at these prewar meetings.

In the years 1935 and 1936 I visited Paris to talk with our French colleagues. On the second occasion Léon Blum was about to become Prime Minister. I had a great affection for him. Tall and handsome, highly cultured and of brilliant intelligence, he possessed great charm. He towered head and shoulders above his colleagues in the French movement, and, indeed, in my view, above all contemporary French politicians. He had a most difficult task in trying to keep together the French Left, with the appeasers on the one side and the Communists on the other. He served France well both before and after the war. A prisoner during the war, by his magnificent defence in the Riom Trial he turned the tables on his accusers.

I had for some years been on friendly terms with Ivan Maisky, the Soviet Ambassador to Great Britain, one of the few Russians who understood Western democracy. He invited me to visit Russia, and I was eager to get a first-hand impression of the Communist regime. Accompanied by John Dugdale and his mother, I sailed from London Docks. We passed through the Kiel Canal, crossed the Baltic, and landed at Leningrad. We had an interesting time, but visited only Leningrad and Moscow, and I think that in the main we saw only what it was intended we should see. Leningrad, with its fine buildings along the quay, was an impressive city but had a curiously dead appearance. There was at that time little motor traffic, while the ill-dressed, depressed-looking people in the streets seemed to be out of place. It gave the impression of a town

on a Bank Holiday during which the usual inhabitants
had gone away, while a number of visitors from a depressed industrial area had come in for a visit.

Moscow was more alive. We saw a number of institutions, including some new schools, which looked to me to
be very jerry-built and the subway, which was very fine.
I did not see Stalin but met a number of the leading men
of the regime. Unfortunately my visit preceded by a few
weeks the big purge, which removed a number of those
whom I had contacted, notably Marshal Tukhachevski.
I had lunch with him and a long talk on the Red Army.
He explained the position of the commissars in the Army
and their function in promoting morale. I could not resist pulling his leg by saying, "They are like Army chaplains." Whereupon he indignantly replied that the priests
were the most despised people in the Czarist Army. I
retorted, "I did not mean your priests. I mean men like
Cromwell's chaplains with the root of the matter in
them." The only apparent survivor among the prominent
people whom I met was Lazar M. Kaganovich, a very able
Jew who was then in charge of transport.

The Soviet was at that time actively supporting the
League of Nations. Litvinov, who was in charge of foreign
affairs, invited me to visit him at his country villa. There
I came into an almost English atmosphere. Madame Litvinov told me that her husband and Maisky were walking
round the farm with the dogs, and I found them feeding
the ducks. After lunch I played billiards with the children. I visited a small town and a village, but I think that
they were really show places and not the least typical. The
biggest impression made on me was the cult of Stalin, his

picture being shown everywhere. This was amusingly exemplified in the War Museum, where great pains had been taken to eliminate every reference to Trotsky. Our guides were anxious to explain that every success had been due to Stalin, every failure to Trotsky.

In November 1936 Roger Salengro, who held the portfolio of Internal Affairs in the Blum government, committed suicide as the result of a particularly vile press attack. I went to Lille to represent the Labour party at the funeral. It was a dull cold day, and we marched for what seemed many hours round the *pavé* streets. In the evening I dined with Herriot as the guest of the Prefect of the Department du Nord and had a long talk with the French statesman.

Two months later I again visited France. As I have mentioned, I contributed articles to various continental newspapers under the ægis of Paul Reves. He also arranged lectures in foreign capitals. I spoke to a large audience at the Salle des Ambassadeurs in Paris on the League of Nations and collective security. I had lunch with the brilliant writer André Maurois, and had a most interesting talk with him.

A month later I was fraternal delegate to the annual conference of the Czech Social Democratic party, visiting Prague for the second time. I was met at the Wilson Station by the president of the legislature, a tall, bearded man, who, somewhat to my embarrassment, kissed me on both cheeks. He was subsequently tortured to death by the Nazis. I had a long interview with Beneš. The threat from the Nazis was already developing, but Beneš, as always, displayed great optimism. He always seemed to me in his dealings both with the Germans and later with the Russians to put far too much confidence in his own cleverness. He did not seem to realize how long a spoon was needed to sup with the devil. I had a long drive through the country to lunch with the Deputy Prime Minister, Becyni, in a pleasant village near the Sudetenland. It looked very peaceful, but they expressed their fear that some time the Nazis would come over and raid them.

One of the fruits of the Baldwin government's weak policy was the attack in 1936 on the Spanish Republican government by General Franco, supported by the fascist dictators. There was much misrepresentation on the subject of the Spanish government. It was the result of a popular election and was a coalition of Left-Wing elements, but was not Communist. Liberals and Socialists were the chief elements, but there were also Catalans and Basques whose interests were mainly regional. No doubt it had many failings, but it was the best government Spain had had for many years. We recognized at once that General Franco's movement was part of the conspiracy against democracy, and most Liberals and some Conservatives agreed with us, but, on the whole, the Conservative party tended to regard Franco as a saviour of society. In this they ran true to form, for a hundred years previously they had supported Don Carlos against the constitutional government of Queen Marìa Cristina. I recall reading a speech by Lord Palmerston on the Spanish question of that time which was extremely apposite to the position in 1936. He told the Tories that they supported reaction abroad because they were in favour of reaction at home. Now the

British government supported the policy of non-intervention, and so did the French Popular Front government under Léon Blum. Keeping the ring with a fair field and no favour, on the ground that the struggle in Spain was a domestic matter, might have been a sensible policy; but it became clear that, under the cloak of non-intervention, Mussolini was actively supporting Franco. The French attitude hampered us in bringing pressure to bear on our own government, while the efforts of the Communists to exploit Spanish resistance for their own ends did harm to the cause of freedom. Enthusiasm for the Republic ran very high in all Left-Wing circles in Britain, and I decided to go to Spain to see the position for myself.

In December 1937 in company with Philip Noel-Baker, Ellen Wilkinson, and John Dugdale, I went to Barcelona. I stayed with Prime Minister Negrin, a distinguished scientist and a Socialist. Here we had our first experience of bombing, a very mild prelude to what was to come a few years later. I met many of the leaders of all the elements of the Left except the anarchists, who were numerous in Catalonia. I talked with leading Catalans on the subject of their particularist aims, and also met Aguirre, the Basque leader, a devoted Catholic and a very fine man.

I saw young troops in training and talked with their officers, and was reminded of the early days of Kitchener's Army in 1914. On the way to Madrid we stopped to dine at a corps headquarters where a Yugoslav commander was supported by a staff of many nationalities. I also inspected the British contingent of the International Brigade; this was an impressive scene in a Spanish village by torchlight. The Brigade had saved the republican cause in Spain. Serving in its ranks were men of diverse views, but animated with courage, self-sacrifice, and devotion, and united in the fight for freedom. It was tragic that all the time the Communists were intriguing and seeking to divert the contest into a battle for communism.

We went into the trenches in the University City and visited General Mijaka in his underground headquarters. I recall very vividly one incident. There was a reception at Madrid. Among others, a British consular officer was introduced to Ellen Wilkinson. She, rightly or wrongly, believed that he was very pro-Franco. She drew herself up to her full height (which was not great) and, looking at him with blazing eyes, repeated his name twice. She then made a very deep curtsy and turned away. It was most impressive, suggesting Queen Elizabeth receiving the French Ambassador after the massacre of St. Bartholomew's Eve.

We flew to Valencia, the only other large town in the hands of the Republic. Flying back to Barcelona, we came very low over the sea close to the shore. I realized that there were Franco planes after us, but my companions were blissfully unconscious of the danger. In fact, the fascist aircraft were just too late.

On my return to England I was criticized for returning the salute of the Spanish Forces with the clenched-fist sign on the ground that I was thereby approving of communism. This story constantly meets me on the public platform. In fact, at that time this salute was commonly used by all supporters of the Republic, whether they were Liberals, Socialists, Communists, or Anarchists. The Spanish struggle was the occasion for a very determined attempt by the Communist party to get into the Labour movement by devious methods, but the majority of the party was too experienced to fall into the trap.

The only real holiday visit that I had abroad was in the summer of 1938. The chairman of the Workers' Travel Association called on me one day to tell me that the association had decided that I needed a holiday and offered to provide one for my wife and myself wherever we should choose to go. I selected Denmark and, together with my wife, flew via Hamburg to Copenhagen. This was my wife's first air journey. We were met at the airport by one of the Danish Ministers, Alsing Andersen, who was a friend of mine, and by the W.T.A. representative. The latter was an excellent courier and looked after us well during our stay. We were greatly struck by the general impression of happiness and contentment that radiated from these democratic people. I much enjoyed, too, seeing some of the social services of which I had often read. We visited the old castle at Elsinore and crossed for a few hours into Sweden. We also made the acquaintance of the parents of a very pleasant Danish girl who was helping to look after our children. It was horrible in later years to think of this civilized people being overrun by the Nazis.

❀   XII   ❀

Labour and Defence

IT IS, I think, fair to say that until 1935 the Parliamentary Labour party had given little or no serious attention to defence problems. The party had held office in a
minority government on two occasions, but these were in
the period following the First World War when it had
been laid down that there was no danger of war for ten
years. There were, indeed, no potentially hostile powers
of any military strength, while, at the League of Nations,
all the emphasis was on disarmament. In these circumstances it was natural that no consideration should be
given to technical problems of defence. MacDonald's Secretaries of State for War had no particular qualifications
for the position except that they were leading party members for whom places in the cabinet had to be found.
Lord Thomson, the Secretary of State for Air, was a
regular soldier, but at the Admiralty, MacDonald placed
Lord Chelmsford, an ex-Indian Viceroy, who would, he
thought, be able to deal with admirals. Four of the junior
ministers had served in the war, and one of these, A. V.

Alexander, became a cabinet minister in MacDonald's second cabinet and was a very active First Lord of the Admiralty.

As I have stated, the party had split on the war issue in 1914. Reunited in 1919, it naturally contained a very large pacifist element. The Independent Labour party had always been strongly pacifist, and one of its points of difference with the Social Democratic Federation had been the latter's support for a citizen army, designed to make impossible the overthrow of democracy by a capitalist dictatorship. Socialist pacifism was a product of the optimistic Victorian era when the British Navy ruled the seas and when the idea of a world war seemed remote. Liberals and Socialists held to this idea. Looking back, one can see that the Social Democratic Federation was more realistic in its attitude, but in the early days of the century the idea that liberal democracy could be overturned by men such as Hitler and Mussolini seemed very far-fetched.

The First World War was a rude awakening, but many were slow to learn its lessons. Most people hoped that four years of war would have caused such a revulsion that people all over the world would refuse to engage again in war, and optimistic hopes were placed in the League of Nations. The general campaign for "No more war" in which I joined, like many others who had served in the war, was in tune with the prevailing sentiment. This was still the mood when I was appointed to serve as Under Secretary of State for War in 1924. I set myself, however, to learn as much as I could about defence problems, for I realized that, whatever might be done in the field of disarmament, there was bound to be the need for an army for policing the widespread territories of the British Commonwealth and Empire.

It always appeared to me that some of my pacifist friends, in their insistence on the wickedness of warfare, considered an inefficient army less wicked than an efficient one, a point of view to which I was unable to subscribe. On the other hand, the party stood for fair treatment for the men in the fighting forces. There is no doubt that formerly poverty had been one of the chief recruiting agencies for the Army. Britain had maintained an army on the cheap. Pay in the ranks was low, while officers were expected to have private means to supplement their quite insufficient pay. It was a satisfaction to me that the wartime government and the Labour government effected vast improvements in these respects.

In the years that followed the first Labour government I intimated to MacDonald that some study might be given to the question of defence, and I think he went as far as to suggest that Sir Charles Trevelyan and I might look into the subject. However, nothing came of it and I was shortly afterwards plunged into consideration of the Indian problem.

After 1931 the party in the House was small; most of those who had been in the Service Ministries were defeated. The Disarmament Conference was still functioning, and our Leader, George Lansbury, was a very strong pacifist. By this time, however, there had been a development of party policy. Mainly under the inspiration of Arthur Henderson, the party had officially accepted the policy of collective security. The conception was that of a

League of Nations strong enough to deter any would-be aggressor. Support of this necessarily entailed the United Kingdom's making its contribution towards armed forces of the League. The majority of the party supported this, but a minority still maintained their old pacifist attitude. The Parliamentary Labour party, therefore, in debates on defence and on the Service Estimates, took up the position that while ready for Britain to make its contribution to collective security it was opposed to purely national armaments.

It had always been the custom in the House of Commons for Liberal and Labour parties to vote against the Service Estimates. This had always been understood to be a vote either against the level of armaments or against the policy of the government of the day, but not as a vote against all armaments. It was left to the coalition governments to make this a cause of attack on the Labour party. The party, in view of this misrepresentation, was perhaps unwise and pedantic in continuing this old established practice. The aggression of Japan against China was the first blow to the authority of the League of Nations. Subsequently the rise of Hitler and the aggression of Mussolini in Abyssinia caused growing apprehension in the Labour movement, and especially among the trade unionists who had witnessed the destruction of German social democracy. It was on the issue of support for sanctions against Mussolini that division arose in the party which resulted in the resignation of George Lansbury and my election as Leader in 1935.

As soon as the new 1935 Parliament met I determined to take steps to create a better knowledge of defence prob-

lems in the party. There were now back in the House a
number of men who had had experience in the Service
Ministries: Alexander and Ammon in the Admiralty;
Lawson, Shinwell, and myself at the War Office; and Mon-
tague in the Air Ministry. There were also those who,
like Hugh Dalton, had served in the First World War. I
accordingly formed a Defence Committee, which met regularly and discussed defence problems. We got able officers
to address us on various points. We made a very careful
study of air warfare, and we employed a very able man
to engage in research on this vital question. At a later
stage (in 1938) we presented our conclusions to Neville
Chamberlain and held a number of meetings with Sir
Kingsley Wood, the Secretary of State for Air, at which
we were able to put a number of searching questions.
Some of us were acquainted with high-ranking officers in
the three Services. The result was seen in the far more
informed contribution Labour men were able to make in
Service debates.

I was myself particularly interested in the higher direction of defence. In a debate on a Private Member's motion in favour of the creation of the Ministry of Defence
I made a speech in February 1936 in which I formulated
my ideas. These met with general acceptance in the
House and led to my being invited to address the Imperial Defence College, the Naval Staff College, and other
Service gatherings. It was a satisfaction to me that years
later, in 1946, I introduced into the House of Commons
a Ministry of Defence Bill, which, though slightly modi-
fied by experience gained in the Second World War, was,

in essence, the same proposal I had adumbrated ten years before.

The first major speech I made in Parliament after my election to the leadership of the Parliamentary Labour party was on the subject of foreign policy and defence. Early in October 1935 Italian troops crossed the River Mareb and invaded Abyssinia, and on the first day after the reassembly of Parliament after the summer recess, the Foreign Secretary, Sir Samuel Hoare, made a statement on the attitude of the government during the events that had led up to the war and the policy adopted by Britain's representatives at Geneva. In my reply to Sir Samuel Hoare I restated the party's policy and attitude towards aggression. "When in office," I said in the course of my speech, "we supported and endeavoured to enhance the League of Nations' authority, and in Opposition we have unremittingly urged the government to make support of the League the whole basis of its policy. I emphasize the point, the whole basis of its policy, because to my mind you cannot follow at one and the same time the system of the League of Nations and the system of old-fashioned imperialism. We base our policy on the facts of the modern world, which, in our view, lead imperatively to subordination of national sovereignties to the League and ultimately to a cooperative commonwealth of the world. We believe that in a state of the world so closely linked together as is the world of today you must have some authority other than the will of individual powers." I went on to inquire what the government meant by declaring their neutrality in the Italian question. "The whole conception of neutrality," I continued, "passed away with the coming of the League. With the declaration of an aggressor nation, that nation could not be treated as if you were purely neutral. You are not neutral. You are engaged in applying sanctions. . . . We support economic sanctions. We support the League system. But what we want to know from the government is what is their general foreign policy besides this immediate matter." Thus the policy of the Labour party was made unequivocally clear.

Four months later, in February 1936, we initiated a debate in the House of Commons on the application of oil sanctions against Italy, and after criticizing the continued postponement of the sanctions I prophesied that concession to Italy would be followed by further concessions to every aggressor. Again, my final words emphasized where the Parliamentary Labour party stood on the question of rearmament. ". . . Whatever arms are required they must be for the League policy, and the first condition for any assent to more arms is that the government shall be following a League policy. . . . I say most emphatically, speaking on behalf of this party, that we shall never agree to piling up armaments and following a policy either of imperialism or of alliances, but only collective security through the League."

Both in the House and in the country I condemned the occupation, in the spring of 1936, of the demilitarized Rhineland Zone by German troops, and three months later, when the Baldwin government announced their intention to advocate the termination of sanctions against Italy at the coming Assembly of the League, the Labour party tabled a Vote of Censure. I told the House that in my opinion the government had "destroyed the League of Nations as an effective instrument for peace. . . . None of the small states of Europe are going to trust any more in collective security under the League if they know that the League will not stand by them." My warning was to prove only too true. A few weeks after the debate civil war broke out in Spain, and as the months went by there was a steady deterioration of the international situation, particularly in the Far East, where the Japanese Army had achieved very considerable successes and the bombing of Canton and other open towns had caused heavy loss of life. In a debate in the House in November 1937 I asked once again what were the government's plans for defence. I inquired about air-raid precautions, plans for evacuation, anti-aircraft guns, our Air Force, and the location of industry from the point of view of defence. But we got little satisfaction from the government about their preparations for these conditions, which, as I told the House, were "the creation of their inept foreign policy."

When Anthony Eden and Lord Cranborne resigned from the Chamberlain government early in 1938 as a protest against the Prime Minister's decision to open conversations with Mussolini whilst Italy was carrying on intervention in Spain and anti-British propaganda, I told the House that the policy of the government was "an abject surrender to the dictators" and that "the government, instead of trying to deal with the causes of war, had always been trying in a feeble way to play off one dictator against another. That is a policy which sooner or later leads to war."

The attitude the Parliamentary Labour party took on

these all-important questions of defence and the international situation was fully supported by the Annual Conferences of the Labour party. When my colleagues and I spoke in the House of Commons we knew that we were voicing the hopes and fears of millions of people, both in Britain and abroad. At the Edinburgh Conference in 1936 a resolution was adopted by an overwhelming majority supporting collective security and declaring that "the armed strength of the countries loyal to the League must be conditioned by the armed strength of the aggressors."

In August 1937 the National Council of Labour (the Labour party, the Trades Union Congress, and the Co-operative party) issued a statement on the war in China that expressed apprehension of the danger of another world war and concluded, "The National Council of Labour urges the British government to endeavour to concert measures with other governments in the League of Nations or under treaty obligations to China, particularly the United States, to secure respect by Japan for international law and treaty rights." A comprehensive document entitled "Policy and Defence" was accepted by the Annual Conference of the party in Bournemouth in the autumn of 1937. The report expressed the conviction that war could be prevented, the arms race stopped, and the League made powerful again if a British government came to power which based its policy on that of the Labour movement. Such a government, in the present state of the world, should be strongly equipped to defend the country and play its full part in collective security, and "until the change in the international situation caused by its advent had had its effect, would be unable to reverse the present programme of rearmament." The statement concluded, "The British Labour movement, fully conscious of the dangers which today threaten our civilization, refuses to accept the doctrine of the inevitability of war, and will continue to exert all its influence to promote a durable peace based upon friendship and justice between nations and respect for international law."

When, with Austria in his possession, Hitler opened his campaign against Czechoslovakia in the late spring of 1938, I was much concerned. I had many friends among the Czech Socialists, and I also knew Dr. Beneš and Jan Masaryk very well. Czechoslovakia was the only real democracy among the Succession States.

I did not believe that Hitler could be argued out of his plan to absorb this key strategic state into the German Reich. We in the Labour party were violently opposed to fascism. We had seen with horror the persecution of the Jews and the Socialists in Germany.

Chamberlain informed me of his intention to fly to Germany to see Hitler, which he thought was a possible way of averting war. I told him I had little faith in the venture, but I could not oppose his action provided he stood firm on principle. He informed the House of his intention just when we were about to debate foreign affairs. I said that no chance should be neglected of preserving peace without sacrifice of principle. But it was just this sacrifice that was made. On his return from Munich with a piece of paper we realized that the pass had been sold, and we sat silent while the majority of the Tories stood up and cheered.

It was on October 3, 1938, that Chamberlain reported

to the House of Commons on his visit to Munich. I recall that before the Prime Minister made his statement, Duff Cooper made a personal explanation of the reasons that had led him to resign from the government the previous day. Following immediately after Chamberlain, I spoke at some length, and perhaps the line I took can be summed up in a couple of sentences early in my speech: "The events of these last few days constitute one of the greatest defeats that this country and France have ever sustained. There can be no doubt that it is a tremendous victory for Herr Hitler."

As winter gave way to spring the international situation went from bad to worse, and in April 1939 the government introduced a measure of conscription. Both the Labour party and the Opposition Liberals voted against this change of policy, which was a contravention of a pledge given by Baldwin not to introduce conscription in peacetime. Speaking for the party, I based my opposition on the argument that the voluntary system, which had not been fully tried, could give better results than compulsory service, and that the new measure would create dissension and not unity at home. Looking back, I think that our attitude was a mistake, but, in the event, the issue was of little importance as a few months later we were at war, when a far more comprehensive measure of compulsory service had our support.

I had for some time been conscious that sooner or later I should have to undergo an operation, but I had postponed doing anything about it until the international sky was clearer. However, when I went to Southport at Whitsun for the Annual Conference I was taken ill. In my absence from the conference (I only addressed the gathering briefly towards the end of the week), Dalton presented a comprehensive and constructive report entitled "Labour and Defence," which was adopted by a very large majority. The document dealt with Labour and the Armed Forces (with special reference to the democratization of the forces and improvements in conditions, the setting up of a Ministry of Supply, and how a Defence Ministry should be constituted). During my brief address to the conference I emphasized that Labour's policy of socialism and peace was a whole and could not be divided into unconnected compartments. "You cannot have one policy for foreign affairs and run a policy at home on entirely different principles," I said. "I want us to devote ourselves to making people realize that if they want peace they must have social justice at home."

✦ **XIII** ✦

War and Downfall of Chamberlain

WHEN I returned from Southport I had to enter a nursing home and underwent two operations for prostate trouble. I was warned that it would be some months before I should be fit to undertake full responsibility. I went with my family to Nevin in North Wales to recuperate, and it was while I was there that Hitler's invasion of Poland took place, which led to the entry of Britain into the war. While I was ill it occurred to a few people that this would be a good opportunity to change the leadership of the party, but this move got little support. Meanwhile I kept in close touch with Arthur Greenwood, who led the party with great ability during my absence.

I warmly approved the line taken by the party in supporting the firm stand against Hitler, and especially Greenwood's strong speech when the call came from the other side of the House, "Speak for England." He rose finely to the occasion.

I also thought that the party was quite right in not entering the government, for in the ranks of Labour there was no confidence in Chamberlain and his immediate associates. Furthermore, in the conditions obtaining there was much to be said for having an alternative administration available.

At the same time we offered our full support in the war effort, as indeed we had done prior to the outbreak of war. Alexander had worked actively in the organization of food supplies, and a number of my colleagues had become regional or deputy regional commissioners for Air Raid Precautions.

Although I came up to the House on a few occasions I was not able to resume my full responsibilities as Leader until the late autumn. We were then in the period known as the "phony war." We were critical of the measures taken by the government, which we did not think were nearly vigorous enough.

Early in 1940 I broadcast to the nation on the reasons that had led the Labour party, in spite of its hatred of war and distrust of the Chamberlain government, to support the successful prosecution of the war against Hitlerism. I said:

> I want this evening to stress the importance of the moral issues involved in this war. When the war of 1914 to 1918 ended, everyone hoped that it would be the last. The setting up of the League of Nations was the expression of the desires of ordinary men and women for peace and for the establishment of moral principles in international relations. The Labour party, knowing well not only the cruelty and horrors of war, but also the loss which it brings especially on the poorer sections of the community, did its utmost to make the League a success. When the late Arthur

Henderson spoke for this country at Geneva there were high hopes of achieving this. Germany was back in the comity of nations. Disarmament seemed likely to be attained. But the old evil forces under the stress of the breakdown of the world economic system reared their heads again. During the last nine years the world has, step by step, moved towards war until it has reached the present position. I believe this has been due to the failure to act on moral principles. When aggression and the use of armed force as an instrument of policy began again, a stand was not taken. The evil was condoned. Peace was destroyed.

Successful violence bred more violence. Ruthless cruelty became rampant. We are now faced with the danger of the world relapsing into barbarism. Nazism is the outstanding menace to civilization, not only because of the character and actions of the men who are in absolute control of a great nation, but because of their ideas which are openly in conflict with all the conceptions upon which civilized life is based. They do not accept as valuable the virtues which are in this country accepted as desirable by all, even by those who honour them with very little in their actions.

Our Western civilization has been built up in the main on the acceptance of the moral standards of Christianity. Even those who find themselves unable to accept Christian dogma accept in the main its ethical standards. In our everyday intercourse we assume that most men are honest, truthful, and kindly, and in general we are not disappointed. We do not expect that we shall be violently attacked or maltreated by our neighbours. This mutual confidence is the foundation of a civilized peaceful life.

At no time in history have these standards been fully maintained in the relations between states.

There have always been those who have been prepared to put apparent national interests before
moral principles, but they have done it shame-
facedly. Bad faith, lying, and injustice have often
marked international relations, but it has been left
to the German government to make them its regular
practice and to glory in them.

Similarly, there was formerly a definite world conscience which revolted against cruelty and atrocities.
The wholesale murder of innocent men, women, and
children was regarded as the mark of a barbarous
people. Where such things happened under pro-
fessedly civilized government there was an outcry
in all countries, including the one whose government
was responsible for the outrage. One can recall instances in our own history, such as the Amritsar
massacre. Today in Germany, Czechoslovakia, and
Poland the German government is indulging in
wholesale massacre and torture of unoffending people. It not only admits it, it glories in it. At home
and abroad, brutal cruelty is the mark of the Nazi
regime.

It is essential to remember that civilization takes
long to build and is easily destroyed. Brutality is in-
fectious.

But there is something more than these outward
expressions of the return to barbarism in the Nazi
regime. There is a denial of the value of the individual. Christianity affirms the value of each individual
soul. Nazism denies it. The individual is sacrificed to
the idol of the German leader, German state, or the
German race. The ordinary citizen is allowed to hear
and think only as the rulers decree. The basic idea
of democracy is thereby rejected. The Labour party
owes its inspiration not to some economic doctrine or
to some theory of class domination. It has always

based its propaganda on ethical principles. We believe that every individual should be afforded the fullest opportunity for developing his or her personality. The founder of our party, Keir Hardie, always made his appeal on moral grounds. He believed that the evils of society were due to the failure to put into practice the principles of the brotherhood of man.

The struggle for the freedom of the individual soul takes different forms at various periods. Here in Britain we have achieved freedom of conscience, freedom of thought, freedom of speech and action within the law, freedom for workers to combine together. They are victories which we will not allow to be reversed, but the fight for freedom continues.

The Labour party is the expression of the revolt of men and women against a materialist system of society which condemns to a narrow and stinted life the majority of our citizens and gives rewards to the greedy and acquisitive. The Labour party's object is the building of a new world on the foundation of social and economic justice. During its existence it has done much to preserve and extend the rights won by its predecessors. It has done much to modify and humanize the capitalist system itself. It has seen many of its ideas accepted by those who formerly scoffed at them. These successes are often ignored by the younger generation, who do not realize what were the conditions a few decades ago.

But all this achievement of the workers is threatened by the rule of the Nazis. The German workers who had built up a great structure of trade unionism, cooperation, and social services have seen it destroyed. They have lost all their democratic rights. Wherever nazism is, there is cruelty, tyranny, and the rule of the secret police. The Labour party, therefore, had taken its stand with the rest of the country to stop this evil thing spreading although we have our own quarrel with the present system of society.

Its position might be compared to that of a man inhabiting a house which is not his own and is seriously defective, but which affords shelter to what he holds dear. He wants a better house, but is bound to defend what he has against those who seek to destroy what it contains. Western civilization, with all its faults, holds within it the heritage won for us by our forefathers.

The victory of nazism would destroy all our hopes for many years to come.

I believe that in this contest we are fighting for something greater than the safety of our own country. We are fighting the battle of civilization against barbarism. To do that successfully we must bring to our aid the spiritual forces in all countries. We must see to it that in this contest we do not allow the evil things against which we fight to master our own souls. Our aims must be such as commend them to the conscience of mankind. If we seek a peace wherein moral principles are to prevail, we must carry out those principles ourselves. If we are conscious all the time that our practice is not in accordance with our precepts we shall be weakened. I want you to consider some of those causes of weakness.

The rulers of Germany assert that the Germans are a special race with the right on account of their qualities to rule over others. They make special claims for Germany for what they call living room. They demand recognition as an imperial power and seek for colonial territories, not because there is much that they can get from them but because their possession is, in their view, due to their position.

I think that the majority of people in this country have now abandoned the old boastful imperialism,

but it was not so long ago in my own lifetime when
our press used to be filled with the same kind of ar-
rogant boasting which one hears from Hitler. We did
pursue a policy of what was called expansion and
brought under our sway great tracts of territory. I
think that we have now realized the falsity of such
ideals, but we still continue to retain the fruits of
that policy. We have accepted to a large extent the
principle that all colonial territories should be held
under trusteeship for the native inhabitants. We
have gone a long way in giving self-government to
the people of India. We have relinquished our hold
on Egypt and Iraq, but on the other hand we have
had the Ottawa policy of economic imperialism.

If we then want to persuade others that we wish
for a world free from imperialist domination, we
must put ourselves right. We must press forward the
policy of extending self-government wherever that is
practical. We must abandon any claim to special
rights. We must be prepared to bring all our colonial
territories under the mandatory principle and to extend and widen the scope of international control.
We must rid ourselves of any taint of imperialism.
Only so can we put ourselves into a position to ask
for a world organized on the democratic principle.

But it is not enough to put in practice moral principles in our relations with those outside our own
boundaries. We have to moralize our social relations
at home.

If we really believe in the supreme value of every
human individual, and this is the core of our democratic faith, we must change a system of society which
does not express this in its institutions. We still live
in a class society. The recognition of equality of opportunity for all has yet to be attained. If in this contest we allow the rigours of war to press most hardly

on the weakest, on the aged, the crippled, and the dependants of our fighting men, we shall be betraying the principles for which we fight. If we permit, as in the last war, inequality of sacrifice so that at the end the gulf between rich and poor is greater than ever, we shall have failed in our task. If we really wish to build a new world wherein justice, mercy and truth shall replace brute force, wherein equality and good neighbourliness shall take the place of violence, aggression, and domination, we must also build a new Britain worthy to lead the world away from anarchy and strife into the paths of peace.

In January 1940 I was invited by Lord Gort, Commander in Chief of the British Expeditionary Force, to pay a visit to his headquarters. I flew to Amiens and was met there by Lord Munster, Lord Gort's aide-de-camp, and we motored to G.H.Q. I toured our defence line on a very cold winter's day, and the general plan was explained to me. Our defence line seemed to be pretty strong but was necessarily sited on the Belgian frontier. Belgium, despite the precedent of 1914, still hoped to remain out of the war. Clearly, however, if Belgium was attacked there would have to be a swing forward of the left of the Allied line, which would mean that we should have to fight in largely unprepared positions. Inevitably, in view of the smallness of our contribution, we had to accept the over-all plans of the French High Command. I was not very happy about this, for I had not a high opinion of French generalship, and I was disturbed at learning that there was not an adequate reserve to reinforce the sector of the line on which an attack developed. The French had the Maginot Line mentality.

My nephew Patrick was commanding an anti-aircraft battery in the neighbourhood of G.H.Q. Someone had discovered this and very kindly invited him to dinner during my stay. I must say that I admired his complete lack of embarrassment at dining with these eminent soldiers. A little later I flew to Scapa and stayed a couple of days with the Fleet. I thoroughly enjoyed this visit, as it was the first opportunity I had had of this kind.

In February I went to Paris with Dalton, Noel-Baker, and Mrs. Ayrton-Gould to discuss matters with our French comrades. This was a most depressing meeting. Most of those whom we met were either pacifist or defeatist. Léon Blum and Grumbach were the outstanding exceptions.

A little later the Labour party held a big conference in London in the course of which I outlined the party's general views on the kind of settlement that we would wish to see at the end of the war. The Russian alliance with Hitler had given a very severe jolt to the Left Wing of the party, which had been prominent in the movements of the Popular Front. The attack on Finland in particular had made a big impression. I think my speech met with general approval.

Meanwhile there was growing criticism of the government, not only from the Labour and Liberal parties, but from many on the Conservative Benches, especially among those serving in the Armed Forces. There was a feeling that there was a lack of drive and inspiration. I recall many talks at this time with various people. A number of small gatherings were held, often under the auspices of "the other Clem"—Clement Davies—who is now the Leader of the Liberal party. He was in touch with a number of Conservatives, notably Lord Salisbury, the father of the present Lord President of the Council. These discontents came to a head in May 1940. The Norwegian campaign had been a failure, while the strange quiet on the Western Front remained. A debate had been arranged just before the Whitsun adjournment. I followed Chamberlain on the first day and did not confine my criticism to the Norwegian campaign, but made a broad attack on the government's handling of the war situation at home and abroad.

The debate on May 7 showed that the revolt against the Chamberlain Government was more widespread than I had thought. Many members serving in the Armed Forces had come up for the debate. Accordingly, next day I recommended to the party that we should vote against the motion for the adjournment. I told them that it must be clearly understood that this was a Vote of Censure and that if it brought the government down we must be prepared to assume responsibility. There was general and enthusiastic support for this action, except, curiously enough, from one or two people normally regarded as extremely Left Wing and anti-fascist. On May 8 Herbert Morrison, supporting our criticisms, announced this decision. Chamberlain replied but was not effective. In particular, his appeal to "his friends" was ill judged and annoyed the House. Members felt that the safety of the country was at stake and that personal friendships were irrelevant. There were very strong speeches from the government side. Admiral Keyes was unusually lucid; Lloyd George told Chamberlain that the best service he could do to the country was to resign; and Amery, quoting Cromwell, said, "You have sat there too long: in God's name go." Churchill made a valiant effort to restore the situation, but in vain. At long last some Conservatives had made up their minds to revolt.

It was a dramatic moment. Into the Lobbies with the Labour party went forty Conservatives, many of them in uniform, having come up specially to vote. Many others abstained. The government majority, usually well over 200, had shrunk to 81, and some of those who voted with the majority did so reluctantly.

On Thursday, May 9, the day after the debate, Chamberlain asked Arthur Greenwood and me to call at Downing Street. We found him with Lord Halifax and Churchill. I told him that I knew the views of our party in the House and in the country and I was perfectly certain that they would not consent to come into a government of which, in effect, he was the head. It was not a pleasant task to tell a Prime Minister that he ought to go, but I had no option but to tell him the truth. I was then asked whether Labour would take part in a coalition of which someone else was the head. I said that I thought they would but that as the party was holding its Annual Conference at Bournemouth I would go down and ask the delegates. It was accordingly agreed that I should put to them two questions:

    (1) Would they enter a government under the present Prime Minister?

    (2) Would they come in under someone else?

I would telephone "Yes" or "No" to these two questions.

Next day I travelled to Bournemouth and met the Executive of the party in the afternoon. There was unanimous agreement to answer "No" to the first question and "Yes" to the second. I telephoned the result and caught a train back to town. I was met by a naval officer and Maurice Webb, then political correspondent for the *Daily Herald,* and was informed that Chamberlain had resigned and that Churchill had been given the King's commission to form a government. I was asked to go to see him at the Admiralty. I had discussed appointments with Greenwood so I was ready with suggestions.

Churchill was anxious to get the war cabinet and the Service Ministers announced as soon as possible. It was agreed that night that there should be a war cabinet of five—Churchill, Halifax, Chamberlain, Greenwood, and myself—and that the Service Ministers should be Alexander, Eden, and Sinclair. At further meetings on the Saturday other appointments were agreed. This was quick work, but at this very time the big German offensive which was to knock France out of the war was developing. I remembered how at a critical stage in the Dardanelles campaign in which I had taken part, vital decisions were delayed because of the long-drawn-out bargainings between the Conservatives and the Liberals over the formation of Asquith's coalition in 1915. I was resolved that I would not, by haggling, be responsible for any failure to act promptly.

The day after I had agreed to Labour's entry into Churchill's wartime government I drove to Bournemouth again and met the party Executive, who approved my action. I also met the Trades Union General Council, who were in session. They promised full support. On the Monday morning I addressed the party conference. I recall here my closing words:

> Friends, we are standing here today to take a decision not only on behalf of our own movements but on behalf of Labour all over the world. We have to stand today for the souls in prison in Czechoslovakia, in Poland, yes, and in Germany. We have to stand for those whose freedom is threatened all over the world. We have to fight for the freedom of the human spirit. I have no doubt at all as to what the feelings of our people are. I believe that every one of us knows what is the thing of most value in life, what we prize above everything else. Life without liberty is not worth living. Let us go forward and win that liberty and establish that liberty forever on the sure foundation of social justice.

The resolution approving the action of the Executive was carried by an overwhelming majority.

Before the vote was taken I had left for London, and was present in the House when Churchill made his famous "Blood, toil, tears, and sweat" speech. Thus began this famous war government with Bevin as Minister of Labour and National Service, Morrison as Minister of Supply, Dalton as Minister of Economic Warfare, and Grenfell as Secretary for Mines. I became Lord Privy Seal, Greenwood became Minister without Portfolio, while Labour also filled the Solicitor Generalship and a number of Under Secretaryships. Though I was not at this time formally appointed Deputy Prime Minister, it was part of my work to relieve the Pime Minister of as much detailed administration as possible.

Wartime Government

GREENWOOD and I set about reorganizing the government machine. There were a great many committees—ministerial and official—many of which we found to be unnecessary. While the committee system is of the greatest value, there is always a danger that Ministers will spend too much time on committees to the detriment of their departmental work. Excessive resort to committees tends to slow down action by discussion of matters that should be decided by Ministers themselves. In fact, it may tend to a reluctance by Ministers to take decisions in matters within their own field.

It was vital that the war cabinet should not be snowed under by reference to it of any questions not of overriding importance. We instituted the Lord President's Committee, which consisted of a few senior Ministers who took decisions on a whole range of subjects, especially those relating to the Home Front, without troubling the cabinet. Chamberlain was its first chairman, then Sir John Anderson (now Lord Waverley), and later myself. There is no doubt that it was a very useful piece of machinery.

The only committee over which the Prime Minister presided was Defence, of which I was vice-chairman.

I had long been persuaded that a small cabinet was essential in time of war. We started with five. The subsequent numbers varied but never rose above eight. I was not appointed Leader of the House formally, but, in fact, Churchill came down only occasionally when it was necessary to report on the war situation or to make speeches thereon, and it fell to me to arrange for the ordinary business of the House.

Also, more often than not, I answered questions put down to the Prime Minister. One of my first duties was to introduce into the House the most drastic bill ever put forward by a government, giving it the widest powers over persons and property. It passed through all its stages in one day.

The formation of the Coalition government of all three principal political parties raised a problem as to how the business of the House was to be carried on, for its functioning depends on the existence of an Opposition. Outside of government supporters, there were only the four Independent Labour party Members and the single Communist. The problem was solved with that practical illogicality which is one of the virtues of the British character.

In making my recommendation to the Prime Minister I had thought it necessary to leave out some of our older leaders. They were therefore available to lead the party in the House. By tacit consent, first Lees-Smith and, after his death, Pethick-Lawrence (now Lord Pethick-Lawrence)—although both were wholehearted supporters of the government—performed the duties of a Leader of the Opposition, asking questions as to the business of the House and so on. The Labour party continued to sit on the Opposition Benches. The Front Bench was filled by leading members of both parties who were sometimes found in temporary alliance. The situation was typified by the cooperation on occasions of Shinwell and Lord Winterton, which was described by a witty Lobby journalist as "Arsenic and Old Lace," from the title of the popular play running in London at that time.

At Churchill's request I had gone into No. 11 Downing Street, traditionally the residence of the Chancellor of the Exchequer, who occupied only the ground floor. I little thought then that this was the beginning of an eleven and a half years' residence in that famous street. My family continued to live at Stanmore, and I went there when possible at weekends.

Events on the Continent were now becoming increasingly critical with the breakthrough in the Ardennes. I recall very clearly informing Léon Blum, who was visiting England, of this news and advising him to get back to France as quickly as possible. As the spearheads of the Panzer Divisions penetrated farther and farther towards the Channel ports, the situation became more and more menacing. The French Army seemed to be unable or unwilling to take any countermeasures, while the position of the British forces became more and more precarious.

On May 31 I accompanied the Prime Minister, the Chief of the Imperial General Staff—General Sir John Dill—and General (now Lord) Ismay to Paris. We were escorted by Spitfires and had to fly by a circuitous route over the Channel Islands. We stayed at the British Embassy. In the garden the archives were being burned.

I shall never forget that meeting. Present were Paul Reynaud, the Prime Minister; Marshal Pétain, sitting inert, like some old image; Admiral Darlan, looking like a bluff sailor; General Weygand, small and nervy; and, in the background, General de Gaulle standing with General Spears. Weygand outlined his plans but did not give the impression of having any confidence. Churchill made a magnificent speech in indifferent French, helped out at times by English words, but extremely effective. I think I said a few words indicating the solidarity of Britain. Churchill's speech gave a momentary fillip to the French government, but it did not long survive our departure.

I remember driving round Paris with Major General Spears, who was the Prime Minister's personal representative with the French government. I recall the curious silence and almost deserted look of the city, which obviously had already decided on surrender.

The next few months were full of great anxiety and grave decisions had to be taken. The French were very insistent on our committing all our air forces to the battle. To this we could not agree. Had we done so we should have been left defenceless when the German attack on Britain developed. It was clear that there was no real determination to resist in the French government and it would have been folly to sacrifice our air forces for no good result.

There followed the episode of Dunkerque. The question arose as to how much of our army could be got away. Military authorities were pessimistic, especially Sir John

Dill. For myself, I never took so gloomy a view. Having taken part in the evacuation of Gallipoli, where an almost equally gloomy view of our prospects had been taken, I was inclined to think that we should get the men away. In the event, my optimism was justified by the great adventure of the little ships.

However, we expected that we should soon be invaded, and although the men had been saved, equipment had been lost. I recall our anxiety as to whether an American ship carrying rifles and small ammunition would get through. It would not have been of much avail, but at least we should have had some weapons with which to fight. I remember, too, going round our beach defences on the south and east coasts. This was the time when the Home Guard was raised and when every available airplane was got ready for the coming fight.

And so, as the weeks and months went by, mobilization of the country for all-out war went forward, inspired by Churchill's leadership. Ernest Bevin was mobilizing manpower. The people rose to the occasion, and there was a wonderful unity in the country. The only exceptions were the Fascists and the Communists. It is well to remember that until Russia was invaded the Communists did all they could to obstruct the war effort, which they denounced as a capitalist war. It is well to remember and to remind them that when freedom was at stake they were supporting the Nazi-Soviet Alliance.

The great victory in the Battle of Britain removed the fear of immediate invasion, but brought no relief from our many pressing anxieties. The Battle of the Atlantic, a much longer-drawn-out affair, was to follow. We had also to deal with the Middle East, where Mussolini hoped to gain an easy triumph. People sometimes forget, in thinking of the later victory at El Alamein, how greatly Wavell's victory over the Italians raised our spirits when things everywhere were very dark.

It also required some determination on the part of the government to keep our forces in North Africa supplied when it might have been thought that every bit of strength was needed at home.

The spirit of unity in the nation was reflected in the government. We were all united in the great task of ensuring our national survival. Labour and Conservative Members worked wholeheartedly together, and differences on party lines did not arise. There was also unity between military and civilians. In the First World War there had been a constant clash between the soldiers and the politicians. That was not so in the Second World War. We had a Prime Minister who understood war and a high proportion of Ministers had served in the First World War, and this in itself made for greater understanding. We were also fortunate in having three outstanding Chiefs of Staff—Pound, Alanbrooke, and Portal —who served together for the greater part of the war. They were men of outstanding ability and, what is not so common when the three Services are concerned, worked together as a team. Ismay, the Secretary of the Defence Committee, was an indispensable link between civilians and military. Sir John Dill, who became the British representative with the Joint Chiefs of Staff in Washington, did an outstanding service in promoting cooperation between the British and Americans. We were indeed fortunate in finding two such men.

Another feature of the Second World War was the wholehearted cooperation of organized labour. Throughout the war the Trades Union Congress played a great part. Undoubtedly the presence in the government of Bevin was a principal factor in securing this result, but it must also be remembered that there was far greater unity on the war question than in the First World War. Opposition was almost confined to the discredited Communists and Fascists, while the position of conscientious objectors was largely met and the numbers were much smaller.

One of the most difficult problems in war is to maintain civil liberty while ensuring the safety of the country. Herbert Morrison, as Home Secretary, had to carry this burden. Although there was some criticism of the operation of Defence Regulations there is no doubt in my mind that the balance was well and truly held, and that Morrison did an outstanding service in a very difficult office.

After the victory of the Battle of Britain and the passing of the invasion danger came the Blitz. The development of our defences against air attack had been the work of Sir John Anderson, and when the time came the organization stood the test. It was a signal example of voluntary service under government guidance. In this work all parties were united. Two of my Parliamentary colleagues were prominent in their regions—Tom Johnston in Scotland and Jack Lawson in Durham.

After a short stay at the Ministry of Supply, Morrison

took over the Home Office and Home Security from
Anderson, and on him fell the heavy responsibility of
dealing with Civil Defence. As the first blow fell on London it was fortunate that so eminent a Londoner was in
charge. He had Ellen Wilkinson as Under Secretary, and
she showed here, as on other occasions, outstanding courage.

Throughout the war there was a steady development
of our defences against air attack. Fighter defence, anti-
aircraft batteries, smoke screens, and balloon barrages
were coordinated with the Civil Defence organization,
and although the loss of life and damage to property was
very heavy, it was less than had been anticipated when we
discussed the matter before the war.

When the Blitz came I was told to seek a safer sleeping
place than the first floor of No. 11 Downing Street. I was
thereafter, until the last year of the war, accommodated
in various buildings which were supposed to be safer.
They were not always so. In fact, one I occupied for some
months was subsequently found to be protected only by
a thin crust of roadway. Ultimately I returned to No. 11,
and went down occasionally to a shelter under No. 10.

I recall an occasion when the late King George VI was
dining with the Prime Minister and several of his colleagues. We were all ordered down to the dugout—King,
Ministers, and domestic servants. The King took it as a
matter of course and was amused at the experience.

My wife, meanwhile, remained at Stanmore, where she
was commandant of the local Red Cross. We had a shelter
in the garden into which we put the children when they
were home from school, but we preferred to stay in the

house. Like everyone else, in time we got so used to raids that I used to sleep through the heaviest gunfire. We were fortunate in having only two bombs near us, and both times I was at home. On the first occasion we were sitting in the drawing room when a bomb fell on some neighbouring houses and our windows were blown in. On the second occasion we were out for a walk and returned to find that a bomb had dropped just across the road and had made a deep crater in the London clay; but again it only blew in our windows and knocked down a couple of chimney stacks.

During the period of the raids I used to go around fairly frequently to see how things were going in Stepney and elsewhere. As everyone knows, the Londoner stood up magnificently to the attacks with his customary courage and humour. I shall always remember going into a big shelter in Limehouse just before Christmas. Outside it was dark and cold and the enemy airplanes could be heard overhead, but down below, the shelter had been decorated for Christmas and there was warmth and light and good fellowship.

I recall a characteristic remark when I was visiting a street that had had a very bad attack the night before, with many houses destroyed. A man called out to me, "Do you know the fun of it? The very first bomb he dropped was on Oswald Mosley's headquarters"—for the Fascists had been busy in Stepney fomenting anti-Semitism. I remember another man saying, "Hullo, Major, old Hitler's bombed me out of Eastfield Street and has bombed me out of Maroon Street, but he's b—— well not going to bomb me out of old Stepney."

I also visited a number of the blitzed cities, such as Liverpool, Birmingham, and Glasgow. Everywhere was the same fine spirit. I think that the bombing did more than anything else to break down class barriers. One West End businessman made a shelter at his own cost and attended there every night, serving at the canteen. He was a strong Conservative politically, but his chief helper was a man whom I had last seen in Spain, where he had been fighting for the Republic in the Foreign Legion.

Downing Street was never actually hit, although there was a nasty incident in the Treasury, and there were various bombs on the Horse Guards Parade. I recall coming in one morning and seeing that all the windows had been smashed in the Cabinet Room. We did not, however, allow that to prevent us from meeting there later in the day. The previous government had made elaborate plans for evacuating the government and Parliament, but we decided at once that our place was in London. With wise forethought we had fitted up Church House as an alternative meeting place in case the House of Commons was bombed. We had one or two practice meetings there, a precaution which some Members derided, but which the event justified when the old House of Commons was destroyed. We used Church House until the Lords kindly lent us their Chamber, but this prevision prevented Hitler from boasting that he had stopped the working of democratic institutions even for a day.

❀   ❀   ❀   ❀   ❀   ❀   ❀

❀   X V   ❀

Wartime Journeys

O NE OF the few international organizations that had
continued to function despite the war was the
International Labour Organization, in which British representatives—government, employers, and workers—had
always taken a very prominent part. Its headquarters had
moved from Switzerland to Canada, where it was enjoying the hospitality of McGill University. I had known its
former directors, Albert Thomas and J. G. Winant, very
well.

A meeting had been arranged in New York, and the
cabinet decided that it was important that Britain should
be fully represented. Bevin was heavily occupied with all
the problems of wartime mobilization of labour so that
he could not attend, and I was invited to lead the British
delegation. This was to be my second visit to America,
my first having taken place in 1907. Accompanying me
were Ralph Assheton, the Conservative Under Secretary
in the Ministry of Labour; Sir Frederick Leggett of the
Ministry of Labour; and my Parliamentary Private Secretary, Arthur Jenkins. We embarked on a flying boat on

October 21, 1941, and made our first stop at Lisbon. As is
not unusual in air journeys, we were delayed at our port
of call. The Ambassador, Sir Ronald Campbell, was an
old schoolmate of mine, and we were very well looked
after. I had time to see something of Lisbon. Our next
stop was Bermuda, where I had the opportunity of meeting the Speaker of the legislature, and of having a talk
with the Governor. Thence, with a heavy load of passengers, we proceeded to New York.

The proceedings were held at Columbia University,
and we were entertained to lunch by its celebrated president—Nicholas Murray Butler. Here, also, I found an
old schoolfellow, Roger Howson, the librarian of the university, who showed me round Manhattan and Brooklyn
and took me up the Empire State Building. I enjoyed
many talks with Miss Frances Perkins, the Secretary of
Labor, and she showed me a number of social institutions in New York City. Together with an employer and
a worker, Miss Perkins and I took part in a broadcast on
the conference.

The actual business of the conference was interesting
but it did not occupy all my time. I was able to see something of American industry—visiting a big airplane factory in New Jersey and going to Philadelphia to see the
Navy Yard. I must say I was greatly impressed by American efficiency. There was a great contrast between the
Navy Yard's spacious layout on the wide river and the
cramped position of British shipyards on the narrow
waters of the Clyde and the Tyne.

I flew to Washington and stayed with our Ambassador,
Lord Halifax, who had so recently been a colleague in the

cabinet. While there, I visited most of the members of the United States cabinet and had a very interesting talk with Chief Justice Stone on the judicial systems of our two countries.

President Roosevelt invited me to accompany him in his yacht for a cruise on the Potomac. He was a charming companion, a brilliant raconteur, and was full of ideas. It will be remembered that the United States was not yet in the war, but it was clear to me that he thought that it was inevitable that she would sooner or later have to join Britain in saving civilization. He had no illusions as to the nature of nazism. I recall particularly how, when we were discussing the probable course of the war, he took down an atlas and, putting his finger on Algiers, said, "That is where I want to have American troops." It was a remarkable piece of prevision, especially when one considers how reluctant were the American military authorities to undertake operations in North Africa. But Roosevelt had had experience in the Navy office and his mind took a broad sweep of world strategy.

I was present at one of the President's Sunday lunches with his family and enjoyed his reminiscences. He called to mind the villages in the mountains of Kentucky and Tennessee where old English words and phrases, long since fallen into desuetude, were still in use.

The members of the International Labour Organization came down to Washington and were addressed in the White House by the President. The room was so hot that even our friends from Asia and Africa wilted. I had a talk with Philip Murray of the Congress of Industrial Organizations, and William Green, the secretary of the American Federation of Labor, two fine men who died in 1952 within a few days of each other. I thought that they were both considerably more advanced than most American trade unionists whom I had met at conferences. American trade unionism seemed to me to suffer from a lack of the idealist spirit that adherence to the socialist creed brings with it. The general outlook at that time appeared to me to be materialist, differing little from that of other acquisitive groups. I also met the redoubtable John L. Lewis, the leader of the miners—a tempermental Welshman with, I thought, "too much egoism in his cosmos"—to quote Rudyard Kipling.

At Washington I had my first experience of a big American press conference. All the principal newspapermen in the city—American and foreign—were present, and after lunch I was bombarded with questions; some were handed in, others were put straight from the floor. House of Commons experience enabled me to deal with them at great speed without difficulty, and this seemed to surprise some of the audience. I gather that I did not drop any bricks or tread on any corns.

I then went by train to Ottawa, where the Governor General, the Earl of Athlone, and Princess Alice most kindly entertained me. Here I was introduced to the leading citizens, among whom persons of Scottish extraction predominated. I addressed a number of meetings and was entertained by Mackenzie King and his government at dinner at a country club. This started a friendship with him that endured until his death. It was also my privilege to address the Canadian House of Commons.

On our way home we stayed again at Lisbon, which

was, of course, full of spies. It was curious to see Germans walking about the town and a German plane on the airfield. No special precautions were taken to look after us, but I expect the Germans valued this listening post.

When Churchill had formed his government he had asked Cripps to go to Moscow as Ambassador. He had accepted and had carried out a difficult and delicate mission with great skill. With the invasion of Russia, however, the Prime Minister wisely decided to utilize Cripps's great abilities in the government. I warmly welcomed this, for I looked forward to future cooperation with him. He took my place as Lord Privy Seal and became Leader of the House of Commons. Although a brilliant parliamentarian, this was not the work for which he was most suited, and after a few months he was transferred to the Ministry of Aircraft Production, to succeed the dynamic but erratic Lord Beaverbrook. Cripps's work there was outstanding. It was a great pleasure to me to have him as a colleague.

Another accession of strength to the Labour contingent in the government was the appointment of Tom Johnston as Secretary of State for Scotland. The Prime Minister had been impressed by the high ability he had shown as Commissioner for Civil Defence. In his new office he showed great ability in getting all sections to work together, and imagination and enterprise in such work as the development of the Highlands through hydroelectrification. I think that it would be generally agreed that he was the most outstanding Secretary of State that Scotland ever had. It was a great regret to me that he decided at the end of the war to retire from political life.

I now became Deputy Prime Minister and Secretary of State for the Dominions. In the former capacity I acted for Churchill on the fairly numerous occasions when he was absent from the country at various conferences. This gave me valuable experience for the future. It fell to me not infrequently to have to announce bad news to the House of Commons, notably the unexpected fall of Tobruk, though I call to mind one occasion in the later stages of the war when my task was more agreeable.

I had not held a departmental office since I was Postmaster General. The Dominions Office is more akin to the Foreign Office than to other departments. There was much to be done in keeping in close touch with the other countries of the Commonwealth. I used to meet the High Commissioners every day, and I kept in constant communication with our own representatives in the Dominions. I also met the Commonwealth Prime Ministers.

One of the problems I encountered at the Dominions Office was that of the future of Newfoundland. The island had enjoyed self-government as a Dominion, but, owing to financial difficulties, the constitution had been suspended and a Commission of Government now ruled. At the time, owing to the creation of an American base, Newfoundland was enjoying a temporary prosperity. I had visited Newfoundlanders serving in the Armed Forces and on lumber work and was much concerned at what would happen after the war. No Secretary of State had ever visited the island, so I decided to make a new start.

Accordingly, in September I and my Parliamentary Private Secretary flew to Gander and proceeded to St. John's to stay with the Governor, Vice-Admiral Sir Humphrey Walwyn, a very cheery retired sailor. It was almost a tradition to have a sailor as governor. In the early days of the colony, the skipper of the first ship that arrived in the colony became governor for the time being. There we had talks with leading citizens and with the members of the Commission of Government. We visited the American base and were amazed at the standards of accommodation. The barracks were more like a superior club. We visited a number of fishing villages, which are scattered round the coast; these were rather reminiscent of Cornwall, though without its picturesqueness. The people were simple and charming but with little or no idea of cooperating for civic purposes. We were lent the Governor's train and journeyed round the island, calling in at various small towns. The capital, St. John's, was a depressing place. I was told that one visitor returning from a visit to the town said that he was appalled at the slums. His host said, "But have you seen Water Street?" "Yes," he said, "that is just where I have been." Water Street was the business quarter where the merchants had their offices. These merchants had the fishermen in a pretty close grip. The fishermen were in debt to the merchants and had to buy all their supplies from them and sell them their fish. Naturally they did not do very well. Belle Isle, where iron ore is mined, was also pretty bad by our standards. The picturesque villages too were very slummy. The great contrast was the two paper-making towns run by companies—Grand Falls and Cornerbrook. Here very fine social work had been done. The housing and amenities were excellent. At the former town I found Sir Vincent Jones, an Old Haileyburian who had been in charge for

many years and had built up the town. I came to the conclusion that the ills from which the island suffered were
partly due to the fact that its economic resources were not
sufficient to allow it to stand on its own feet and partly to
the lack of public spirit, which had in the past resulted in
a good deal of corruption. Besides this, the island was
dominated by a group of capitalists who monopolized
trade.

We crossed safely to Sydney, Nova Scotia, by steamer,
but the next vessel was torpedoed and lost.

At Ottawa we stayed with the High Commissioner,
Malcolm MacDonald, an old friend who was doing very
fine work. I enjoyed further talks with Mackenzie King
and also met a number of leading members of the Canadian Civil Service. These formed an impressive group of
very able men, equal to the best in Whitehall.

On my return to England I sent out a goodwill mission consisting of three Members of Parliament—Charles
Ammon (now Lord Ammon), Derek Gunston (now Sir
Derek Gunston), and A. P. Herbert (now Sir Alan Herbert)—to visit the island and report their conclusions.
They spent some time there and made valuable and interesting reports.

Later, when I became Prime Minister, I departed from
previous practice by the appointment of a man of political experience as governor. My choice was Gordon Mac-
Donald (now Lord MacDonald), a popular miners' M.P.,
who left Parliament to help with the coal situation
during the war. He fully justified his selection. In 1949
a popular vote resulted in the decision by the people of

Newfoundland to join up with Canada, which was, in my view, the only possible solution to the problem.

In August 1944 I took advantage of the Parliamentary Recess to pay a visit to the Italian theatre of war. George Hall (now Viscount Hall), who was Under Secretary of State for Foreign Affairs, and my Secretary, J. T. A. Burke, accompanied me. We went by air and stopped for breakfast at Gibraltar, where the Governor showed me over the colony—in particular, the caverns in the rock full of stores and workshops. From there we went to Algiers, where we stayed with Duff Cooper (later Viscount Norwich), who was our representative with the French National Committee, which united the anti-Vichy elements in French political life. I had an opportunity of talking with them. There were some experienced politicians among them, and I wished that they were with General de Gaulle in London, for the gallant general's patriotism was unfortunately accompanied by a complete political ineptitude.

From Algiers we went to Caserta, where we lunched with General Wilson (now Field Marshal Lord Wilson), the commander in chief. Thence we drove to Naples. I was much impressed by the skill with which the Navy had got the wrecked port into operation again. While we were there Prime Minister Churchill arrived. This was the first and only time we were both out of the country together. I remember, in discussing this with the Prime Minister, he said, "That's all right, we can leave it for a day or two to the automatic pilot"—meaning that very able administrator, Sir John Anderson. He had been the outstanding civil servant of his generation, and his great experience and his judicial mind were a tower of strength. I remember General Smuts saying to me, "Don't let Churchill send Anderson away. Every war cabinet needs a man to run the machine. Milner did it in the First World War, and Anderson does it in this." Anderson's nickname in Whitehall was, owing to his Olympic calm, "Jehovah." I once remarked to a committee that was waiting for him, "Here we all are—Jehovah's witnesses."

While in Naples we went across to Capri and saw the famous Blue Grotto. I then went to Rome by car. On the way I stopped at Monte Cassino and was taken over the ruins of the famous monastery by a monk, and was able to produce an apposite quotation from Dante: *Che la diritta via era smarrita.*

In Rome I saw the sights and had half an hour's conversation with the Pope. We met at dinner the leading Italian politicians, and I sat next to the Communist leader, Togliatti. There was an amusing incident between him and George Hall. Hall asked him a series of questions such as, "Which was the country that declared war on Hitler without being attacked?" "Which was the country that, though hard pressed, sent munitions to Russia?" "Which was the country that came to the help of Greece when she was attacked?" In every case he had to answer "Britain," whereupon Hall remarked dryly, "You might think of that a bit."

I also talked with the Socialist leaders, Pietro Nenni and Giuseppe Saragat. Nenni told me that he had got a firm agreement with the Communists. I warned him that all experience showed that the Communists would be sure to stab him in the back, a prophecy that was abundantly justified, for when next I met him they had just left him in the lurch. Signor Saragat seems to have taken my warning more seriously. Nenni is now a mere fellow traveller.

From Rome I flew to Siena and stayed with General Alexander. I was impressed by the way in which his staff of British and American officers was completely integrated. He lent me his plane to fly across to the Adriatic Front. On the way back we circled round Perugia, which recalled happy memories of my visit in 1921. We stayed the night in a caravan at General Leese's headquarters and next day went up the line. I had tea with two relations— a cousin, Major General Walsh, Chief of Staff Eighth Army, and a nephew, Sergeant Fletcher of the Signals Corps.

Lord Tweedsmuir took me in a jeep right up to the front line where he was in command, and we saw some newly captured Germans—very young and unpleasant-looking—the products, I fancy, of the Hitler Youth Movement. We returned covered with yellow dust.

From Siena I drove out to visit General Mark Clark, who was commanding the Americans. I inspected a guard of honour, feeling very small beside the general, who is of great height.

I drove into Florence and saw again the Duomo and other well-loved buildings, and also saw the destruction wrought by the Germans on the bridges over the Arno. After that I flew back to Algiers, where I was hospitably entertained by an American Admiral and, in due course, rejoined George Hall. We had intended to go to Gibraltar but a heavy mist came down. Our pilot first tried to find Gibraltar by flying low and then tried to see the point of the Rock. He asked, "What is the height of it?" and I was relieved when he decided to make for Rabat instead. From there, after tea with the British Consul, we flew back to England.

During the same month I paid a visit to Normandy. I saw the artificial harbour busily at work, and was especially struck by the procession of DUKWs coming in and discharging their loads, which were picked up by lorries. The whole thing worked like clockwork.

I visited Caen and Bayeux, towns I had known in more peaceful days. At Caen I met an officer of my regiment who was in command of a labour battalion which was building a bridge over the canal. I was glad to see him. I had a year or two before intervened to prevent his being given a "bowler hat" on account of his having used strong language to some officers who had grossly failed to look after their men. He was, I knew, a first-class fighting soldier.

I spent the night in a tent near Bayeux and then had a long drive in a jeep to visit General Bradley's Chief of Staff. It provided an opportunity for seeing something of the American troops. I visited General Montgomery, who was in his caravan in a wood. He described his plans, and showed me how closely what had actually happened coincided with the forecast he had made.

As the tide of Nazi conquest rolled back, the cabinet were anxious as to what would happen in the freed countries; more especially were they concerned with the food problem. The position of the Dutch was very critical. I was charged with the task of looking into this and kindred problems. We made careful plans for sending in food in case of emergency—if possible, by land and sea, but, if necessary, by air.

I visited Allied Headquarters at Versailles and saw Paris looking very shabby after its long occupation. On the way to Belgium by car I saw Aachen; the whole town was flat except for the cathedral and a small area round it. I was also taken in a jeep along the Siegfried Line; thence to Brussels, which looked very smart compared to Paris, and on to Antwerp, upon which V-1s were still dropping.

I had a long drive to Walcheren Island, which was still flooded. I saw the breaches in the dykes and the place where the Marines had landed. Flushing was rather a pitiful sight; there were streets on the outskirts lined with pleasant little houses but with water up to the first floor. I was taken in a DUKW to Middelburg, which stood out like an island in a lake. There were raised duckboard tracks in the streets at first-floor level, for the lower parts of the houses were under water. I went along them and talked with the leading citizens and was struck by their courage. Their beautiful island was ruined for some years. We had had to do it in order to open the way for ships to go to Antwerp. They said, "Our island has been flooded several times in the last thousand years. It is better to be free even if our land is under water." I saw the efforts being made to mend the dykes. It was a race against time, as it had to be completed before winter set in.

There was a sequel to this when my wife and I later

visited the island to take part in the ceremony of planting trees to replace those that had been destroyed by the floods. On this occasion we flew to The Hague and stayed with the Ambassador, Sir Nevile Bland. We went by train to the island, being joined en route by Princess (now Queen) Juliana and Prince Bernhard of the Netherlands. The proceedings were delightfully informal. We drove round the island and then took part in the ceremony of tree planting, the trees being held in position by little girls in old Dutch costumes. The whole island was keeping festival, and it was pleasant to see how much had been done to restore the war damage. We also attended a service in the Cathedral at Flushing.

XVI

The End of the Wartime Government

THE INCREASING prospects of an early end to the war in Europe brought about a growing strain on the Coalition government. I had hoped that the comprehensive schemes of social reform that had been formulated by members of the Conservative and Labour parties, and agreed upon, might be passed into law. In particular, there was the implementation of the Beveridge Report, on which a vast amount of work had been done. There was great pressure from the Labour party for legislation. It became clear to me that Churchill had other views. I think that he conceived a Conservative Social Reform government coming into power and carrying out over a period of five years the programme of reforms we had worked out. In other respects the administration would be Conservative. This was quite natural, for he had never been returned at an election as the leader of a victorious party and he would have liked to have followed up his success as a war leader by showing that he could also be a great Prime Minister in peace. I found, therefore, that it was more and more difficult to get postwar projects before the cabinet.

Agreements arrived at after long discussion by a committee, in which both parties were fully represented, were blocked by the opposition of certain members of the government who evinced a quite new interest in subjects hitherto outside the range of their attention. It was, indeed, becoming clear that the Coalition government formed to win the war would not survive its success.

It was in these circumstances that I was asked to be a member of the delegation to San Francisco, to take part in the founding of the United Nations. Anthony Eden, as Foreign Secretary, was to head the delegation, and although I was Deputy Prime Minister I had no hesitation in accepting his leadership. Lord Salisbury was the other principal delegate, but there were a number of junior ministers from all three parties, including—from our side —George Tomlinson and Ellen Wilkinson. John Dugdale, who was now a Member of Parliament, came with me, having taken over the position of my Parliamentary Private Secretary from Arthur Jenkins, who had joined the government as an Under Secretary.

We set off in May 1945 and flew by way of the Azores across the Atlantic. We broke our journey across the United States at Denver, Colorado, where we were most hospitably entertained. During our stay there we had a very fine drive into the Rocky Mountains. On the way we saw people playing tennis, while higher up winter sports were in full swing. Proceeding on our journey, we flew over the Rockies and landed at San Francisco. This was my first visit to the West, and I enjoyed our stay in this lovely city with its steep streets and magnificent harbour.

Most of our time was taken up with the conference and I met many interesting people. The American Secretary of State, Edward Stettinius, presided, and was supported by Republicans and Democrats, notably Senator Connally, Senator Vandenberg, and Harold Stassen. Much of the work was done in private meetings of the heads of delegations. Molotov led the Russians, and in those days he was quite cooperative and used to echo the "Okay" of the Americans and British. It is a pity that it later dropped out of his vocabulary. I remember we went round the Kaiser shipyard and Molotov asked a worker what was the badge on his coat. He said it was his trade-union badge. Molotov asked his wages and was rather startled to learn how high they were.

We British formed a harmonious team, meeting daily under my chairmanship to discuss the work of the day and to report what had been done by our members on the various committees on which they served. There were also frequent meetings with our friends of the Commonwealth delegations. The photographers were very much in evidence at the conference: in fact, on the one occasion when a vote was taken and we were asked to stand up, I said that it was obvious that the cameramen were in the majority.

Among the delegates was Field Marshal Smuts, who played a prominent part in the conference. He was the only leader who had taken part in the founding of the League of Nations. The preamble that was adopted declaring the aims of the United Nations was based on a draft he put forward.

While we were at the conference the news came through that the war against the Nazis had ended. We gathered to celebrate the event in a room at the top of a skyscraper. In San Francisco the Japanese war was nearer and of greater concern to the citizens than the European contest, and we were sorry not to be at home for the celebrations.

I spent a weekend with Dugdale at the town of Stockton, staying with some of his friends. We drove round the old mining camps, now semi-derelict, but full of memories of the old days described by Bret Harte. We also saw the great redwood trees. Dugdale and I visited an old friend who used to be my neighbour in Limehouse. The press made much of the fact that we insisted on sharing in the washing-up after supper.

The biggest issue at the conference was the question of the veto in the Security Council. We agreed with the Americans and the Russians that the veto was necessary, but many delegates of the smaller powers, especially Peter Fraser of New Zealand, opposed it strongly. It was clear to me that the veto was essential, but the assumption was that it would be used very sparingly. Its subsequent misuse by the Russians was quite contrary to the spirit in which it was accepted. Another matter of some controversy was that of trusteeship, in which powers with colonial possessions found themselves at variance with those whose views were based on admirable sentiments but great lack of practical knowledge of actual conditions.

Meanwhile political events had been moving at home, and as all major decisions at San Francisco had been taken it was agreed that Eden and I and some of the delegates should return, leaving Lord Salisbury and Lord Halifax, British Ambassador in Washington, in charge. The coming General Election was already casting its shadow. We flew back by a southerly route round the Rockies and across the Southern states and arrived in London after an uneventful journey.

Bevin and Morrison informed me of the talks they had had with Prime Minister Churchill as to the future of the government, and I then also discussed the whole question with him. We considered the possibility of the government's carrying on until the end of the Japanese war, which, it was then thought, might continue for many months. I did not know then that the atom-bomb project was about to come to fruition, for knowledge of it had been restricted to a very narrow circle. It looked at that time as if the Japanese would have to be dislodged piece-meal from the wide area they occupied.

After a day or two I sensed that there was very heavy pressure from the Conservatives to "cash in" on victory. It will be remembered that the formation of the wartime government had coincided with the Labour party Annual Conference at Bournemouth, which had enabled me to get the full backing of the party for entering Churchill's government. Fortunately the same thing happened in 1945. The issue of continued participation in Churchill's administration came to a head at Whitsun when the party conference was to meet at Blackpool. There was therefore a full opportunity for discussing the whole matter with the Executive and the party leaders and of obtaining the opinion of the supreme party authority.

The conference, over which Ellen Wilkinson presided,

was united and enthusiastic. After full consideration of all the issues, it was decided that the time had come for the party to resume its independence. On May 21, 1945, I wrote a letter to Churchill setting out our position very fully:

> I thank you for your letter of May 18. I have, with my colleagues, given the most careful consideration to the proposal which you make that we should continue together until the end of the Japanese war and seek a further extension of life for the present Parliament. The Labour party, on entering the government, set no particular date for the termination of the partnership. It has, however, been recognized that a General Election must necessarily bring the partnership to an end if the electors are to have full and free opportunity of expressing their views on future policy.
>
> The need for bringing to an end, when conditions allowed, a Parliament, the life of which has been prolonged year after year, has been recognized by all of us, and by no one more emphatically than yourself. You stated that the prolongation of the life of the existing Parliament by another two or three years would be a very serious constitutional lapse. It is for that reason that my colleagues and I have always held that there should be an interval between the time when conditions permitted an election to be held and the election itself. Recognizing the possibility of prejudice to the party holding power during this interim period, we have been prepared to share the responsibilities of government up to the time when an election was declared. An autumn election would provide a more complete and effective register than that now in force and would give to the Service electors the opportunity of more fully ac-

quainting themselves with the candidates' standing
and the issues involved in the election than would be
available in July. Service candidates would also have
a fair chance of making themselves known to the
electorate. My colleagues and I do not share your
view that the country's interests would be prejudiced
by a continuance of the present government until the
autumn. On the contrary, we think that there would
be great advantage in the government which has successfully brought the nation through the war continuing for a short time in order to deal with the
immediate problems in the international field, and
especially to help bring to a successful conclusion the
San Francisco Conference. We can rely on our members in the House to do all they can to maintain this
unity.

The increasing success of our arms warranted you,
when introducing the last Prolongation of Parliament Bill, to assume the probability of the defeat of
Germany. As you said: "We must look to the termination of the war against nazism as a pointer which
will fix the date of the General Election." Political
parties and the country generally shared your justi-
fiable faith in victory this year, and have, therefore,
accepted from you the end of the present session as
the terminal date for a General Election. It has been
the view of the Labour party, which I think you
share, that a rushed election like that of 1918, before
the electorate, and especially those serving overseas,
have had a fair opportunity of considering candidates and policies, would be utterly wrong and
would gravely weaken the authority of any government resulting from such an election at a time when
public confidence would be especially necessary. We,
therefore, consider that the fair and just solution of
the problem is an election in the autumn. You sug-

gest, as an alternative, that we should continue together until the end of the Japanese war. It is unnecessary for me to assure you that, whether in or out of the government, the Labour party will give its fullest support to the war until Japan is defeated. But when this will be is uncertain. We hope it may be soon, but if it were to be prolonged we see arising in a much more acute form all those difficulties which you apprehend at the present time in the domestic sphere and which you give as an objection to continuing to the autumn.

It is precisely on the problems of the reconstruction of the economic life of the country that party differences are most acute. What is required is decisive action. This can only be forthcoming from a government united on principle and policy. A government so divided that it could take no effective action would be a disaster to the country. My colleagues and I do not believe that it would be possible to lay aside political controversy now that the expectation of an election has engaged the attention of the country. To give a guarantee of agreement to carry on for an indefinite period is not in my power, nor, I suggest, in yours.

I do not think that it would be right or possible to obtain from Parliament another prolongation of its life. I could not consent to the introduction into our national life of a device so alien to all our traditions as the referendum, which has only too often been the instrument of nazism and fascism. Hitler's practices in the field of referenda and plebiscites can hardly have endeared these expedients to the British heart. For the reasons which I have given your present proposal is unacceptable.

It has been my desire, publicly expressed, that the long and honourable association of the parties in the government which has brought the country through so many perils to victory under your leadership, loyally supported by your Labour colleagues, should be brought to an end by common agreement and without controversy. I am sure that this would be your own wish, but I am bound to state that the reasons for rejecting an autumn election seem to me to be based not on national interests but on consideration of party expediency. It appears to me that you are departing from the position of a national leader by yielding to the pressure of the Conservative party, which is anxious to exploit your own great service to the nation in its own interests. I would earnestly ask you to reconsider your decision to hold an election under circumstances which are bound to cause bitter resentment among the men of the fighting Services. Should you, however, decide on an election in July despite all the disadvantages to the electors set out in this letter, with which you are familiar, the responsibility must and will, of course, be yours.

The conference enthusiastically approved the election programme. Perhaps the highlight of the conference was a very fine speech on foreign affairs by Bevin, who at that time had no idea that in a few months he would be in charge at the Foreign Office.

Harold Laski became chairman of the party Executive, a fact that was to be of some importance in the immediate future. The position of chairman of the Executive is not always well understood. He or she is elected for a year only by the Executive from among their own number. It has become the practice to choose the member with the longest service who has not occupied the chair. It is rather a curious custom and has at times resulted in the chair being occupied in difficult times by a person not very well qualified. The duty of the chairman is to preside over meetings of the Executive and at the Annual Conference. The Leader of the Labour party, on the other hand, is the chairman of the Parliamentary Labour party, elected to that position annually by the members of the Parliamentary Labour party in the House of Commons. In the early days of the party in the House the chairmanship was frequently changed, but for the last eighteen years I have held the position. Harold Laski, who seemed to me to be always uncertain as to whether his role was to be that of a leading figure on the political stage or an *eminence grise* operating influentially behind the scenes, appeared to incline to the first role when he became chairman.

The Labour Ministers resigned their offices in May 1945 and returned to the Opposition Front Bench for the short time before the election to face the "Caretaker" government Churchill had formed.

In the Honours List that followed the ending of the wartime coalition I was made a Companion of Honour.

It seems appropriate here to say something of the wartime government and of its leader. I have often paid my tribute to Churchill's great leadership. Undoubtedly the hour found the man and the man found his hour. The hour was one of mortal peril. Our Allies had been struck down and we stood alone, facing a formidable enemy across the Channel, able to mobilize against us the greater part of the resources of a whole continent. Our armies had escaped with the loss of the bulk of their equipment. There was no immediate prospect of help from any quarter. We were under no illusions as to these dangers. We lived on faith, but that faith burned clear in the whole nation. Churchill was supremely fitted to give that faith expression. He said in unforgettable phrases what people had in their minds. He inspired everyone. Britain was, I think, fortunate to have at hand a man who, besides his personal qualities, held a peculiar position. He had been at odds with the Conservative party and was thus free from the taint of Munich. This made it possible for Labour Ministers to work under him, which they could not have done so easily with a regular supporter of Chamberlain. He was, on the other hand, a Conservative. I doubt whether any Labour leader would have been accepted by the Tories.

Leadership in war requires exceptional qualities. Two men in our time had them to a marked degree—Lloyd George and Churchill. Both of them had the power of injecting into the whole administration and, indeed, into the life of the nation, the sense of urgency that success in war requires. Both of them had minds receptive to new ideas and strong wills to overcome inertia and the opposition of the hidebound. History will no doubt give her verdict as to which of these two war leaders was the greater. In my view, the balance lies on the side of Churchill, though, of course, my judgment may be affected by personal experience. Churchill had the great advantage over Lloyd George of having studied military matters for many years. There was not, therefore, in the Second World War, that constant clash between the military men and the politicians which comes out so vividly in the histories and diaries that tell of the 1914-1918 war.

He had also the advantage of having had the experience of office in the First World War and of having fought in the field.

Churchill's wide knowledge of history and his ability to see the present as a stage in the unfolding of the drama of the ages made his outlook more spacious than that of Lloyd George. He kept a close eye on all that was going on under his government, but was content to repose a good deal of responsibility on his colleagues, especially on home matters, although at any moment he might make an incursion into fields with which he was not closely concerned. He was fertile in ideas—some good, some bad. Lloyd George once said to me apropos of some matter, "There's Winston—he has half a dozen solutions to it and one of them is right, but the trouble is he does not know which it is." This is putting the matter extremely, but I think that Churchill does need men around him who, while ready to support a good idea, however novel, are prepared on occasions to take an emphatic line against a bad one.

The wartime government contained a number of very able men. Perhaps the two most outstanding were Sir John Anderson and Ernest Bevin, but there were many others who played no inconsiderable part in winning the war. I have very pleasant memories of working with my colleagues in the government. It was very seldom that any party issues arose to divide us until the last stage, when I think they were designedly fomented by certain persons. Usually, applying our minds to the actual problems facing us, we came to an agreement as to what was the best course. Quite naturally, in war, where the public good must take precedence over private interests, the solutions had a strong Socialist flavour.

During the war I got to know Lord Portal very well, and I and my family experienced much kindness from him and Lady Portal. He did extremely good service, especially in relation to the procurement and allocation of raw materials. I was very indignant when, in the last year of the war, he was extruded from office. He was one of the ablest of the businessmen who joined the government. Extremely generous and public-spirited, he won the hearts of Labour by his work for the distressed areas before the war.

The short session of Parliament that intervened between the resignation of the wartime government and the General Election was devoted to clearing up outstanding business and to debates in which the speakers had their eyes turned more to the constituencies than to the House of Commons. Very careful arrangements had been made to ensure that those serving in the field should have full opportunity of registering their votes. Special arrangements had also been made to hold the election later in certain Lancashire towns because their holiday Wakes Weeks coincided with the General Election date. The collection of the votes of the men and women in the Armed Forces involved a delay of three weeks between the close of the poll and the declaration of the results.

Broadcasting has made a great difference to the way in which General Elections are fought. In the old days even the most active leader was heard by only a few score thousand. Nowadays, the leader speaking on the radio may have an audience of millions. Nevertheless there are still

those who like to go to public meetings. Some desire to
see as well as hear some prominent person. Others go in
order to feel the glow of enthusiasm that a big meeting
evokes. The influence of the radio has, I think, operated
to make election audiences more thoughtful and more
desirous of listening to solid reasoning.

My own constituency of Limehouse had been devas-
tated by bombing and was reduced to about sixteen thousand voters. My supporters were confident that I should
have no difficulty in retaining the seat and willingly set
me free so that I might undertake an electoral tour
throughout the country. Before this, however, I had to
deliver the first of the Labour speeches in the B.B.C. electoral series—following Churchill. I had prepared a
speech that was intended to be a careful exposition of
the Labour programme, with very little party polemics in
it. The unexpectedly violent attack by the Prime Minister on his late colleagues and on all that they stood for
raised the question as to what line I should follow. I decided not to alter my original script but only to add a few
words of comment on the line taken by my opponent. For
example, on the question of traditional British freedom,
I said:

> The Prime Minister made much play last night
> with the rights of the individual and the dangers of
> people being ordered about by officials. I entirely
> agree that people should have the greatest freedom
> compatible with the freedom of others. There was a
> time when employers were free to work little chil-
> dren for sixteen hours a day. I remember when em-
> ployers were free to employ sweated women workers
> on finishing trousers at a penny-halfpenny a pair.

There was a time when people were free to neglect
sanitation so that thousands died of preventable dis-
eases. For years every attempt to remedy these crying
evils was blocked by the same plea of freedom for
the individual. It was in fact freedom for the rich
and slavery for the poor. Make no mistake, it has only
been through the power of the state, given to it by
Parliament, that the general public has been protected against the greed of ruthless profit-makers and
property owners.

After sketching the events that had led up to the election
and outlining some aspects of Labour's policy at home
and abroad, I concluded my broadcast with a reference
to the representative nature of the party:

> Forty years ago the Labour party might, with some
> justice, have been called a class party, representing
> almost exclusively the wage earners. It is still based
> on organized labour, but has steadily become more
> and more inclusive. In the ranks of the Parliamen-
> tary party and among our candidates you will find
> numbers of men and women drawn from every class
> and occupation in the community. Wage and salary
> earners form the majority, but there are many from
> other walks of life, from the professions and from the
> business world, giving a wide range of experience.
> More than a hundred and twenty of our candidates
> come from the Fighting Services, so that youth is
> well represented.
>
> The present government is Conservative. I do not
> suppose that the Prime Minister expected anyone to
> take seriously his claim that, in addition to the Con-
> servative majority, a few Independents who are stay-
> ing on as temporary caretakers, and some tame
> Liberals who owe their seats to Tory votes and obey

strictly the Tory Whip, really make his government "National." It is Conservative. The Conservative party remains as always a class party. In twenty-three years in the House of Commons I cannot recall more than half a dozen from the ranks of the wage earners. It represents today, as in the past, the forces of property and privilege. The Labour party is, in fact, the one party which most nearly reflects in its representation and composition all the main streams which flow into the great river of our national life.

Our appeal to you, therefore, is not narrow or sectional. We are proud of the fact that our country in the hours of its greatest danger stood firm and united, setting an example to the world of how a great democratic people rose to the height of the occasion and saved democracy and liberty. We are proud of the self-sacrifice and devotion displayed by men and women in every walk of life in this great adventure. We call you to another great adventure, which will demand the same high qualities as those shown in the war—the adventure of civilization.

We have seen a great and powerful nation return to barbarism. We have seen European civilization almost destroyed and an attempt made to set aside the moral principles upon which it has been built. It is for us to help to reknit the fabric of civilized life woven through the centuries, and with the other nations to seek to create a world in which free peoples living their own distinctive lives in a society of nations cooperate together, free from the fear of war.

We have to plan the broad lines of our national life so that all may have the duty and the opportunity of rendering service to the nation, everyone in his or her sphere, and that all may help to create and share in an increasing material prosperity free from the fear of want. We have to preserve and enhance

the beauty of our country to make it a place where
men and women may live finely and happily, free to
worship God in their own way, free to speak their
minds, free citizens of a great country.

I think that it was a tactical error on the part of Churchill to take the line he did. I considered that he had probably been ill advised by Lord Beaverbrook and said so in
my broadcast. I feel that the line I took was more in accord with the mood of the electors. I have been told that
this broadcast had a considerable effect on the campaign.
Instead of an election manifesto my article, "An Appeal
to the Nation," was issued to all our candidates. In my
election address to my own constituents I was careful to
warn them that the postwar years would not be easy, and
I struck the same note in my speeches in the country.

A very extensive tour had been arranged for me with
seven or eight meetings a day. I was to go up through the
West Midlands to Lancashire and down through New-
castle, Yorkshire, the Eastern Counties, and so back to
London. It was a campaign even more strenuous than
that of 1935. On this occasion, as on that, I was accompanied by H. R. S. Philpott of the *Daily Herald,* who was
invaluable in dealing with the press and in reporting the
meetings. This time my wife drove me in our own car. It
was her responsibility to see that I got to all the meetings
in time, and she never failed to do so. Our rather unosten-
tatious method of travel contrasted with the elaborate
procession that accompanied Churchill on his journey.
Quite unintentionally, this turned out to be somewhat of
an asset, as it was given a great deal of prominence in the
press.

Everywhere we went we received an enthusiastic reception and great crowds attended the meetings. I spoke about seventy times in all, and practically all of my speeches were extempore, as I dislike speaking from notes. At all the places I visited I was assured that we should score a great victory. Having fought many campaigns, I did not allow myself to be too optimistic about the result, for I knew that electoral fights are not won by crowded meetings. I knew, too, that Churchill was having what was described as a triumphal progress and also how great was his popularity. I recalled how Lloyd George, as "the man who won the war," had swept the country in 1918. On the other hand, by-elections had shown a big swing to the Left. During the war, under the terms of the electoral truce, the Labour party could not put up candidates. Indeed, I then wrote letters asking our members to support Conservatives. There had, however, been formed a Commonwealth party with a programme very like our own, and, despite their lack of organization, several Commonwealth candidates had been returned for what were usually safe Conservative seats. I concluded my campaign with a number of meetings in London and a final rally in Limehouse.

In the course of the campaign an issue arose which the Conservatives endeavoured to develop into an election scare. This was not tactically very wise because we had warned our people assiduously of the likelihood of something of the sort occurring and they were therefore pretty well scareproof. The matter arose thus. A conference was to be held at Potsdam between Britain, the United States, and Russia. In view of the uncertainty of the result of the election, Prime Minister Churchill, wisely in my view, invited me to accompany him as one of the British representatives. After consulting leading colleagues, I accepted. Laski, whose political judgment was not very good, made a very indiscreet statement in which he suggested that I should go to Potsdam only as an observer. He issued this statement as chairman of the Executive, although he had no authority to do so. The chairman of the Executive does not make authoritative pronouncements of this kind. The Prime Minister—also, I think, unwisely—took this up in a series of letters to me designed to show that I was a mere tool in the hands of a non-Parliamentary body, the National Executive of the Labour party. I explained patiently what was the actual position, but he was very persistent. All the correspondence was published. Sometimes his letters reached me at a late hour at night, but I always contrived to get my replies into the press the same day as his letters appeared. I was generally thought to have had the better of the exchanges. The authors of *The British General Election of 1945,* McCallum and Readman, stated that I had the air of a sound and steady batsman keeping up his wicket with ease against a demon bowler who was losing both pace and length. Laski, incidentally, had tried very hard to substitute Morrison for me as Leader of the party but failed to get any response.

On July 5 I saw the electors of Limehouse walking to vote through wide open spaces which had once been streets crowded with people. Three weeks of suspense followed.

❁   ❁   ❁   ❁   ❁   ❁   ❁

❁   XVII   ❁

Labour in Power

IMMEDIATELY after the end of the election I flew to
Potsdam to join Churchill and Eden in the talks with
our American and Russian Allies. Lord Woolton kindly
released my old Secretary, J. T. A. Burke, to accompany
me. We landed at the airport near Potsdam and drove to
a villa near a lake where we were to stay. It had been the
property of a German engineer whose library consisted
of German technical and fascist books but included,
oddly enough, Miss Mitford's *Our Village.*

I suppose that in most countries the idea that the two
leaders in a hotly contested election should be able to
meet again on easy terms, and to cooperate, would seem
strange, but we had so recently been colleagues that we
experienced no difficulty.

We were in the Russian Zone and, except in our immediate vicinity, Russian soldiers, whom I saw for the first
time, were plentiful and the safety precautions taken
were complete. I recall that once, while driving to dine
with Stalin, we were held up for some time by a Russian

officer with whom we could not converse and who was full of suspicion.

Our meetings took place in the Cecilienhof, a Stock-Exchange-Gothic mansion which belonged to the Crown Prince and was full of English books. Stalin presided with Molotov as his chief assistant. President Truman and Secretary of State Byrnes led for the Americans. There was a host of advisers, civil and military, including General Alexander (now Field Marshal Earl Alexander) and Marshal of the Royal Air Force Lord Tedder.

The discussions were difficult as the Russians were out to get all they could in the way of territory and reparations and insisted on the very big concessions they had got at Teheran and Yalta. We sought to get a reasonable settlement which would allow Germany some prospect of becoming, in time, a member of the European community of nations. We were also acutely aware of the combination of Russian old-time and Communist modern imperialism which threatened the freedom of Europe. I thought that the Americans had an insufficient appreciation of this danger, and indeed of the whole European situation. They suspected the British of being old-time imperialists and were inclined to think of Russia and America as two big boys who could settle things amicably between them. This was no doubt partly due to the fact that Roosevelt had managed to get on fairly good terms with Stalin at Yalta.

We attended an impressive parade of British troops in the Unter den Linden. One of our interpreters elicited from some Russian officers, who were looking on, that what struck them most was the way in which Churchill and I walked about without any guards and the fact that the uniform of our officers was so little different from that of the men. In Berlin, which presented an appalling scene of destruction, I went over the wreck of the German Chancellery where Hitler spent his last days.

Generally, our relationship with our Russian Allies was friendly, and I talked with Stalin and Molotov on various social occasions. Molotov's smile never seemed to go beyond his lips, but Stalin had a lively sense of humour. I remember, after a long controversy about Spain in which he had denounced Franco and all his ways, the question of a meeting place in another connection came up, and he blandly said, "Well, why not Madrid?" On another occasion, when he had been venting his distrust about our retention of Hess, he enjoyed Bevin's remark, "You can have Hess but we'll charge you his keep for two years."

Our talks were interrupted in order that we might return home to hear the result of the General Election. I got back to Stanmore on the eve of the count. My wife, who always acts as a counting agent at elections, had already seen the opening of the boxes of the Service voters and had a good idea of how the land lay, but kept it to herself. We drove to Stepney with my daughters, Janet and Felicity, to be present at the count. It very soon appeared that much of the interest would turn on the loss or saving of deposits.[1] In Whitechapel both Liberal and Tory lost theirs. My opponent, Lieutenant A. N. P.

---

[1] Candidates for election to Parliament must deposit £150. This is returned if the candidate is elected or if he polls more than one-eighth of the total votes cast; otherwise the deposit is forfeited to the Crown.—*Ed.*

Woodward, a pleasant young man, saved his, but my majority was 6,789 out of a poll of 10,006.

The only drawback was the loss of Mile End to a Communist. During the count rumours of Labour victories began to come in. We drove through the City and picked up at Waterloo my daughter Alison, who was returning from school, and went on to Transport House. There seemed to be much excitement outside and crowds of photographers. We were greeted with great enthusiasm and found that there was every indication of a landslide in our favour. Conservative Ministers were losing seats and we were making a clean sweep of the big towns. As the day wore on country results confirmed our victory, and by the middle of the afternoon it was clear that we had won a great victory.

Lord Portal, who was chairman of the Great Western Railway, gave the family tea at Paddington, and presently I was told by Prime Minister Churchill that he was resigning. A summons to the Palace followed. My wife drove me there and waited outside for me. The King gave me his commission to form a government. He always said later that I looked very surprised, as indeed I certainly was, at the extent of our success. We went to a Victory Rally at Westminster Central Hall, where I announced that I had been charged with the task of forming a government, looked in at a Fabian Society gathering, and then returned to Stanmore after an exciting day.

The Potsdam Conference was awaiting the return of the British representatives, and I had only a short time to form the nucleus of a government. Fortunately there was a strong team available. There were those who had been

Ministers in the wartime government, the original members having been reinforced by Tom Johnston and Stafford Cripps, who had now rejoined the Labour party. Cripps had left the party owing to his advocacy of a Popular Front with the Communists. There were also those who had served as Under Secretaries, the original seven having increased to fifteen during the course of the war. There were also survivors of the 1929 government who had not been in the wartime administration, notably Addison, Pethick-Lawrence, and Stansgate, and, in the Commons, Shinwell and Lawson. There was, therefore, no lack of experience, while I was aware that there was a great deal of ability among the new members, some of whom were ripe for office. I limited myself to six appointments before leaving for Potsdam. The filling of the other posts could wait.

Neither Churchill nor Eden wished to return to Potsdam, so Ernest Bevin, the new Foreign Secretary, and I returned alone. Our arrival created somewhat of a sensation. Our American friends were surprised to find that there was no change in our official advisers and that I had even taken over, as my Principal Private Secretary, Leslie Rowan, who had been serving Churchill in the same capacity. Molotov kept saying, "But you said the election would be a close thing and now you have a big majority." I said, "Yes, we could not tell what the result would be." But he kept repeating the same phrase. He could not understand why we had not known the result. I am sure he thought that Churchill would have "fixed" the election. The change-over by democratic process was a great shock to him.

Bevin at once gave proof of his remarkable ability by the speed with which he picked up all the threads of the subjects under discussion and appreciated what were the attitudes of the Americans and the Russians. We had our distinctive position on a number of points but very often found ourselves in a minority. There was, for instance, the discussion as to the eastern boundary of Germany. In our view, the Russians were asking too much when they demanded the Oder-Neisse line for Poland, thus expelling the Germans from lands almost wholly inhabited by them. We were obliged to accept the position pending a peace settlement, but it was obvious that, once settled in this sense, it would be difficult to change the boundary. We also had to concede more on reparations from Germany to Russia than we thought either just or feasible. We did our utmost to try to secure that the people of Poland should choose what regime they wished to have. There were two rival Polish organizations—one that had been in London and under whose leadership the Polish Armed Forces had fought so gallantly; the other called the "Lublin Poles," who were the creatures of Russia. Bevin and I met the latter and gained a very disagreeable impression of them. Eventually a joint government was formed, but the Communists, supported by Russian arms, soon liquidated their colleagues of other parties.

I recall very well President Truman's telling me that the atom bomb had been tried out successfully at Los Alamos and how he informed Stalin of this. Stalin made no comment though it must have given him a bad shock.

The agreement made at Potsdam for a quadripartite administration of Germany would have worked all right given goodwill, but after a fairly favourable start it became plain that here, as in so many other fields, the will to cooperate was wanting.

On my return from Potsdam I had to complete the government—a difficult task at any time. I was fortunate in that we were a united party, a great contrast to the position that had obtained after the First World War. I was therefore able to draw on all the talent available, and I think I got together a very strong government.

The first task of the Labour government was to complete the winning of the war against Japan, and it was generally anticipated that this might prove to be long and difficult. A very large part of Southeast Asia had been overrun and occupied. The Japanese might well have decided to carry on the war in these widespread areas until the last of them had been hunted down in the jungles, but the use of the atom bomb at Hiroshima brought the war to a sudden end. It was, of course, an immense relief, but it brought with it very difficult immediate problems. Instead of a gradual redeployment of our forces from the Western to the Eastern theatres of war, we now had to deal with demobilization on a much larger scale than had been anticipated. Fortunately, plans for demobilization based on simple, just, and understandable principles had been worked out, largely under the inspiration of Bevin when Minister of Labour during the War, and these plans we adhered to. We were very mindful of the chaos and near mutinies that had occurred after the First World War. Despite the unwise pressure of the Leader of the Opposition for a more rapid demobilization, we stuck to our well-laid plans and were helped not a little by the personal visits Jack Lawson, the Secretary of State for War, paid to the troops overseas. The whole process was effected with remarkably little friction and discontent.

The economic effect of the end of the Japanese war was far more serious. Our whole economy had been geared to the war effort. We had allowed our export trade to decline. We were closely integrated with the United States economy through the operation of Lend-Lease, and this had meant that we had not had to worry about our supplies of food and raw materials or about our overseas payments. Now, in a moment, all this was brought to an end. I do not know whether President Truman could have continued Lend-Lease for a reasonable period in order to give us time for redeploying our industry, but in fact he did not. I doubt if the American administration realized how serious was the blow it struck. We were faced at once with an acute crisis. Loans were essential to tide us over a very difficult period. In due course, these were negotiated with the United States and Canada, and we sent, as our principal negotiator, Lord Keynes, who brought all his remarkable ability to the task.

Although I became Prime Minister at a time of great difficulty, and in the midst of all the international problems which arise at the end of a world war, I was, in other ways, very fortunate. With only a very short intervening period, I had been in office for five years. I had been Deputy Prime Minister and was therefore acquainted not only with all the outstanding problems, but with the course of events out of which they had developed. I had had a full experience of high and responsible office, understood the machinery of government, and knew personally the leading figures in the Civil Service and in the Fighting Services. I had many experienced colleagues and I was backed by a large and solid majority in the House of Commons, while I had a good team in the House of Lords.

How different had been the position of MacDonald in 1924 when, with no experience of office and with only three or four ex-Ministers, he had to take office in a minority. Even in 1929, though his support in the Commons was greater than five years earlier, he still lacked a majority and was short of experienced Ministers.

For many years I had given a good deal of thought to the problem of the machinery of government, having realized that the old pattern needed reforming in the light of the wide extensions of government activity and the inevitable increase in the number of departmental Ministers. In 1940 it had been thought right, for war purposes, to have a small cabinet. This was in accordance with the precedent set in 1916 after experience had shown the need for it. The question I had to answer was, "What should be the size and composition of the cabinet in peacetime?" After the First World War there had been a return to prewar practice of a cabinet composed of twenty or even more Ministers. Its composition was largely on traditional lines. Certain offices were held to carry cabinet rank, and therefore the holders must be included. Sometimes holders of the offices were included because of their personal standing. But there was no definite theoretical basis.

I was aware that there was a view held in some quarters that a cabinet should be composed of only a few members without departmental responsibilities—a cabinet of "overlords"—its function being essentially that of dealing with large matters of policy. It was to be an instrument of decision. I had myself been attracted by this idea though I was well aware that considerations—both political and personal—would make it difficult to adopt in its entirety. Having had experience of the working of a system in which senior Ministers were given a general oversight over a range of functions, and being aware of the crucial problem of securing supervision without blurring the responsibility of departmental Ministers, I approached my task of forming a government with all these considerations in mind.

Cabinets in the past had been composed of the holders of certain offices. Some, such as the Secretaries of State, had always been included; others, such as Postmaster General, Chancellor of the Duchy of Lancaster, and First Commissioner of Works, had sometimes been excluded. The great offices of State, such as Lord President of the Council and Lord Privy Seal, which carry practically no departmental responsibilities, have almost always been cabinet offices, although the Lord Privy Seal has been on one or two occasions omitted from the cabinet. The result of this had been that, not infrequently, an office—for instance, that of Secretary of State for War—was held by a man, not on account of his fitness for it, but because his position in the party hierarchy demanded his inclusion in the cabinet. There had been a good deal of clearing of the ground by the Act of 1937, which removed anomalies of remuneration and restrictions on the number of Ministers who could sit in the House of Commons. In the wartime government new posts had been created, for in-

stance, that of Minister of State. There had also been
evolved the device of Minister of cabinet rank, equal to
a cabinet colleague in status and salary but outside the
cabinet. There was now a good deal more room for ma-
nœuvre than previously. I had always felt the need for
making very full use of senior non-departmental Ministers for the supervision of particular groups of Ministers
and to have men in the cabinet free from absorption in
departmental detail and available for considering major
policy.

In my view, the inclusion of other Ministers in the cabinet must be decided by two considerations—the personality of the holder of the office and the importance, for
the time being, of the subject dealt with by him. I was,
of course, aware of the views of the permanent officials,
who set considerable store by the status of the Minister
whom they served.

As I have said, when I formed my administration the
war with Japan was still raging and it was necessary to
include the three Service Ministers in the cabinet. I was
fortunate in having at hand A. V. Alexander, who had
had seven years' experience as First Lord of the Admiralty; Jack Lawson, who had served in the First World
War and had held office as Under Secretary of State at the
War Office; and Lord Stansgate, who had a very fine record as an airman and had been a cabinet Minister. It was
my intention before long to set up a Ministry of Defence,
when the Service Ministers would cease to sit in the cabinet. Herbert Morrison was Lord President and Arthur
Greenwood was Lord Privy Seal, thus providing for two
senior Ministers whose duties would be coordination.

The former was also to lead the House of Commons. Lord Addison became Secretary of State for the Dominions and Leader of the House of Lords, and there could have been no better choice. Although getting on in years he had a young spirit, and had the quality of tact and sweet reasonableness essential for a Leader in a House with a large Opposition majority.

It is already known that I hesitated for some hours as to whether Bevin should take the Exchequer and Dalton the Foreign Office, or the reverse. Various reasons impelled me to my final decision, which was, I think, justified in the event. Tom Williams was the obvious choice for Minister of Agriculture, and it might have been thought that Chuter Ede would be chosen for Education, for he had great experience, but I needed a man of particular quality for the Home Office, which is a post where mistakes can easily be made. Ellen Wilkinson had done well as a junior Minister, and I knew she was an enthusiast for education. George Hall had had experience in several offices, but I chose him for Colonial Secretary. There were two positions which would be of great importance in view of our legislative programme and of the urgency of the problems to be faced by their occupants—Fuel and Power, and Health. Shinwell had had experience in the former department and had plenty of vigour. For Health I chose Aneurin Bevan, whose abilities had up to now been displayed only in opposition, but I felt that he had it in him to do good service. Stafford Cripps took another key office—the Board of Trade. Another major problem was that of India, and for that I chose Pethick-Lawrence, who went to the Lords. He was well known by Indians for his keen sympathy with their aspirations, and he also brought to the cabinet his great knowledge of finance. George Isaacs (an experienced trade unionist) as Minister of Labour, and Joseph Westwood, as Secretary of State for Scotland, completed the team, making a cabinet of nineteen, of whom four were in the House of Lords. In my view, this was larger than was desirable, but, even so, important Ministers, such as those dealing with Food and Transport, remained outside.

Nowadays, it is inevitable—if cabinets are to be kept to a reasonable size—that important departments should not be included. In theory it is, I think, right that Ministers in charge of purely administrative departments, such as the Post Office, Supply and Works, should not be in the cabinet; but as far as possible they should have the same status and pay as their cabinet colleagues. Of course, such Ministers are summoned to cabinet for particular items of business, but there is the danger that a Minister in charge of a department may feel himself left out of discussions on policy and, indeed, feel neglected. To a large extent this has been met by the development of a system of cabinet committees. I had had a good deal of responsibility for arranging committees during the war-time government, and the experience so gained stood me in good stead when making arrangements for governmental machinery in the Labour administration.

It was unavoidable that, at the start, the general age level among Ministers was rather high. There was a great deal of ability among the large number of new Members brought into the House by the General Election, but, clearly, time was required to find out where this new ability lay. However, I brought into the ranks of the junior Ministers as many young men as possible. I took for the English Law Officers two able young barristers without previous Parliamentary experience. I also included among the Under Secretaries two new Members and a number of younger members of the party who had come into the House only recently.

The choosing of Ministers is, I think, the most difficult of all the tasks which fall to the lot of a Prime Minister, while their dismissal is the most distasteful. Yet it is essential, if a party is to live, to bring on the younger members. On a number of occasions I had to tell Ministers that the time had come when they must give place to younger men and, in one or two instances, to tell them that I thought that they were not quite up to their jobs. I should like to record that, with the exception of one person who was clearly unfit, all of my colleagues took my decision with complete loyalty and never displayed the least resentment. Nevertheless, it is a most distasteful thing to have to say to an old friend and colleague that it is time for him to make room for a younger man, and I am eternally grateful to my colleagues for their magnanimity.

William Jowitt, who had served as Attorney General in the second Labour government and as a Law Officer and Minister in the wartime administration, became Lord Chancellor. As I have already related, he had been put in my charge when he was a new boy at my preparatory school. Lady Jowitt had lived next door to us at Putney. I recall quite clearly sitting next to them at a big service in St. Paul's Cathedral and thinking how surprised my mother would have been if she could have seen what happened to these three children.

Two of my former Parliamentary Private Secretaries were included in the government—Arthur Jenkins as Under Secretary for Education, and John Dugdale as Parliamentary Secretary to the Board of Admiralty. I therefore had to find someone else for this post, which is one of great importance. It is essential for a Prime Minister to keep in touch with all members of the party and to have early knowledge of currents of opinion. This a wise Parliamentary Private Secretary can do. He is also largely responsible for seeing people and thus sparing the Prime Minister's time. There was a wide choice, but, other things being equal, I saw no reason why I should not select someone from my old school. For the first time there were Old Haileyburians in the Labour party in the House of Commons. One of these, Christopher Mayhew, had already been taken by Herbert Morrison, though Morrison was soon to lose him to Ernest Bevin, who wanted him as Under Secretary. I chose Geoffrey de Freitas, who had had somewhat the same background as myself—as barrister, social worker, and municipal councillor—together with war experience, scholarship, and athletic distinction; he was an air officer and a Cambridge man. He very quickly acquired a knowledge of his job and did his work admirably, but after a few months it was clear that he would be well suited to fill a vacancy that had occurred at the Air Ministry. He was succeeded by a trade unionist, Arthur Moyle, who is with me still and has been described with justice as the ideal Parliamentary Private Secretary.

It is not without interest to recall that, after the 1931 election debacle, with the very strong feeling that had naturally arisen against MacDonald in the Labour party, proposals were made to restrict the powers of any future Labour Prime Minister. He was to have colleagues selected by the party to act with him in choosing members of the government. The passage of time and further experience has led to these proposals being tacitly dropped. In my view, the responsibility of choosing the members of the government must rest solely with the Prime Minister, though in practice he will consult with his colleagues. If he cannot be trusted to exercise this power in the best interests of the nation and the party without fear, favour, or affection, he is not fit to be Prime Minister. I am quite sure that the method of the Australian Labour party, whereby a number of members are elected by the Caucus and all that is left to the Prime Minister is to fit the pieces into a jigsaw puzzle as best he may, is quite wrong.

XVIII

Family Life

MY ELEVATION to the premiership necessarily
brought with it a change of residence, and for the
next six and a half years we were to live at 10 Downing
Street. My wife had to bear the brunt of this change, because, immediately after the election, I had to go to Potsdam. She had the task of making the arrangements for
the change-over. On the first floor there is a very fine
suite of rooms, beautifully furnished, but, in our view,
not very suited to family life in the present age. My wife
took counsel with Mrs. Churchill, who kindly helped her,
and decided to turn the top floor, which had in earlier
days been used only by domestics, into a family flat. It
was just the right size for the family, with a drawing
room and dining room, while my study was on the floor
below. A kitchen was also installed, as the one in the
basement was a huge, old-fashioned affair. We used the
State Rooms for formal occasions, such as dinners and receptions, but the flat was our real home.

While alterations were being carried out I lived in a
flat in Storey's Gate, while the family remained at Stan-

more. In view of the shortage of housing accommodation, it would have been wrong to have kept the Stanmore house. Furthermore, we would have to reconsider our requirements when the time came to leave office. Accordingly, we got the Ministry of Health to settle what was a fair price for Heywood and then found a purchaser.

We settled into 10 Downing Street and found it very comfortable. Actually I saw more of my family during the period of my premiership than ever before, as now I was living on the job instead of having to leave home early and return late at night. My eldest daughter, Janet, had joined the W.A.A.F. on leaving school and had, after service in the ranks, become an officer. At the end of the war she obtained a post in Bristol. My second daughter, Felicity, had been trained in the Margaret MacMillan College and worked in a nursery school in Bermondsey. My son, Martin, was a cadet in the Merchant Service and rejoined us on his periods of leave, while our youngest girl, Alison, was still at school. We did a good deal of modest entertaining, and my wife became interested in a large number of societies of one kind and another, especially the Margaret MacMillan Memorial Fund and the Victory Club. Many charitable meetings were held in the State Rooms at No. 10. I got to know St. James's Park very well, as on most mornings I used to take a walk with my wife and her dog before starting work.

We used to go to Chequers every weekend unless I had some engagement out of town. Although the house is full of beautiful and valuable things, it is not a museum but a friendly house in which to live. We made very full use of it. In the summer we played a lot of tennis and croquet, and in the winter we took many walks in the country. We fell in love with the Buckinghamshire countryside; so much so that when we had been in office four years and it became necessary to make provision for eventualities, we sought for a house in the Chilterns and were lucky enough to find our present dwelling place, Cherry Cottage, Prestwood, some six miles from Chequers. My wife furnished it, and we let it to tenants with a special provision for notice to quit as soon as an election was declared.

Chequers was an admirable place for entertaining visitors. Besides personal friends and colleagues in the government, we had many distinguished statesmen from the Commonwealth and foreign countries to stay for the weekend or to come for a meal. I always thought that the historical continuity of Chequers impressed those who came from younger countries. The house is Elizabethan, but the family who built it had been there for some centuries previously, while on the grounds is a mound marking the site of a castle of King Cymbeline. A daughter of Oliver Cromwell married into the family, a sister of Lady Jane Grey was imprisoned there, and the property marches with the lands formerly owned by John Hampden. As I have noted elsewhere, I have always been a lover of history and responded enthusiastically to this environment.

Among our pleasant memories of Chequers are the children's parties that we gave every year on Boxing Day, attended by children from the neighbourhood and by the sons and daughters of Ministers and Private Secretaries.

We had two outstanding family events during those years. One was my eldest daughter's marriage, which took place in the country with a reception at Chequers, and the other was the celebration of our Silver Wedding in 1947, when we were the recipients of much kindness and of many presents, including those from my colleagues in the government and from the party in the House.

The question of staffing a great house is no easy one to answer in these days, especially as we frequently entertained very important persons from abroad. The solution was found by having a detachment of A.T.S., W.R.N.S., and W.R.A.F. in succession. Under the guidance of Mrs. Hill, the housekeeper, they looked after us well. It was one of the intentions of the Lees in founding the Trust that Chequers should be a place of rest, not only for the Prime Minister but for his wife, and it was, I am sure, a very good thing for my wife to have all domestic cares removed during the weekends and on holidays. We have memories of much kindly service from our friends in the Women's Organizations.

A Prime Minister also has two detectives to look after him. We were greatly indebted to our good friends from Scotland Yard—Chief Inspector Hughes, Inspector Busbridge, and Sergeant Green—who were real friends to us. They all had the art of never being in the way but always being there when wanted and always ready to help.

The weekends were, of course, never free from work, but generally a few hours would dispose of it; while the private telephone line to Downing Street made it possible to communicate easily with my colleagues. It seems curious that, until the advent of Churchill, there was no direct communication with Downing Street and no provision for secret conversations: only a telephone in the butler's pantry. I gather, too, that Chamberlain managed to do without secretarial assistance at the weekend, whereas, except at Christmas, I found it essential always to have a Secretary present.

During my term of office I spent most of my holidays at Chequers, but paid three visits overseas. The first was to Eire. Although I had once visited Belfast, I had never been in the South and I welcomed the suggestion of one of my Secretaries, Mr. Bevir, that we should occupy his house in Newport, County Mayo, for a holiday. We flew to Dublin, where we were welcomed by Lord Rugby, the High Commissioner. I called on President O'Kelly and was entertained by members of the Government and saw something of the city. We then motored right across the island to the west coast, where we enjoyed the lovely scenery and the very kind hospitality extended to us. The Foreign Secretary, Mr. MacBride, was staying in the neighbourhood and showed us much kindness. We played golf, sailed and fished in the bay, and motored round the country. We also paid a visit to Sir Basil and Lady Brooke at Brookeborough, County Fermanagh, in Northern Ireland. I had the rather unusual experience of being cheered on both sides of the border.

The second holiday we spent in France. We took our own car with us and drove to Chartres. I was surprised to find that my wife felt no difficulty in driving on the right-hand side of the road, as I always feel a bit offside myself. We had our own detective and one from the Sûreté who was driven in a separate car. I had always wanted to see the chateaux of the Loire and we had a very fine time visiting not only those which are regularly open to the public but some which are still inhabited by old families. We paid a visit also to Paul-Boncour, the distinguished French statesman.

In 1951 my wife and I were invited to be the guests of the Norwegian government for a week. We flew to Edinburgh and embarked at Queensferry on a frigate, the *Widemouth Bay*. The frigate was a training ship for young sailors and was cruising in the North Sea, and the Admiralty kindly gave us this opportunity of a sea voyage. We stopped at Bergen and continued up the Sonerfjord, calling in at little towns on the way. We were very kindly received everywhere. Later, we motored into the mountains, staying at a very pleasant hotel at Elvasaeter, and so came down to Oslo. There I had the opportunity of talking with Prime Minister Gerhardsen and his cabinet and of seeing the fine Town Hall. We also lunched with King Haakon VII on board his yacht, and then returned by frigate to Scotland. We had rather a rough passage back, which my wife enjoyed, as it gave her an opportunity to see how good a sailor she was. The trial was satisfactory for her but not so for most of her fellow voyagers, including myself. This was the first time that I succumbed to seasickness since before the First World War.

XIX

Work of the Labour Government

AS I HAVE already stated, the project for making an atom bomb had been a secret confided to very few people. It had been one of our apprehensions during the war that possibly the Germans might have got ahead of us. Had this happened I do not see how we could have avoided defeat. In the event, the close cooperation between American and British scientists resulted in the Allies being successful. The immediate result was the ending of the war in the East and a change in the balance of power in the West. The immense forces of Russia that threatened to give her complete power in Europe were held in check by this terrible weapon in the hands of the West.

It had been realized that atomic energy might be used not to destroy but to aid mankind, although this might take time. An agreement for partnership in the atomic field between the United States, Canada, and Britain had been reached at the Quebec Conference in 1943, but the industrial use of atomic energy had been specifically conceded to the United States. The agreement in itself was loosely worded, and it was clear that the position would need to be clarified. Although British scientists had contributed very greatly to the development of atomic energy the actual work had been done in America, owing to war conditions.

Sir John Anderson had been the Minister principally concerned with this project, and at my request he continued in a special capacity to deal with it after the change of government. I decided that it was time to clarify the position with the Americans and arranged for Sir John and myself to go to Washington. I had to speak at the Lord Mayor's Luncheon on November 9, 1945; I went direct from the Mansion House to the airfield and landed at Washington at 9:30 the next day. We went at once to the White House, where I was to stay. There President Truman, Mackenzie King, and I began our talks. There was a State Dinner in the evening at which Mackenzie King, Herbert Evatt of Australia, and the other Commonwealth representatives in Washington were present; also leading members of the United States government and the Senate.

On the following day I went with the President to attend the Armistice Day celebrations in Arlington Cemetery, where I laid a wreath on the tomb of Sir John Dill, the wartime British representative on the Chiefs of Staff Committee who had earned the affection of all those who knew him. In the afternoon we had a conference on Secretary of the Navy Forrestal's yacht on the Potomac. This meeting place is convenient for evading the attentions of the press. On Tuesday I had the privilege of addressing both Houses of Congress, and I also spoke at a very big luncheon given by the Press Club. On Thursday morning at the White House, President Truman, Mackenzie King, and I signed a joint statement. During this visit I met many leading Americans, including the most prominent trade unionists.

Accompanied by Mackenzie King, I then went by train to Ottawa, where we were met at the station by a number of members of the cabinet and were conducted out of the station by a kilted M.P. playing the bagpipes. I stayed with the High Commissioner, Malcolm MacDonald. After laying a wreath on the Canadian War Memorial, I addressed both Houses of Parliament, introducing an apposite French sentence on peace which, curiously enough, came from Rabelais. I then returned home by air.

We had reached what Sir John and I both thought was a satisfactory agreement for future cooperation in the field of atomic energy. But, as sometimes happens in dealing with our American friends, the administration proposes but Congress disposes. The action of Congress in passing the MacMahon Bill made cooperation difficult, and the unfortunate affair of Dr. Fuchs, which occurred shortly afterwards, set everything back. However, all this time there was steady progress in research and development in England, and the project was never hampered by lack of money. I was anxious for full cooperation with the United States but was not prepared to leave Britain fully dependent in this sphere on our friends across the Atlantic.

The Labour party came to power with a well-defined policy worked out over many years. It had been set out very clearly in our election manifesto, and we were determined to carry it out. Its ultimate objective was the creation of a society based on social justice, and, in our view, this could be attained only by bringing under public ownership and control the main factors in the economic system.

Nationalization was not an end in itself but an essential element in achieving the ends we sought. Controls were desirable not for their own sake but because they were necessary to gain freedom from the economic power of the owners of capital. A juster distribution of wealth was not a policy designed to soak the rich or to take revenge, but because a society with gross inequalities of wealth and opportunity is fundamentally unhealthy.

It had always been our practice, in accord with the natural genius of the British people, to work empirically. We were not afraid of compromises and partial solutions. We knew that mistakes would be made and that advance would often be by trial and error. We realized that the application of socialist principles in a country such as Britain, with a peculiar economic structure based on international trade, required great flexibility.

We were also well aware of the especially difficult situation of the country resulting from the great life-and-death struggle from which we had emerged victorious. But, in our view, this did not make change in the socialist direction less necessary. On the contrary, it was clear that there could be no return to past conditions. The old pattern was worn out, and it was for us to weave the new. Thus the kind of reproach levelled at us by Churchill that, instead of uniting the country by a programme of social reform on the lines of the Beveridge Report, we were following a course dictated by social prejudice or theory left us completely unmoved. We had not been elected to try to patch up an old system but to make something new. Our policy was not a reformed capitalism but progress towards a democratic socialism. Furthermore, our experience in the war had shown how much could be accomplished when public advantage was put before private vested interest. If this was right in wartime it was also right in peacetime. I therefore determined that we would go ahead as fast as possible with our programme.

When I formed the government I told Dalton that it would be his task to nationalize the Bank of England, as well as to deal with the financial position of the country. It would be Shinwell's business, in addition to getting the mines to work and dealing with the problems of the coal, gas, and electricity industries, to prepare legislation for nationalizing the fuel and power industries. Similar instructions were given to Alfred Barnes in relation to transport, and John Wilmot for iron and steel. Aneurin Bevan had to deal with the housing problem and also had to get ready a scheme for a National Health Service; and James Griffiths had to bring forward a comprehensive scheme of National Insurance.

An order of priority was adopted. It was obvious, for instance, that the coal industry was more urgently in need of reconstruction than iron and steel. National Insurance was in a more advanced stage of preparation than the National Health Service. First things had to come first. It was also the case that every Minister had urgent immediate problems needing solution. Care was taken that present needs were not subordinated to long-term policy, but, equally, present needs must not prevent progress being made with major schemes.

While Ministers were fully responsible for their departmental work, senior Ministers holding non-departmental offices undertook the work of coordination—as did Greenwood in the field of the social services and Dalton and Cripps in the economic field. Morrison, in addition to leading the House of Commons, also undertook much coordinating work.

The system of committees was so arranged that full attention could be given to current administration and also to legislation. While the cabinet necessarily took final responsibility, broad economic problems were dealt with by a special committee of Ministers of high rank.

I assumed the office of Minister of Defence because, at the start, the war with Japan was still to be won and there were also many urgent Service matters to be dealt with—in particular, the redeployment of our forces after demobilization. I formed a Defence Committee based on certain views I had held for many years and on wartime experience. In 1946 an act was passed setting up a Ministry of Defence, and I relinquished the post to A. V. Alexander.

The legislative programme on which the 1945 Labour government embarked was much more extensive than that launched by any peacetime government, and it undoubtedly made a heavy demand on the House of Commons. It would certainly have astonished Members of Parliament of the days before the First World War, when one major measure in a session was thought to be quite enough. The verdict of the electors had, however, been sufficiently decisive to prevent the Opposition from indulging in obstruction.

Members of the wartime government now in Opposition were also committed to support the broad principles of our social-reform legislation and had accepted full employment as an objective for any government. This fact strikingly illustrates the change of outlook since the days when I was a rank-and-file Member. Then unemployment was not considered a matter that concerned governments.

There was also not much real opposition to our nationalization policy. It was realized on all sides that the problem of the coal industry had been shockingly mishandled in the past and that if men were to be got to work in the pits a new start was necessary. Electricity and gas had already to a large extent passed into public ownership, while the Conservatives had themselves been forced by the logic of facts in 1931 to carry through Morrison's London Transport Bill. It was perhaps surprising, in view of the fury the banks had caused in the past, that nationalization of the Bank of England went through with the minimum of opposition. Of all our nationalization proposals, only iron and steel roused much feeling, perhaps because hopes of profit were greater here than elsewhere.

There was, of course, a great difference in the make-up of the Parliament of 1945 as compared with that of 1918, in which wartime profiteers had formed so large a part. Undoubtedly the experience of the Second World War, in which the whole nation was mobilized and exposed to danger, had done much to change the mental climate in the Conservative party. In the Second World War there had been far more equality of sacrifice than in the First World War. Profiteering had been repressed, rationing had been better managed, high rates of interest had not been allowed, and very heavy taxation had been imposed.

It was difficult to argue that what had been done in war with such good results should not be continued in peace, especially in view of the situation in which the country was placed. On the other hand, unless there had been a government with a clear policy and a resolute will we might well have slipped back to the evil conditions of the past. No doubt we made many mistakes, but there has been a remarkable advance in many directions. I am far from claiming all the credit on behalf of the Labour government. Much was done during the war to equalize conditions, but I always feel cheered when I look at the children and babies of today and compare them with those of past times.

In 1953 a Canadian wrote to me saying that he had visited Britain from time to time since 1911. He had just paid a prolonged visit during which he had been to many parts of the country, mostly on foot. He said that nowhere had he seen such fine children. He had not seen one child underfed or ragged, and this testimony has been borne by many observers and is fully supported by vital statistics.

In fact, during these years a peaceful revolution has taken place. Broadly speaking, there has been a great levelling up of conditions. The great mass of abject poverty has disappeared. Full employment and the development of the social services are, of course, the principal factors in this, but there are many others. One, in particular, is of special interest to me as an old resident in the dock area—the de-casualization of dock labour initiated by Ernest Bevin. This has changed the whole outlook for many families. The housewife can now reckon on a steady income coming into the home. One of the chief elements in creating a mass of poverty and ill-paid labour has gone.

Inevitably there has been a worsening for some people. The big country house with its retinue of servants is disappearing. Domestic labour is hard to come by, and this has meant a pretty drastic change in the way of life for many middle-class families. Victorian England has gone. But I have met many people who, reared in the comfort of former days, do not resent the change but acknowledge that the old class system was bad and make the best of the new.

There is also, today, a far wider range of opportunity. Capable persons, no matter in what stratum of society they were born, have a far better chance of getting a full education and of developing their faculties. Here the foundation was laid by the Education Act of the wartime government, but it fell to the Labour government to see that it was implemented.

We had always anticipated that when Labour came into power there might be difficulties with the House of Lords and we had accordingly stated in our election programme that we should, if necessary, take action to ensure that the popular will prevailed. I recalled how the great liberal majority of 1906 had been frustrated by the Upper Chamber. I held the view that Prime Minister

Campbell-Bannerman ought to have taken action while his mandate from the country was fresh. However, things had changed since the great fight over the Lords' veto in 1910. The Peers had in Lord Salisbury a wise leader, and we had in Lord Addison a skilful and conciliatory spokesman. Thus for our first three years we experienced no trouble. The House of Lords fulfilled a useful role as a debating forum and a revising chamber.

It was, however, clear that the Iron and Steel Bill would not get through the Lords without the use of the Parliament Bill. In my view, the period of delay imposed by this measure before the will of the elected chamber could prevail was too long. Accordingly, it was decided to introduce a measure shortening the period by which measures passed in the Commons could be held up, and in November 1947 a bill to amend the 1911 Act was introduced by Morrison. This bill said that any measure rejected by the Lords would become law if it had been passed by the Commons in two successive sessions instead of three (as under the 1911 Act) and provided that one year (instead of two) had elapsed between its first appearance for the second reading and its passage through the Commons for a second time. The Conservatives naturally put up strong opposition, but were somewhat embarrassed by the fact that the best shots in our oratorical locker were provided by extracts from the speeches of their own Leader when he was a Liberal. The bill was rejected by the House of Lords in June and September 1948, but was reintroduced in July 1949 and passed into law over the heads of the Peers.

In the course of this controversy the question of the

reform of the House of Lords, which had been adumbrated in the preamble to the 1911 Act, was raised. The Conservatives themselves had recognized the weakness of the House, owing to the existence of five or six hundred Peers who never attended but whose voting power was a potential menace to any government. Lord Salisbury's father had for some years endeavoured to secure an alteration in its composition.

The Labour party had formerly been in favour of a single-chamber government, but of recent years many of its members had realized the practical advantage of a revising chamber provided that it had not the power of defeating the popular will. Accordingly, when we were invited to discuss the subject with Opposition leaders, I agreed very willingly. In fact, we reached substantial agreement as to the composition of a reformed House. We had no mandate to come to a decision but we were prepared to recommend the acceptance of the scheme provided that we could be satisfied as to the powers to be entrusted to the reformed House. It was on this that the conference broke down. The Conservatives now regarded the Parliament Act of 1911 as the Ark of the Covenant and were not prepared to relinquish the power of the unrepresentative House to thwart the Commons. I think that they lost a very good chance of reaching an amicable settlement of a vexed question. As it is, the power of the Lords has been restricted without reform.

Foreign Affairs

IT WILL, I think, be convenient to depart from chronological order and to treat the subject of foreign affairs in a single chapter. I shall not attempt to deal with them in any great detail, but will indicate only my own part. Foreign affairs are the province of the Foreign Secretary, and it is, in my view, a mistake for a Prime Minister—save in exceptional circumstances—to intervene personally.

There is a current idea that international questions can be settled by intimate talks between a few leading statesmen. Such meetings are seldom successful unless the ground has been well prepared. Where they have been so prepared they usually register, with a certain amount of publicity, agreements that have been worked out through the usual channels.

"If you have a good dog, don't bark yourself" is a good proverb, and in Ernest Bevin I had an exceptionally good dog. On the other hand, I am quite opposed to leaving Foreign Affairs to be dealt with as something outside the ordinary business of government, a mystery to be touched only by the initiates. Foreign and economic affairs are so much interwoven in these days, and the relationship between home and foreign affairs so close, that it is essential that all the members of the cabinet should be kept fully informed. Bevin realized this and reported fully to his colleagues. He kept in daily touch with me.

The disturbed international situation was a constant anxiety during the whole of our period of office and the work of the Foreign Secretary was very exacting. The great number of conferences and meetings—most of them overseas—put a heavy strain on Ministers, and it was necessary to add a Minister of State and an additional Under Secretary to cope with the work, while for the special commitment of the German Occupation successive Chancellors of the Duchy of Lancaster were employed. Philip Noel-Baker, Hector McNeil, Christopher Mayhew, Kenneth Younger, and Lord Henderson served in the Foreign Office under Bevin with great distinction, but, necessarily, the Secretary of State carried the heaviest burden. Bevin knew his own mind, was a first-class negotiator and administrator, and evoked loyal cooperation from all. He was very conscious always of the economic issues that underlay so many international questions and worked in close cooperation with successive Chancellors of the Exchequer. Our economic weakness was a great handicap to him in his work. I often heard him say that a few million tons of coal at his disposal would have made all the difference to the outcome of some of his negotiations.

Following on from San Francisco and Potsdam, our policy was based on support for the United Nations and an honest endeavour to work in close harmony with the

United States and with Soviet Russia. Unfortunately we experienced opposition everywhere from the latter. The work of the quadripartite administration in Germany was frustrated constantly by Russian intransigence, while at the United Nations the Russian representative soon showed his intention of abusing the veto.

As the friction with Russia increased, Britain naturally drew closer to the United States. This was helped by a change in the attitude of the administration, which realized what the assumption of responsibility in world affairs entailed. Many Americans shed their old isolationism and, with it, some of their long-seated prejudice against Britain as a predatory imperialist power. They were also disillusioned with Soviet Russia. The two English-speaking countries began to see that their close cooperation was essential to world peace and prosperity. The holding of the Secretaryship of State by General Marshall and by his successor, Dean Acheson, was an important factor in the promotion of good relations. Perhaps the decisive event in establishing the new alignment was the Marshall Plan. It was Bevin who, by his quick follow-up of General Marshall's speech, made it a prime event; no one was more aware than he of the need to buttress peace by economic reconstruction. When Poland and Czechoslovakia accepted the idea of Marshall aid, his hopes for the integration of Eastern and Western Europe rose high. The withdrawal of these acceptances at the orders of the Kremlin dashed this hope. It was, in fact, a declaration of the "cold war."

The making of the Brussels Treaty and of the Atlantic Pact, which was the work of Bevin, was a recognition of the fact that before Russia would consider reasonable relations with the free world there must be a building up of strength. Strength was the only factor the Russians considered.

A few weeks after becoming Prime Minister I presented the Charter of the United Nations to the House of Commons. Approval and ratification was readily given—*The Times* commenting that it was discussed "in the spirit of a Council of State." In January 1946 I addressed the opening session of the General Assembly of the United Nations in the Central Hall, Westminster. In the course of a brief speech of welcome I sought to stress the importance of the nations not making the mistake that led to the breakdown of the League of Nations. On this point I said:

> The United Nations Organization must become the overriding factor in foreign policy. After the First World War there was a tendency to regard the League of Nations as something outside the ordinary range of foreign policy. Governments continued on the old lines, pursuing individual aims and following the path of power politics, not understanding that the world had passed into a new epoch. In just such a spirit in times past in these islands great nobles and their retainers used to practise private war in disregard of the authority of the central government. The time came when private armies were abolished, when the rule of law was established throughout the length and breadth of this island. What has been done in Britain and in other countries on a small stage has now to be effected throughout the whole world. We must all now today recognize the truth proclaimed by the Foreign Minister of

the U.S.S.R. at Geneva, "Peace is indivisible." Looking back on past years, we can trace the origins of the late war to acts of aggression, the significance of which was not realized at the time. Failure to deal with the Japanese adventure in the Far East and with the acts of aggression of the fascist rulers of Germany and Italy led inevitably to the breakdown of the rule of law and to the Second World War. In the last five years the aggression of Hitler in Europe drew eventually into the contest men from all the continents and from the islands of the sea. It should make us all realize that the welfare of every one of us is bound up with the welfare of the world as a whole, and that we are all members one of another.

I am glad that the Charter of the United Nations does not deal only with governments and states or with politics and war, but with the simple elemental needs of human beings whatever be their race, their colour, or their creed. In the Charter we reaffirm our faith in fundamental human rights. We see the freedom of the individual in the state as an essential complement to the freedom of the state in the world community of nations. We stress too that social justice and the best possible standards of life for all are essential factors in promoting and maintaining the peace of the world.

I concluded my address with reference to our ultimate aim as, "Not just the negation of war but the creation of a world of security and freedom, of a world which is governed by justice and the moral law."

The Brussels Treaty and the Atlantic Pact were both designed to strengthen and to unify the Western democracies. They were a recognition of the fact of the changed balance of power in the world. It is hard for those whose

memories go back to the nineteenth century to realize
that Western Europe, so long the dominant factor in the
world, is today a collection of disunited elements lying
between two great continental powers—the U.S.A. and
the U.S.S.R. Germany is potentially a great power, but
France is unlikely ever to occupy again the position she
once held. A realization of this has created a demand for
some form of federation, but without Britain such a
grouping would not be strong enough to hold its own. On
the other hand, Britain has never regarded itself as just a
European power. Her interests are world-wide. She is the
heart of a great Commonwealth and tends to look out-
wards from Europe, though maintaining a close interest
in all that goes on in that Continent. Indeed, the advent
of air power has made her connection with the Continent
a greater necessity than in the days of naval power, when
splendid isolation was a possible policy.

As a general proposition it is obvious that a closer association of the West European states is desirable; indeed,
I am on record as having said, "Europe must federate
or perish," but to bring such ideas into the region of the
practical is a very difficult proposition. Every state has its
old traditions and its special ideological setup. Some of
our American friends did not always realize this. They
did not appreciate the difference between European federation of old-established communities and the federation
of the thirteen American colonies.

As a government, we favoured every effort to effect
greater European integration, such as the Benelux Agreement and the setting up of the coal and steel organization
under the Schuman Plan, but we could not enter into

engagements to the full extent possible to the continental powers.

The issue arose in an acute form over the proposal to create the Council of Europe as a move towards federation. We took part in its formation, but we were unable to accept the views of the extreme federalists. The composition of the Assembly of the Council of Europe from members of all parties gave Churchill an opportunity he was quick to seize. He appeared at the Assembly, spoke with great enthusiasm, encouraging the continentals to expect a wide measure of participation by Britain. Returning to Westminster, he attacked the Labour government for dragging its feet instead of marching forward boldly. However, as soon as his return to 10 Downing Street gave him another stage on which to perform, his interest disappeared and he was less forthcoming than the Labour government. For the time, however, he thought he had a useful stick with which to beat the government. Whether or not the Council of Europe will develop into something more than a debating society has yet to be proved.

A critical phase in the relations between Soviet Russia and the West was reached when the Russians imposed what was in effect a blockade on Berlin. This was an act in the "cold war." It was defeated by the very remarkable achievement of the American and British Air Forces in keeping Berlin supplied by air. In March 1949, in company with Lord Henderson, I flew to Berlin in bitter weather to see this great effort at first hand, and was welcomed by an American Guard of Honour. The continuous stream of planes landing at Tempelhof was an impressive sight. This was my first visit to Germany since Potsdam, and I met the British, American, and French members of the Control Commission and also leading Berlin citizens. I was able to see the progress made in German recovery. A few weeks later the Russian attempt to starve Berlin into submission came to an end.

The Middle East presented us with a very difficult problem. The Sudan, Egypt, the Arab States, Palestine, and Iran all had their own special problems and represented an area of possible conflict as well as an area of political and economic weakness—providing tempting bait for any power that wished to fish in troubled waters. Britain had a long connection with this region, and vital strategic interests to sustain, interests that also concerned the Commonwealth. France had a sentimental interest in the Levant, while the United States, in dealing with the problem, had to face very heavy pressure from the Jewish population in America. It was our thankless task to try to reconcile many competing interests.

We recognized that Egypt had a real grievance in the occupation by British troops of the citadel of Cairo, and we early took the decision to withdraw them. We also sent a cabinet mission to Egypt to try to settle amicably all outstanding questions. Ultimately negotiations broke down over the claims of the Egyptian government in the Sudan. We had to regard susceptibilities and the real interests of the Sudanese people, and we were not prepared to hand the latter over to the ruling class in Egypt. Many times we came near to settling the questions of our defence interests in Egypt, but the Sudanese question remained an unsolved problem.

The Palestine problem continually impinged on the Egyptian aspect of the matter. We were faced with a legacy of the past in the incompatible assurances that had been given to Arabs and Jews. The sufferings of the Jews under the Nazi regime, the romantic adventure of the Palestine experiment, and the wealth of sentiment for the Jewish national home enlisted great support for the Jews, whose influence extended widely throughout the world. On the other hand, the Arabs, as the inhabitants of Palestine for centuries, had a case which was sometimes ignored. They commanded support throughout the Moslem world, and there are many Moslems in the British Commonwealth and Empire.

Transjordan and Iraq owed their existence to Britain, who had delivered them from the Turk and Syria, and the Levant States were but recently freed from French tutelage. In Iraq, Iran, and elsewhere there were vitally important oil supplies.

The weakness in all the Arab countries was a backward economy and a very low standard of life for the masses. It was our view that it was essential to take steps to try to raise the standard of life of the masses in all these countries, and Bevin worked hard to this end. In dealing with the Palestine question we sought to hold a fair balance between the rival claimants to this little territory and, as usual, got small thanks from either side. It took a long time before the United States realized the importance of the Middle East in the world. They were inclined to attribute the difficulties to British imperialism, though gradually they came to understand the situation better.

A difficult problem arose during the latter period of

the Labour government in relation to Iran and the Anglo-Iranian Oil Company. It illustrated the kind of problem that arises when insurgent nationalism comes into conflict with old-established commercial interests. Bevin, who was always prescient in such matters, had done much to get the Anglo-Iranian Company to improve the living conditions of the workers in the industry, and, indeed, they were much superior to conditions elsewhere in Iran. On the other hand, the company remained an alien capitalist enterprise that made very large profits that went out of the country. The attitude of the company generally was, I think, contemptuous of the Iranian government, and not without reason, for it was both inefficient and corrupt. Iran was ruled by a selfish and antisocial landlord class, and the Shah, who was well intentioned, had great difficulty in effecting reforms. There was also a Communist-influenced Tudeh party, able to exploit nationalist sentiment in the ultimate interests of the U.S.S.R. We were met by a demand for the nationalization of the undertaking, a demand we could not resist, provided that proper compensation was paid. We had, however, to deal with an intransigent government dominated by a fanatical nationalist. The situation was potentially dangerous, and we had to make preparations for sending in armed forces in the event of danger to our nationals. On the other hand, any attempt to coerce the Iranian government by the use of force was out of the question. Such action would no doubt have been taken in former times, but would, in the modern world, have outraged opinion at home and abroad. We endeavoured to negotiate a reasonable settlement, but without success. We had, therefore, to submit to heavy losses and to the closing down of the refinery and the evacuation of our nationals. For this, of course, we were blamed by the Opposition, but up to date they have failed to find any way out of the difficulty. The case is interesting both in itself and for the moral that can be drawn from it. In my view, the day is past when commercial undertakings from industrialized countries, having obtained some concession, can carry on their business without regard to the feelings of the people of the country in which they are operating. It is not merely a question as to the proper allocation of the profits of the enterprise but as to right human relationships. The local people feel that there is a loss of self-respect in the exploitation of the resources of their country by an alien agency. The Anglo-Iranian Oil Company showed a lack of sensitivity in not realizing this, and I think that successive British governments, including the Labour government, did not make enough use of the power which the government's holdings in the enterprise gave them to make changes in good time.

I think wherever European or Western enterprises are operating, an endeavour should be made to bring the local people into cooperation, so that the enterprise, instead of being that of an alien power, is accepted as belonging in part to the country concerned. In 1953 in Burma I talked with British businessmen who had grasped the necessity for this and had brought in Burmese directors and were training young Burmese to take their part in management and in technical operation, with very happy results. No doubt this is troublesome but it is well worth while, and indeed, I think, essential if Western capital and technique are to play their part in raising the standard of life of the less-developed parts of the world.

Commonwealth Relations

AS I LOOK back over the period of my prime minis-
tership, one of my most interesting memories is that
of my relationship with my fellow Prime Ministers of the
Commonwealth. It is sad to realize that of those who were
in office in the early years I alone survive, while out of the
three Asians, who for the first time took their seats as free
and equal members, only Jawaharlal Nehru is still living, although Sir Godfrey Huggins of Southern Rhodesia,
who was a frequent attender, still holds his position. I was
certainly fortunate in having such outstanding men as colleagues.

Field Marshal Smuts was the doyen and the only one of
us who had taken part in the conduct of the First World
War and in the negotiations for peace. His long experience and fine judgment were allied to great personal
charm. More than any other statesman of his time, he
understood what a great thing is the British Commonwealth of Nations. He had seen the whole thing grow and
develop, and he used to say that British imperialism died
with the South African War. I believe that this is true

and that we ought always to recall with gratitude Campbell-Bannerman, for it was his enlightened policy towards South Africa that was the turning point in this development. Smuts was a great South African, but, in my view, he was greater on the wider stage of Commonwealth and international affairs. His mind had a very wide sweep, and I had always noticed how, even from far-away South Africa, he had a just appreciation of the wide strategy of the war. So it was in peace.

Another veteran was Mackenzie King. In contrast to Smuts, he had for the greater part of his career been apprehensive of being dominated by the government of the United Kingdom and had been almost morbidly fearful lest Canada should be drawn into European entanglements without her consent. Undoubtedly the war years had effected a considerable change in his outlook, due also to the consciousness that Canada was playing a very big part in the war and that her position as a very important power was fully recognized. He was, however, still apt to be rather non-committal and to be unwilling to make pronouncements when away from his cabinet. It was pleasant to have him to stay at Chequers for he had a very keen interest in history and archæology. He was a great Canadian statesman and throughout the war played a big part as a connecting link between the United States and the United Kingdom, to which his personal relations with Roosevelt and Churchill contributed not a little.

In all my relationships with my fellow Prime Ministers I have never known any line of cleavage develop on account of our particular political affiliations. Commonwealth relations are above and outside party politics. I had, however, great pleasure in getting to know the Prime Ministers of Australia and New Zealand. Joseph Chifley, an Australian-born railway worker, was a man of great character, respected by all. His contributions to our discussions were always brief and to the point, and he had a thorough grasp of essentials and a broad outlook. I had known Peter Fraser for some years. We had the same political beginnings; prior to his departure for New Zealand, he and I were members of the Independent Labour party, and to the end he gave evidence of this. He had worked as a docker and had come up the hard way. He was a most lovable character with a very human outlook, and he had plenty of courage. He was a fitting representative of the New Zealand people. In peace, as in war, he was always ready to do all he could to help the old country. His idealism was tempered by realism; his natural temperament would have led him to be a pacifist, but his sense of reality enabled him to lead his people in war. He, like his Australian colleague, had earned the affection and respect of his political opponents as well as of his supporters.

Nehru, who united great charm with high abilities, brought a very distinctive viewpoint to our discussions. Despite his long and strenuous opposition to the British Raj and his years of imprisonment, he had no bitterness. He is entirely free from the spirit of hatred which sometimes possesses the nationalist.

The first Prime Minister of Pakistan, Liaquat Ali Khan, was a very fine man, and Pakistan was fortunate in having him as leader in the first difficult years of the new state. He was singularly free from prejudice, and despite the differences that arose between him and the Prime Minister of India, he remained his friend. It was a tragic misfortune for his country that he should have been struck down by the hand of an assassin.

The Prime Minister of Ceylon, D. S. Senanayaka, was a man of great charm. Wise and experienced, he was the right man to guide his country in the new era, and he felt keenly the exclusion of his country from the United Nations. He has a worthy successor in his son.

I very much enjoyed these meetings, which it was my object to keep as informal as possible. We were not overburdened with a great deal of documentation. Once general agreement has been reached on policy, details can be dealt with by meetings of officials or even by correspondence. The essence of a Commonwealth conference is, in my view, the meetings of minds and the personal contacts.

After the First World War there had been important developments in the relationship of the members of the British Commonwealth to one another. The colonial conception passed away, a fact that was signalized by the creation of the Dominions Office to deal with the self-governing Dominions. This development had culminated in the Statute of Westminster, which made all the self-governing Dominions free and equal and also implied the right of secession. It was therefore to be expected that further changes would follow the strains and stresses of the Second World War. It fell to my lot to have to deal with these. By the end of my period of office three new Dominions, one of which was a republic, had been added to Great Britain and the four old Dominions. A former Dominion, Newfoundland, had become a province of Canada, while Burma and Eire had severed their connection with the Commonwealth.

India had entered the war without the legislature's being consulted. The Congress party considered, with some justification, that the Indian people had been brought into a European quarrel with which they were not concerned. They were therefore not prepared to cooperate; on the contrary, there was a considerable amount of resistance. The Viceroy, Lord Linlithgow, had a difficult task, as did his successor, Lord Wavell, but, in fact, the war effort was not hampered by nationalist opposition. When Japan entered the war and the attack on Malaya developed, the situation became more dangerous, and with the overrunning of Burma, critical. The eastern frontiers of India had always been considered safe because of the difficulties of the terrain and the absence of any proximity to a military power. The face of India, from the point of view of defence, had always been turned to the northwest.

Although Indian leaders had no sympathy with Japanese imperialism there were men who saw in the Japanese advance the opportunity of throwing off what they considered to be the imperial yoke from the neck of India. Indeed, Subhas Bose of Bengal was busily engaged in forming, from among the Indian prisoners taken by the Japanese in Burma, an Indian National Army. Just as the defeat of Russia by Japan at the beginning of the century had intensified Asiatic nationalism, so it was clear to me that immediately the war ended Britain would be met by a very strong demand for equality on the part of

Asiatics who saw domination of Asia by Europeans in decline.

Successive British governments had declared their intention of giving India full self-government. The end of the war would certainly bring a demand for these promises to be implemented. Furthermore the American people had very strong views, shared by the administration, of the evils of imperialism. Much of the criticism of British rule was very ill informed, but its strength could not be denied. Americans drew a sharp distinction between their own expansion from the Atlantic to the Pacific, involving the Mexican War and the relegation to reservations of the original inhabitants, and British overseas expansion. The absorption of a continent seemed to be a natural process to them, but an empire containing numerous detached portions of land inhabited by various races at different stages of civilization appeared an example of colonialism and rank imperialism.

For all these reasons it was clear that the Indian problem would have to be faced. The wartime cabinet was well aware of this. There was a special committee on India, over which I presided, which contained, in addition to the Secretary of State for India, L. S. Amery, men of great experience—Sir John Simon, the head of the Simon Commission, Sir John Anderson, an ex-Governor of Bengal, Sir James Grigg, a former Finance Member of the Viceroy's Council, R. A. Butler, a former Under Secretary of State for India, and Stafford Cripps, who had close contacts with Indian leaders. The committee kept Indian affairs under close review and gave long and careful consideration to the whole question.

Prior to the war I had had a long talk with Cripps and Nehru on possible lines of dealing with the problem of Indian self-government, and we had sketched out the idea of a constituent assembly to be summoned in order that Indians themselves might decide on their future. A plan of this kind was now propounded by Cripps and accepted by the committee. The plan was a bold one, but was accepted by the cabinet. This decision reflected great credit on those members of the government who were not sanguine as to the feasibility of Indian self-government, and especially upon Prime Minister Churchill, whose views on the subject were very strong. It was decided that the best hope of success was to send a cabinet Minister, and Cripps's offer to undertake this duty was accepted. Meanwhile the number of Indians in the Viceroy's Council had been increased.

Cripps did all that a man could do to achieve success, but despite his great sympathy with Indian aspirations and his outstanding ability he failed to get agreement. The old stumbling block of Hindu-Moslem antagonism and distrust could not be overcome, and Gandhi at this time was not helpful. The mission failed. A number of Indian leaders, including Nehru, were kept in jail; law and order had to be preserved.

Thereafter the tide of war turned. Admiral Mountbatten, as Supreme Allied Commander in Southeast Asia, drove the Japanese out of Burma. The Labour government came into power and the atom bomb brought about the surrender of Japan. India was one of the problems with which the new government, under my direction, had to deal.

I had selected Lord Pethick-Lawrence as Secretary of State for India. He had many friends in that country and was therefore well fitted to inaugurate a new policy, but it was clear to me that the problem could not be handled by a Secretary of State and a Viceroy, however able they might be. Accordingly, it was decided to send out a cabinet mission, consisting of Cripps, Lord Pethick-Lawrence, and A. V. Alexander, to get into personal contact with the Indian leaders. The cabinet mission went out in the spring of 1946 and continued their labours right into the hot weather. Working with the Viceroy, Lord Wavell, they made considerable progress. Hindu and Moslem leaders, including Nehru and Liaquat Ali Khan, entered the Viceroy's Council. Excellent relations were established, but nothing seemed to avail to overcome the communal trouble. Jinnah was now the accepted leader of the Moslems. At one time a worker with the Congress party, he had now got control of the Moslem League and had set his heart on a Moslem state carved out of India.

As a member of the Simon Commission nearly twenty years earlier, I had heard of Pakistan, a Moslem state, composed of the Punjab, Sind, Kashmir, Baluchistan, the Northwest Frontier Province, and Eastern Bengal, but it was talked of then as the idle dream of a communal enthusiast; now it had taken shape and Jinnah was its prophet. Congress, on the other hand, had always talked of the Indian nation and of a state embracing the whole of the peninsula. Nehru hated the idea of a confessional state. He had always sought to bring Moslems as well as Hindus into Congress. Other men, no doubt, thought in terms of a Hindu Raj, a thing abhorrent to the Moslems.

My colleagues and I saw all the difficulties of a division of India into two states—Hindu and Moslem—for any such partition would necessarily leave minorities in both states. We doubted also whether Pakistan, with an important unit geographically separate from the real centre of the new state, was viable. My cabinet colleagues and the Viceroy spent many hours seeking to get a solution that would satisfy both communities. The difficulty did not lie with any unwillingness of Britain to part with power, but with arranging for the succession. Finally the cabinet mission reluctantly returned home, frustrated, though having accomplished much in the creation of good relations, for Indians realized that the Labour government was in earnest in seeking to implement the promises made by Britain.

Meanwhile the machinery of government in India was running down. This was nothing new. The process of Indianization, begun after the report of the Lee Commission just before the First World War, meant that the British element in the Services had been steadily declining. The war itself had meant a cessation of recruitment for India, while the uncertainty as to the future of the Indian Empire naturally deterred men from entering. Lord Wavell had reported very fully on this. I recalled Lord Wavell in order to discuss the whole position with him. No progress had been made since the return of the cabinet mission, and Lord Wavell and his chief Service advisers were despondent and could suggest only a progressive retirement from India province by province, which was, in my view, a counsel of despair. I had a great admiration for Lord Wavell, both as a soldier and a man, but I did not think that he was likely to find a solution. I did not think that he and the Indian could really understand each other. New men were needed for a new policy.

I had already departed from precedent in the appointments made to the governorships of the two great Presidency provinces of Madras and Bengal. To the former was sent General Sir Archibald Nye, a very able soldier who had been Vice-Chief of the Imperial General Staff during the war. He and Lady Nye speedily won the hearts of the people of Madras. To Bengal went Frederick Burrows, who had once been a parcels clerk at a small station in Herefordshire. He had served as president of the National Union of Railwaymen and a member of the Labour party Executive. I knew him to be a man of strong character and great ability. He had served with distinction on the commission that dealt with the Constitution of Ceylon. Here again, the choice was amply justified. Sir John Colville, Governor of Bombay, was, I knew, well liked in that province, and so the three principal governorships were well filled.

But finding the right man to take the place of Lord Wavell was the subject of anxious consideration. I had come to the conclusion that it was useless to try to get agreement by discussion between the leaders of the rival communities. Unless these men were faced with the urgency of a time limit, there would always be procrastination. As long as Britain held power it was always possible to attribute failure to her. Indians must be faced with the fact that in a short space of time they would have responsibility thrust upon them. I did not think that the chances of success were very good, but I felt there was one man who might pull it off. Admiral Mountbatten, a brilliant sailor, had been selected by Churchill to be Supreme Commander of all three Services in the campaign in Southeast Asia. He had had to work with our Allies—American and Chinese; he had had to command troops of many nationalities and had been brilliantly successful; he had imagination, sympathy, and tremendous drive. I knew also that he had, in Lady Mountbatten, a wife who would admirably assist him. I realized that in asking him to go to India I was making a great demand on his sense of duty. He was devoted to the Navy, and here he was being asked to undertake a task of supreme difficulty, the chances of success in which, I frankly told him, were not at all rosy. My colleagues welcomed my proposal, and with great public spirit he accepted this task. He was in entire agreement with the line of policy that it was intended should be followed and welcomed the fact that his task was to end one regime and to inaugurate a new one. He was able to secure the help of General Ismay, who also made a great sacrifice, and Sir Eric Miéville, two men with wide experience of India and of public affairs. Lord Mountbatten is, of course, a member of the Royal Family, and it might have been thought that it was hazardous to send him out on such a mission, but King George VI very warmly approved this choice.

The appointment was generally welcomed, but the decision to set a time limit after which India would be handed over to whatever Indian authorities were available met with a good deal of opposition from the Conservatives, including Sir John Anderson and R. A. Butler. It was, however, notable that three Conservative Members who had lived many years in India supported the government. When it came to a vote in the House of Commons the government had a handsome majority. In the House of Lords the position was much more difficult and at one moment it seemed likely that an adverse vote would be cast, but a very fine speech by Lord Halifax, who, in my view, added another to the many services he had done for India, averted a division.

In March 1947 the new Viceroy took over and soon showed his quality. Indian leaders were constantly reminded that the sands were running out. Hindus and Moslems, however, found it impossible to agree on a single government for the whole of India—the solution we had striven to effect—and it was by the decision of the Indians themselves that a partition was made. Two new Dominions—India and Pakistan, which would be equal in all respects to the other Dominions—were to come into being. In accordance with the Statute of Westminster each would have the right to decide as to whether to stay in the Commonwealth. The cabinet was, of course, kept in the closest touch with all the negotiations.

In July 1947 I introduced into the House of Commons the Indian Independence Bill, which passed through both Houses without a division, and on August 15 India and Pakistan became free and equal members of the British Commonwealth of Nations. Unprecedented scenes of enthusiasm accompanied the declaration. The last British Viceroy had a reception such as had never been given to any of his predecessors, and it was amply deserved. In my opinion no other man could have carried out this tremendous task. It was a great tribute to him that he should have been made, at the request of the Indian leaders, the first Governor General of the new Dominion. Jinnah became the first Governor General of Pakistan. Both countries were fortunate in having two outstanding men as their first Prime Ministers—Nehru and Liaquat Ali Khan —for events were soon to test them to the utmost.

In the first months of the new order fratricidal strife broke out, causing the loss of thousands of lives and driving a great number of people from their homes. The troubles were the legacy of the past in which Hindus and Moslems, in province after province, had been guilty of acts of violence. It is idle to ask who began it, though it must be said that the most serious outbreak was started by the Sikhs. Immense distress resulted, and both governments were faced with very serious refugee problems. Lady Mountbatten played a very notable part in relief work. It was natural that Indians should become Governors of provinces in the new dispensation, but Sir Archibald Nye was reappointed Governor of Madras.

Despite troubles and the graver crisis that arose later over Kashmir, the change-over was successfully made. Great credit was due especially to Liaquat Ali Khan, who had to build up the governmental machine in Pakistan almost from nothing. A very difficult problem was the division of the two great provinces of Bengal and the Punjab. This was decided by an award of Sir Cyril Radcliffe (now Lord Radcliffe). Inevitably, some of the rulings were criticized, but they were accepted.

Lord Pethick-Lawrence, who had laboured so hard, found himself unable to continue his work, owing to the strain on his advancing years, and Lord Listowel took over for the final stages and thus became the last Secretary of State for India. The old India Office now fused with the Dominions Office, which had been renamed the Commonwealth Relations Office. Sir Archibald Carter, who had served so well as one of the Secretaries to the Simon Commission, became Joint Permanent Under Secretary during the period of fusion.

Thus came to an end the direct rule of the British in India, and the King ceased to be Emperor of India. The process of training Indians in self-government had fulfilled its purpose. An evolution, foreseen by many of the greatest of those who served India in the past, had come about. It is not without interest that many of these were trained at the old East India College at Haileybury, the buildings of which subsequently were occupied by the school at which I was educated. Little did I think, when I used to sit in the study once occupied by John Lawrence, that I should be the head of the administration that would hand over the government of India to her own people.

There was one difficult question that had yet to be settled, namely, whether India was to remain in the British Commonwealth. Not unnaturally, in the course of the struggle for Indian independence, the National Congress had declared in favour of republicanism, although that form of government had never been adopted in India, where the tradition of monarchy is very strong. However, in the new Constitution, it had been decided that India should be a republic. The question arose as to whether it was possible for a republic to be part of the Commonwealth, for the tie that unites all its members is allegiance to the Crown. The question was very fully discussed at a meeting of Commonwealth Prime Ministers over which I presided. It had always been held that allegiance to the Crown was one of the most essential ties, and it was not easy for some of those who felt very strongly on this point to accept any change. However, Nehru showed high statesmanship in accepting a new relationship whereby in respect to India the monarch was recognized as head of the Commonwealth. He had to face the critics in his own ranks who held strong theoretical views on independence and republicanism. No less wisdom was displayed by the Prime Ministers of the old Dominions in agreeing to this formula. This solution of a difficult question was accepted by the House of Commons and by public opinion. It may be that had this precedent been set earlier, both Burma and Eire would have remained in the Commonwealth.

Burma offered a different problem from India. I had visited the country with the Simon Commission, and it was upon our recommendation that Burma had been separated from India. The Burmese had made considerable progress in self-government before the war, but there were fewer Western-educated Burmese and not many were in the administration. While Burma was not cursed with a communal problem on the scale of the Hindu-Moslem one in India, she had the problem of primitive peoples and minority communities, such as the Karens and the Indian and Chinese immigrants.

Burma had been invaded by the Japanese and only reconquered after a long and difficult campaign. Some of the Burmese had cooperated with the Japanese, believing that they really intended to give the Burmese their freedom, and had supported a puppet government under Dr. Ba Maw. They were soon disillusioned. A resistance movement, officered by young men under the leadership of Aung San, got into touch with the British Forces and, owing to the wise policy of Lord Mountbatten, cooperated in driving out the invaders. As the country was recovered, a civil affairs administration was set up under a very able soldier, Sir Hubert Rance. Meanwhile a government-in-exile, which had been formed in India under Sir Reginald Dorman-Smith, was making plans for reconstruction. With him were some of the old politicians. I think that we made a mistake in restoring prematurely the form of partial self-government Burma had enjoyed before the war. The young men of the resistance were impatient, while the older men were out of touch with the Nationalist movement that had grown up. It was, admittedly, not easy to evaluate the various trends of opinion. Eventually I decided to recommend that Sir Hubert Rance, who had great knowledge of the country and was well liked by the Burmese, should be made Governor and that a deputation, representative of the various political parties, should come to London to discuss the future of Burma. We had long conferences with them. Some of them had known Cripps before the war, and this was a great help. They were, however, very suspicious at first and could not believe that we were prepared to abide by the choice of the Burmese people. They had unfortunately committed themselves to their followers in favour of complete independence and a republic. They had also to face the Communist party. As the talks proceeded, their distrust disappeared, and I think that some of them —particularly their leader, Aung San, a strong character— began to realize the desirability of remaining in the Commonwealth, though it may be that, like India, they would have opted for a republic. The members were very young and inexperienced; one of them said, "We're just a lot of raw lads." They were a pleasant lot, except for one representative of a minority party—U Saw. I had met him before the war and, indeed, during the war when he came to England, but it was discovered that he was trying to make contact with the Germans in Lisbon, and he had to be interned. I regarded him as a man who would "smile and smile and be a villain."

We invited the whole party down to Chequers for lunch, and my wife little thought that she was entertaining a prospective murderer and his victims, but so it was. Not long after their return to Burma, Aung San and most of his fellow Ministers were murdered by U Saw. It was due to the prompt action of the Governor that this plot went no further. Thakin Nu, with great courage, took over the governorship, and U Saw was brought to justice, but the blow to Burma was severe. In my view, Aung San was a statesman of considerable capacity and wisdom, as was shown by his generous proposals for dealing with the minority communities. Had he lived, Burma might well have stayed in the Commonwealth, but, as it was, the Burmese decided on complete independence. In accordance with our principles, we had no option but to grant this request. Since that time the Burmese government has had to cope with serious rebellion both from Communists and others. Prime Minister U Nu and his colleagues deserve great credit for the way they have stood up to all these difficulties.

The achievement of full Dominion status by Ceylon was effected without any difficulty. Although there are racial minorities in the island, the conflict of interest between Singhalese and Tamils has never been acute. Ceylon had learned much under the interim constitution that had resulted from the Simon Commission. There was a wise and trusted leader available in Mr. Senanayaka, and, on his death, his son carried on his father's work.

Our policy in giving full self-government and equality in the Commonwealth to the three Asiatic states has, I think, met with general approval except from a limited number of people—among them Churchill, who regarded it as a betrayal of our imperial heritage. In fact, we have gained the friendship of the Asiatic peoples, which is, in my view, of immense importance to the future peace of the world. Communism, which has little appeal to peoples enjoying a comparatively high standard of life, appears to many of the peoples of Asia as a liberating force. An attempt to maintain the old colonialism would, I am sure, have immensely aided the Communist attack on Asia.

This can be shown by the experience of two other great colonial powers—the Dutch and the French. The great Dutch Empire in the East Indies had been overrun by the Japanese. The Indonesians had seen Europeans beaten by an Asiatic power and were not slow to draw their conclusions. When the war came to an end with the defeat of Japan, nationalist elements at once advanced their claims to self-government. The wiser Dutch statesmen saw that there must be concessions, but there were strong sections of Dutch opinion, both in the colonies and in Holland, who thought that there could be a return to the old regime.

The position in Indonesia was a subject of grave anxiety to Britain in the first two years after the war. Bevin and I had many meetings with Dutch statesmen on the future of Indonesia, and I think that we were not without influence in the decisions that were eventually arrived at, but the delay in granting full self-government was unfortunate. It encouraged disorder and lost the Dutch much goodwill, which a speedier acceptance of the inevitable would have avoided.

The French were still slower to recognize the march of events. In 1953 the French government at last acknowledged the right of the people of Indo-China to self-government. Had this been done earlier, France would have been spared the heavy drain of a long military campaign. The leaders of Viet Minh might have been by now responsible statesmen like Nehru and the late Liaquat Ali Khan. Communism would not have had the opportunity of making itself the champion of nationalism. Colonialism of the old kind, with its virtues and defects, is out of place in the modern world. It behooves all colonial powers to read the lessons of the last eight years. They need to be applied in Africa as in Asia. Here again, I may claim that the Labour government has blazed the trail.

Yet another country to sever the links binding it to the Commonwealth was Eire. True, these links had become very tenuous. Eire was already a republic in fact, with complete freedom. Much of the old bitterness between

English and Irish had passed away, as I found when I visited Eire for a holiday, but the division between North and South was still a rankling sore.

I always thought that Eamon de Valera missed a great chance of unifying Ireland during the war. Eire sent many volunteers to fight for freedom, and I am sure that the spirit of the people was with the Allies, but old memories stood in the way of full cooperation, although, in fact, Eire's neutrality was benevolent. The trouble seems to me to be that neither North nor South has ever set itself to woo the other.

I had several meetings with de Valera and found him very charming. He had, I thought, mellowed with the years. It was therefore ironical that the cutting of the last link with Britain was due not to the man who was considered to be the extremist, but to John A. Costello, who was supposed to be more moderate and whose supporters included men from the extreme Left and extreme Right. He made a speech in Canada—which was, I believe, not premeditated—in which he declared for cutting the last link that bound Eire to the Commonwealth, and could not then retreat from this position. Obviously it was the worst thing to do from the point of view of those who sought the unity of Ireland, for it dug deeper the ditch separating Ulster and the South. Had he had the patience to wait he might have done as India did later. The result would have been more satisfactory than the rather illogical relationship between Britain and Eire which exists today. We had, of course, no option but to accept this decision by Eire, for the days of coercion of a member state of the Commonwealth are gone forever. Northern

Ireland's relations with Britain are conducted through the Home Office. Although the Northern Irish government is Conservative and the Ulster Members predominantly in opposition to Labour in several respects, the legislation of the Labour government has been paralleled in Northern Ireland and both Herbert Morrison and Chuter Ede, when at the Home Office, enjoyed cordial relations with the Northern Irish government and, particularly, with the Prime Minister, Sir Basil Brooke.

The developments in the Commonwealth sector were paralleled by those in the colonial sphere. The successive Ministers at the Colonial Office carried out a policy which had two sides: one, the raising of the standard of life of the people by economic advances; the other, the increase of self-government. In particular, in the Gold Coast and Nigeria a great increase of self-government was achieved. It was clear to me that the wave of nationalist feeling and the desire for an enhancement of the status of the darker-coloured races, which we had had to meet in India, had now spread to Africa. I also knew very well that a failure to meet reasonably these aspirations would lead to an ever-worsening position. I had seen the fruits of delay in French Indo-China and had seen danger only narrowly averted by the Dutch in the East Indies. At the same time it had to be recognized that the African, unlike the Asiatic, had not behind him a tradition of a developed civilization. There was danger in a too rapid transition. However, considerable progress was made.

All this has to be considered in relation to the future of the Commonwealth. The Commonwealth started by consisting solely of member states inhabited by people of

European stock or, as the Union of South Africa, where the European ruled. I have seen the admission of three Asiatic states, and the question arises, "What next?" There has been an assumption that all the colonies are progressing towards self-government. Are they all to become free and equal members?

One must expect a fairly rapid development in Malaya when the present troubles are over. I took steps to have full consideration given to the possibilities of the formation of a West Indies Federation. The West African colonies are already far advanced. One cannot see what will be the developments in Central and East Africa. How will this affect the attitude of the Union of South Africa? What will be the reaction of the other old Dominions to these demands for equality? There is also the question of how the smaller units are to be fitted into this structure. I caused inquiries to be made into this.

I do not pretend to answer any of these questions, but I was always very conscious that some time a solution must be sought, for it is the essence of the Commonwealth that it is not static; there is constant change going forward. The solution of these problems will call for statesmanship of a high order.

❁   ❁   ❁   ❁   ❁   ❁   ❁

❁   **XXII**   ❁

The Labour Government of 1950–1951

AS THE YEAR 1949 drew to a close I had to consider when to advise the King to dissolve Parliament. We had now been in power for more than four years and had carried out the programme we had put forward at the last General Election. We had no reason to think that we had lost the confidence of the country, for we had created a record in having never lost a by-election, despite the fact that some of these had occurred in marginal constituencies and in two instances, owing to the behaviour of the retiring Members, in very unfavourable conditions.

Nevertheless, it is rare for a Parliament in modern times to run its full course, for with the approach of the date when a General Election is inevitable the minds of Members of Parliament are turned to their constituencies, while the Opposition naturally takes every opportunity to cause difficulties.

It is therefore the duty of the Prime Minister to choose the time which, in his view, is the most propitious. In these days the choice is limited. The Budget and the financial year, the local elections and the holiday periods, restrict the choice to late autumn, early spring, or mid-summer. There is always the gamble as to what the weather will be. November and February are notoriously liable to be foggy. Election work is difficult in winter in rural areas generally, particularly in the north. I chose February and was very fortunate in that it turned out to be one of the best months in the year.

A meeting of the party Executive and leading Ministers had already taken place at Dorking, where we had fully discussed policy, the result of which had been the production of a policy statement entitled "Labour Believes in Britain." This was presented to the party conference at Whitsun and approved. It formed the basis on which we appealed to the country. The conference was notable for two very fine speeches by Ernest Bevin and Stafford Cripps.

Labour went to the Election with a great record of work done, but with a full appreciation of the difficulties lying ahead for any government. But, necessarily, there was an accumulation of minor grievances incidental to a postwar period. Indeed, few governments that take office after a war survive the next General Election.

There were certain factors that told against us, the most important of which was the redistribution of seats. The heavy bombing of inner London and of some other great cities had depopulated areas that were formerly Labour strongholds. For instance, in East and South East London eighteen seats were cut down to nine. Elsewhere the tendency for redistribution was to transfer Labour votes from marginal constituencies to solid Labour seats.

Undoubtedly, this most honest attempt to give one vote one value hurt Labour very severely.

We had had also a number of unexpected victories in county areas that were usually Conservative and might be expected to return to their allegiance. The position was complicated by the interposition of no less than 478 Liberal candidates. The Liberals were trying to stage a comeback. They were unlikely to return many Members, but they might take votes from Labour, particularly in the south. On the other hand, we had got rid of the City of London, which was a Conservative pocket borough and the business vote. The University seats, still predominantly a Conservative preserve, had also disappeared.

My own seat at Limehouse was among those that had gone, and now formed part of the single seat for the Borough of Stepney. As it was probable that I should have less difficulty in finding another seat than my good colleague Walter Edwards, the Member for Whitechapel, I decided to go elsewhere and to leave the field to him. I had no doubt about his ability to deal with the Communist who sat for Mile End. I was invited to contest West Walthamstow, from which an old friend, Val McEntee (who became Lord McEntee), was retiring after having held the seat for the greater part of twenty-eight years. The division was a Labour stronghold, an important point for me, because the Leader of a party cannot give as much time as other members to his constituency. It also enabled me to leave the fight to my supporters and to tour the country.

Accordingly, after opening the local campaign, I set off from Downing Street with my wife at the wheel of our car, accompanied by our old companion of past contests, Philpott of the *Daily Herald,* and one detective. A very extensive tour had been arranged, mostly in marginal constituencies, but with some big area rallies. We started with a meeting of over two thousand people at eleven o'clock in the morning at Watford, and this was a foretaste of what we experienced everywhere. Meetings were crowded and enthusiastic. We traversed the East Midlands, with a meeting of thirty thousand in the Market at Birmingham as the highlight, took a number of meetings in Lancashire, and then had a quiet weekend at Wemyss Bay in Scotland. This was very welcome, as I had been doing seven or eight meetings every day. The following is a fair specimen of a day's work:

11 a.m.	West Bromwich
12 noon	Wolverhampton
1:15 p.m.	Walsall
3:30 p.m.	Lichfield
6:30 p.m.	Stoke
8:15 p.m.	Burton
9:00 p.m.	Derby

I then had the rest of the day free to deal with official business with my Secretary. After speaking in Scotland and Yorkshire, I came to the Midlands, ending up with very large gatherings at Bedford, Luton, and St. Albans. My wife drove throughout the tour and never failed to get me to each place on time.

I made the final broadcast in the election series and

then settled down for the last few days of the fight in Walthamstow and in other parts of London.

I had three opponents—a Conservative, a Liberal, and a fellow traveller who had been in the last Parliament as a Labour Member but had been removed from the party shortly before the election. In the result the two latter lost their deposits, the figures being:

C. R. Attlee (Lab.)	21,095
Paul, J. A. (Con.)	8,988
Pim, A. W. (Lib.)	4,102
Hutchinson, H. L. (Ind. Lab.)	704
Majority	12,107

During the count, news had been coming in of losses in the London area, and, although on the first day's results we had a substantial majority, it was clear to me that with most of the county returns yet to come it would be a pretty close thing. Next afternoon I sat in the drawing room at Downing Street listening to the wireless and hearing our majority dwindle. At one time it looked as if the two parties would be equal, for the Liberals were clearly out of it. Ultimately we had an all-over majority of ten. There were nine Liberals, two Irish Nationalists, and, for the first time for many years, no Independents. Labour polled over a million and a quarter more votes than in 1945, a remarkable achievement.

Only one Minister—Arthur Creech Jones—five Under Secretaries, and Sir Frank Soskice, the Solicitor General, lost their seats, while Lewis Silkin had failed to find a seat, so no very great changes were needed in the government. I took occasion, however, to make certain changes. James Griffiths succeeded Creech Jones at the Colonial Office and entered the cabinet, while his place at the Ministry of National Insurance was filled by Dr. Edith Summerskill, thereby giving us a woman Minister again. We had suffered a great loss in the sudden death of Ellen Wilkinson, who had done good work at the Ministry of Education. She was succeeded there by George Tomlinson. Soskice soon got a seat at a by-election. Dalton took over Town and Country Planning, Alexander became Chancellor of the Duchy of Lancaster, while Shinwell re-entered the cabinet as Minister of Defence. The promotion of Patrick Gordon-Walker to the Secretaryship for Commonwealth Relations and of Hector McNeil to the Scottish Office brought two of the younger men into the cabinet, while Hugh Gaitskell became a Minister of State to assist Cripps in the very heavy work of the Treasury. (Gaitskell later succeeded Cripps.) There were also a number of minor consequential appointments, mostly of young men.

It was, of course, obvious that with so slender a majority our position in the House of Commons was going to be very difficult and that we could not embark on any major controversial measures, but the King's government had got to be carried on whatever the difficulties.

My chief source of anxiety was, however, the ill health of the two most important members of the administration —Cripps and Bevin. We had also a number of Members whose health was not too good, so that our nominal majority was seldom reached. The Conservatives were very reluctant to give "pairs" even for Ministers whose duties called them overseas, and they engaged in harassing tactics in order to wear out our Members. It says much for the loyalty of the rank and file and the great devotion of our Chief Whip, William Whiteley, and his assistants that we sustained no major defeat.

Sir Stafford Cripps carried through his Budget successfully though he was far from well. I hoped that after the Finance Bill had been passed he would be able to take a good holiday and be able to return to work, but it was not to be. His doctors said that he must have a rest for at least a year, and accordingly, in October 1950, he retired from the government. This was a very heavy blow. He had not had really good health for many years and had consistently overworked. Only his great courage and sense of duty had carried him through the last months of office. In April 1952 came the sad news of his death. In a tribute to him in the House of Commons I said:

> He came from a remarkable family with a high tradition of public and social service. When he entered this House he had already become a leading figure at the Bar. He united high scientific attainments with a mastery of detail and a power of clear exposition and incisive argument. Many great barristers have failed in this House. Stafford Cripps succeeded at once.
>
> I recall how he had immediately to take part in piloting a difficult Budget and how well he succeeded. In the years that followed he was one of the mainstays of the very small Labour Opposition of those years. Later his enthusiasm, his eagerness, and his impatience led him into paths which the majority of us could not follow, but there was never any

breach of friendship, and there was never any doubt of his sincerity.

Experience, I think, led him to maturer views without in any way impairing his fervent socialist faith. The Prime Minister[1] has spoken of his work in the wartime government, when he led this House and when later he ran a great department. It was a great pleasure to me when he rejoined our party and took office as President of the Board of Trade. Later he became Chancellor of the Exchequer, and most honorable and right honorable Members will remember his lucid speeches when he introduced his Budgets and when he dealt with economic issues. He took a major share in dealing with the very difficult economic and financial problems of the postwar period and in planning the economy of the country.

His high sense of duty drove him to tax his physical resources to the utmost. He worked intolerably long hours, yet retained his serenity. He took his full share in every kind of work of government and he faced his problems with the same courage with which he met criticism. He was never afraid of the unpopular course if he held it to be right. I believe he did immense service to this country.

But foreign affairs and economics are so closely linked in these days that he worked also in the international field. Here he and his fellow West-countryman, Ernest Bevin, two Gloucester men coming from such very different social environments, worked closely and harmoniously together. He was largely responsible for setting up the Organization for European Economic Cooperation. Despite the strong views which he held so tenaciously, he was an admirable colleague, always ready to help others. In

[1] Churchill, who returned to power in October 1951.—*Ed.*

particular, he took infinite pains to encourage and bring forward younger colleagues.

He and Lady Cripps were both deeply interested in China and India. His mission to India during the war and his leadership of the cabinet mission later paved the way for the ultimate settlement of the problem of Indian self-government. Here his close friendship with leading Indians was a great help.

I think that everyone who was brought in contact with Stafford Cripps realized that he was a man of high principle. He was deeply religious, a devout member of the Church of England, and brought to his work the inspiration of high purpose. He was a keen Socialist; his Christianity and socialism were the guiding forces of his life. I think few men have been so little regardful of self. And he was no cold intellectual. On the contrary, he was a very warm-hearted, generous, and lovable man with great personal charm. His interests were wide and his capabilities in many fields were manifold. He suffered constantly from ill health and during the last two years of his life, when this became serious, he met it with unflinching courage, and it was only the positive orders of his doctors that forced him to retire from active life.

I had the privilege of his friendship and worked closely with him for many years. I was bound to him by affection, and I had very many acts of kindness from him. When I saw him for the last time, prior to his leaving for Switzerland, he was still full of hope that a complete cure could be effected, with a further opportunity of service. His strong will and his faith had carried him so far. But it was not to be.

In July 1950 occurred the aggression by the North Koreans on South Korea. I had no doubt that it was our duty to give full support to the United Nations, and in this we had the agreement of the Opposition, but the Korean attack was not an isolated episode. It showed that Communist forces were prepared, if occasion offered, to resort to war. It became necessary, therefore, to strengthen the armed forces of the democracies.

We had to embark on an extensive rearmament programme. We realized that this would put a great strain on the economy of the country, but we were given assurances of American help, especially in maintaining the exchange position. Whether we could carry out our full programme of armaments depended on many factors, particularly on the availability of machine tools and raw materials and the control of world prices. Given these conditions, it was the view of our advisers that we could carry out this programme without an unbearable strain.

Although our military strength was already under considerable strain, owing to our having, in effect, to hold a long line of positions in the Middle East against the Communist threat, we were able to send a brigade to Korea, which, together with other Commonwealth contingents, formed part of the extremely efficient Commonwealth Division.

As the year drew towards its close I became increasingly anxious over the situation in Korea. MacArthur's advance up the peninsula had ended in retreat and had brought North Korea the support of Chinese forces, although these were supposed to be only volunteers. There was considerable support in America for an extension of the war. Some people were anxious for a showdown with Russia. MacArthur was a Republican and a possible future candidate for the Presidency, and this, I think, led to insufficient control of his activities. It always seemed strange to me that he was never called back to America for discussions with the administration. He had not been in America since before the war. The only time that he and the President met was when Mr. Truman went to the East. This appeared to us a curious relationship between government and a general.

Our view had always been that the Far Eastern war should be confined to Korea and that it would be a great mistake to have large forces committed to a major campaign in Asia. We also realized how important it was that a contest between the forces of the United Nations and aggressor state should not become a fight between Europeans and Asiatics. We had recognized the Chinese Republic as being the real and effective government of China, but the Americans continued to support the discredited government of Marshal Chiang Kai-Shek and to protect his forces in Formosa. It was understandable that Formosa in Communist hands would represent a threat to the United States Pacific interests, for it was from there that the Japanese had launched their attacks. Equally, the Chinese government regarded Formosa as a jumping-off place for the counterattack by the old Chinese government. In view of the divergence of outlook between the United States and Britain, it seemed to me that the time was opportune for me to confer with President Truman. Bevin's health was not good and he could not have travelled by air. My decision to go to Washington was welcomed by the House of Commons. The French Prime Minister, René Pleven, and the Foreign Minister,

Robert Schuman, were in London, so that I was able to have a full discussion with them and Bevin before departing. We were also in close touch with opinion in the Commonwealth. I left London in the evening of Sunday, December 3, and reached Washington at nine-forty next morning. Sir William Slim, Chief of the Imperial General Staff, and Foreign Office officials accompanied me, and our Ambassador in Washington, Sir Oliver Franks, joined us for talks. I could not have wished for better advisers.

In the afternoon we began our discussions with the President, General Bradley, and Secretary of State Acheson. I set out our view very fully. The next day Kenneth Younger, our Minister of State, arrived from New York, where he had been attending a session of the United Nations. We lunched on the President's yacht on the Potomac and continued our talks on board. I also talked with several leading senators. In the evening I attended a concert to hear Miss Margaret Truman sing. It was in relation to this that the President wrote a somewhat vigorous letter to a critic who had passed an unfavourable and, to my mind, unfair criticism on her singing.

As the talks progressed I found a general understanding of the British position and agreement on the need for preventing the extension of the war in the Far East. On the question of the recognition of the Chinese government and the position of Formosa we agreed to differ. My own suggestion was that Formosa should be neutralized for a period of years. General Slim's contributions to the discussion were extremely useful. We then explored the difficult question of the allocation and procurement of

raw materials for rearmament by the Allies. We agreed
to set up a number of commodity committees. Unfortunately, in my view, the urgency of the matter was not sufficiently realized in the United States, with the result that
prices were forced up before the committees could get to
work. Altogether, I think the talks were useful and accomplished their object of clarifying the position.

From Washington I flew to New York and stayed with
Sir Gladwyn Jebb, the head of the British delegation to
the U.N., in whose company I visited the United Nations
offices at Lake Success and talked with many of the delegates. Thence I flew to Canada, where I stayed with the
Governor General, Lord Alexander, and met Mr. St. Laurent and his cabinet colleagues. We had good talks on the
Washington meeting and other matters of common concern. I did a broadcast to the Canadian people and then
flew back to New York. I left there at six o'clock on a
Monday and reached London by ten on Tuesday morning.
After seeing the King and presiding over a cabinet, I
made a statement in the House in the afternoon. I then
saw the Leader of the Opposition, worked at some papers,
took part in a vote at ten p.m., and so to bed at midnight.
From all this it will be seen that I am one of those fortunate people who do not find air travel tiring.

The general effect of this visit was good and did something to relieve the anxiety felt by many people. It was
also a useful prelude to the meeting of Commonwealth
Prime Ministers which was held in January 1951. This
was the last of the series of Commonwealth Prime Ministers' meetings over which I presided. My personal relations with the new Commonwealth Prime Ministers were

no less cordial than with their predecessors. Mr. Menzies and Mr. Holland had replaced the Labour Prime Ministers of Australia and New Zealand. Dr. Malan was represented by Mr. T. E. Donges, while Mr. St. Laurent (who had in 1948 succeeded MacKenzie King as Prime Minister of Canada), Mr. Nehru, Mr. Liaquat Ali Khan, and Mr. Senanayaka—all old friends—were present again. We had most useful talks on Middle Eastern and defence problems, and also on the economic situation.

We also had a number of private talks, in which Mr. Menzies took a leading part, in an endeavour to get our Indian and Pakistani friends to agree on the conditions for a plebiscite in Kashmir. Unfortunately these efforts did not succeed. The fact that these talks were unofficial emphasizes the point that these Commonwealth meetings are not intended for the airing of differences between members of the Commonwealth but for dealing with common problems.

Bevin had taken part in this conference, as he had in others with Foreign Ministers, although often suffering acute pain. But his condition was not improving, and he had to be absent on several important occasions. There was growing criticism of the fact that in these critical times the Foreign Secretaryship was held by an invalid. I kept in close touch with what was going on and deputized for him, but it was clear that the position could not continue long. His doctors were, however, hopeful, and I was reluctant, while there was still hope, to remove him from a sphere where his prestige, both at home and abroad, was very high. However, in March 1951, a change became inevitable. The burden was too heavy for him.

He became Lord Privy Seal so that his advice would still be available to the government, and Herbert Morrison took his place at the Foreign Office. I hoped that, freed from the daily cares of a department, Bevin might recover his health. He received a remarkable and unprecedented testimony on his leaving the Foreign Office, in the form of a presentation to which several thousands of the staff of the Foreign Service—from ambassadors to messengers —had contributed. It was a great shock to me when a few weeks later he suddenly died. He was the greatest trade-union leader of his generation, a great Foreign Secretary, and a man of outstanding character and ability. To me he was also a most dear friend and loyal comrade. His ashes were fittingly laid in Westminster Abbey among the great men of his country. I will here quote what I said of him in a broadcast tribute:

Ernest Bevin was first and foremost a great Englishman, forthright and courageous; an idealist, but an eminently practical one. He understood the people of this country, which he loved, and I believe he interpreted the British idea with great fidelity. He was a great Labour leader; he understood instinctively the reactions of the ordinary working man and woman. But his knowledge of poverty did not drive him into a sterile and bitter class-consciousness. He understood and could work with people of all classes. Few men have done so great a service for their fellow workers. I recall that when Bevin began his trade-union work, low pay, long hours, and casual employment were features of the transport industry. Organization was weak and conditions bad. It is largely due to Ernest Bevin that the status of the transport worker is so different today. He would have been the first to acknowledge the work of others; there was no doubt as to the magnitude of his contribution.

But his services to the workers extended beyond his own industry, and indeed beyond his own country. On the Trades Union Congress, at the International Labour Office, and at many international conferences he widened his experience. So when he came to the Foreign Office he brought with him all the knowledge and wisdom that this background of international problems had given him. He had travelled much on the Continent, in the Commonwealth, and in the United States. But his work in the trade-union movement had also given him extensive contacts with the managerial side of industry. He had served on important bodies, such as the Macmillan Committee. He was fully conversant with the economic problems of this country and with international trade and exchange. This background of economic knowledge was invaluable in dealing with the problems of foreign policy of the world today, in which the political and economic factors are so closely interwoven.

I recall very vividly when at short notice he came to Potsdam he showed an immediate grasp of the problems. As Foreign Secretary he had to deal with a Europe in ruins, as a result of the war. His courage and wisdom kept our prestige high in a world where our material power had been diminished by that war. He strove patiently and earnestly to try to preserve the wartime partnership with Soviet Russia, but could not prevail against their intransigence. His immediate response to Mr. Marshall's speech was a measure of his statesmanship. If he had not acted as he did, it is possible that American economic aid for Europe might never have materialized. His enthusiasm, his welcome for that speech, may well have saved

Western Europe from communism. The Russian rejection of Marshall aid marked that country's definite refusal to agree to that cooperation Ernest Bevin had worked so hard to bring about.

It was largely due to his initiative that the Brussels Treaty and the Atlantic Treaty came into being. He rightly regarded the establishment of the Atlantic Treaty as one of his greatest achievements, and history will confirm that judgment. Yet another example of his initiative was the Colombo Conference, which really resulted from discussions on the problem of dealing with the underdeveloped regions of the world. Bevin always stressed the point that prevention of war was not enough. There must always be a positive policy of raising standards of living throughout the world so as to destroy the conditions in which Russian communism thrives.

Despite the heavy burden of foreign affairs, he took a very full share of cabinet work, especially on economic matters, on which he worked very closely with Sir Stafford Cripps. Ernest Bevin always kept his colleagues fully informed on foreign affairs, for he regarded foreign and home policy as complementary. He came to Parliament too late to become really a House of Commons man—not that he could not speak effectively in the House, but his real platform was a trade-union or Labour party conference; his speeches on these occasions were remarkably effective. Ernest Bevin was the soul of loyalty, and he had the power of invoking a loyal service. At the Ministry of Labour and the Foreign Office he enlisted the enthusiastic support of his officials. He, in his turn, was very solicitous for the comfort of those who worked for him. He had also the gift of giving scope and responsibility to his junior Ministers.

For the last five years, save when he was out of the

country, I saw him almost daily. Whatever the subject of discussion, he was sure to make some fruitful suggestion, or to throw new light on a problem. He was, too, a delightful companion, with a vivid sense of humour and a great store of good stories and reminiscences. He was filled with a burning desire to see the foundations of peace firmly established. During the last year, when he suffered from ill health, he fought against it. He was full of hope that the international atmosphere might improve. Despite acute pain, he forced himself to carry through an important conference. His physical courage was as great as his moral courage. I have lost in him a good and loyal comrade, and a very dear friend.

❀ ❀ ❀ ❀ ❀ ❀ ❀

❀ XXIII ❀

I Become Leader of the Opposition Again

I HAD BEEN having trouble for some time with pains in the stomach and also eczema. It seemed that I had a duodenal ulcer and must go to hospital for some weeks. I went into St. Mary's Hospital, where I made good progress towards recovery, but during my absence differences of opinion arose in the government. The immediate cause was a proposal in the Budget to make charges for certain of the Health Services in order to prevent abuse. There were other differences of a more personal nature. I endeavoured to effect agreement, but the disagreement spread to some other matters, notably to the effect on the economy of the level of armaments on which we had embarked. I had, as a matter of fact, pointed out in public speeches that the achievement of our programme was conditioned by various factors such as the availability of raw materials and machine tools, and the level of prices. There was, therefore, in my view, no real difference of principle. However, the upshot was that Aneurin Bevan, Harold Wilson, and John Freeman insisted on resigning from the government. Their places were filled by Alfred

Robens, Sir Hartley Shawcross, and Michael Stewart. Sir
Frank Soskice became Attorney General and Sir Lynn
Ungoed-Thomas, Solicitor General. The government carried on, but a dissension of this kind necessarily weakens
the position of the administration. We continued to be
subjected to harassing tactics by the Opposition, but we
suffered no major defeat in the House.

We had carried on now for eighteen months with an
exiguous majority. The strain on our Members, some of
whom were in indifferent health, was very great. It was
not pleasant to have Members coming from hospital at the
risk of their lives to prevent a defeat in the House. The
Opposition tactics were designed to wear out our Members by keeping them late every night. This was done
particularly by putting down "Prayers" against Orders.
These are one of the ways under the procedure governing
the sittings of the House whereby the debate may be prolonged beyond the customary adjournment time of eleven
p.m. Many of our Members lived in the outer suburbs. It
was easy, therefore, for Conservatives who resided in
central London to keep things going until last buses and
trains had gone. It needed only a breakdown in health
of half a dozen of our Members to put us in a minority.

I had therefore to consider when it would be necessary
to appeal to the country. At the moment we had a favourable balance of payments, but I was well aware
how precarious was the situation. There was the impact of
the heavy rearmament programme, which would inevitably mean some halt in our progress towards a better
standard of life. We required more adequate support in
the House if we were to face successfully these difficulties.

There was a further reason. King George and Queen Elizabeth were to visit Australia and New Zealand in the spring of 1952. It would, I knew, be a constant anxiety to the King if there was a possibility of a fall of the government or a General Election during his absence. There were cogent reasons for having an election in the autumn, and I made up my mind before the House rose for the Autumn Recess. It will be seen that there is no foundation for the silly suggestion of some Tory Members that we had an election in order to get out of our responsibilities.

Accordingly, when the House met again in October, after reference had been made to the King's illness, the dissolution was announced. The party conference at Scarborough was cut down to three days, becoming a pre-election conference. The party programme was approved, and the ranks closed for the contest.

For the fourth time my wife and I set out on an election tour. We started in the Eastern Counties, working round to the Midlands and then to the Southwest. Everywhere we had packed and enthusiastic meetings, the audience sometimes reaching five figures. I recall, especially, one at Nottingham, where the police said there were thirty thousand people in the Square. My nephew, Christopher Attlee, was standing at Eastbourne. We had arranged to have a rest at the weekend at Chequers, but we fitted in a meeting for him. This involved four hundred miles of driving in one day for my wife. The only other occasion she has driven so far was during the King's illness, when I was at North Berwick. She drove me to Edinburgh early in the morning to catch a plane to London, and came on by herself by road, arriving in the evening.

I came to Walthamstow for the closing days of the
campaign, which had been very well organized and run.
A curious incident was the invasion of one of my schoolroom meetings by the Fascists. I never saw a more unpleasant-looking collection of "spivs" and "toughs." However, they did not effect anything.

At this election I had a straight fight with an able young
Conservative, and though my vote increased my majority
was slightly reduced. The actual figures were:

Attlee, C. R. (Lab.)	23,021
Du Cann, E. D. L. (Con.)	11,447
Majority	11,574

This was typical of the country generally. The Liberal party put only 109 candidates in the field, and it was
probable that the issue would be decided by the way the
Liberal electors cast their votes in constituencies where
there was a straight fight between Labour and Tory. In
the event, the Liberals tended in most areas to give two
or three votes to the Conservatives for every one they
gave to Labour. We won two seats in Wales from the
Liberals, but, on balance, we lost nineteen seats—enough
to give the Conservatives a majority in the House.

In spite of this, our vote went up to 13,948,385—an
increase of over 700,000, the biggest vote ever given to
any political party in British history, and more than that
of the Conservatives and their allies. The Liberal party
was reduced to six Members, only one of whom had a
Conservative opponent.

As soon as the result was clear I went to the Palace and
tendered my resignation to the King. A few days later I

was summoned to the Palace, and the King bestowed on me the Order of Merit, the highest honour in his gift. This was only one of the many kindnesses I had received from King George VI. I had served him as Prime Minister for six and a half years and there had never been any difficulty between us. I felt, therefore, a real sense of loss when a few months later he died. I endeavoured to express what I felt in the speech I delivered in the House on February 11, 1952:

> I rise to support, on behalf of all my Friends on this side of the House, the Motions which have been moved in such fitting and eloquent terms by the Prime Minister. I cannot but recall today that it is scarcely more than sixteen years since I spoke in support of similar Motions moved by Mr. Baldwin on the occasion of the death of King George V. It is with deep sorrow that we mourn today the death at so early an age of his son.
>
> Father and son alike served Great Britain and the Commonwealth and Empire with unselfish devotion. Both of them had to face the ordeal of war and earned the gratitude of the nation for the steadfast courage with which in time of great peril they led their people to victory. Both of them in their public and private lives set a noble example to the world and showed what true kingship meant in a democracy.
>
> I admired and respected the great qualities of King George V, but I did not know him intimately. I was privileged to serve His Majesty King George VI as a Minister for more than eleven years, and for more than six of those years I was his Prime Minister, and hardly a week passed in which I did not spend an hour in his company. I feel, therefore, besides the

deep regret which all his subjects have at the passing of a great and good King, a keen sense of personal loss in the death of one to whom I was bound not only by loyalty and respect, but by affection. I received from him at all times the greatest kindness and consideration. The longer I served him, the greater was my respect and admiration.

We offer to Queen Elizabeth, to the Queen Mother, to Queen Mary and to all the Royal Family our deepest sympathy in their great sorrow. We know that Parliament today is truly representative of the feelings of the nation. If any comfort can come to the bereaved in the knowledge that millions in Britain, in the Commonwealth and Empire and in other lands, share their grief, they have it in full measure.

King George VI was not brought up with the prospect of succeeding to the Throne always before him. He had, therefore, the opportunity of leading a freer life than that which is imposed on an Heir Apparent. He was able to mix more widely with the people. He served in the Navy in peace and war, and lived the life of his fellow officers, sharing the same risks and enjoying the same comradeship. He made a happy marriage and, while doing the duties which his birth imposed, took his full part in the games and social activities which this country affords.

He took great interest in social questions, especially in the welfare of industrial workers. He grew to have a wide knowledge of social and industrial problems. He was never happier than when in the camps for boys of all classes, which he organized, and when he joined in their games.

Happy in marriage and in his family life, it might well have seemed that his lot was cast in easy and pleasant places. But in circumstances of great difficulty he was called upon to take up the burden of kingship. He responded to that call with that high sense of duty which was, I think, his outstanding characteristic.

It was his fate to reign in times of great tension. He could never look round and see a clear sky. There were always dark clouds of anxiety. The early years of his reign were overshadowed by the increasing danger of war. Then came the years of war during which he shared to the full in the perils and anxieties of his people. When peace came, it did not bring tranquillity. Through it all his courage never failed. He never doubted that we should win through. He was exposed in London to the same dangers as his subjects. His devotion to duty and his ready sympathy with his people were an inspiration to all.

I know how much he desired peace and how great was his solicitude for his people. He felt, I think, at all times a burden of responsibility for their welfare, yet he was always cheerful. He had the happy faculty of setting people at their ease. Without loss of dignity he could converse with all sorts and conditions of people. He was a delightful host and the personal relationship which he established with so many people from all over the world was of great service to this country.

In all his work he had the help and support of the gracious lady who was an ideal Consort. As Queen and wife and mother, she won a firm place in the hearts of the people.

I have spoken of the King's sense of duty. He was a very hard worker. Few people realize how much time and care he gave to public affairs, but visitors from overseas were often astonished at his close familiarity with all kinds of questions. With this close study went a good judgment, and a sure instinct for what was really vital. During his reign there were developments in the Commonwealth, some of which entailed the abandonment of outward forms which a lesser man might have felt it difficult to surrender, but he was essentially broad-minded and was ready to accept changes that seemed necessary.

His visit to South Africa and the projected visit to Australia and New Zealand, which was frustrated by his illness, were examples of his keen interest in the Commonwealth. In his own person he was a living and invaluable link to bind together the divers peoples of his realms.

When illness came to him he faced it with the same courage that he showed in war. His one concern was lest he should be prevented from doing his work.

When Mr. Baldwin spoke here sixteen years ago, he said very truly that the influence of the Crown was very great and that it was due to the character of the occupant of the Throne. I think he was right. Certainly in these years no two people could have done more to strengthen it than King George and Queen Elizabeth. That Throne is firmly established in the hearts and homes of the people.

Only a few weeks ago we were listening to the King's Christmas broadcast. I am sure that as the years went by people liked more and more to listen to these talks addressed by a King to his own people. They realized that the man who spoke to them was sincere. They could feel in his tones that firm religious faith which was one of the sources of his strength.

In King George we have lost a great King, and a very good man. We turn to offer our loyal service to our young Queen. She comes to the Throne with the goodwill and affection of all her subjects. She takes up a heavy burden, but I am confident that she will sustain it. It is our hope that Her Majesty may live

long and happily and that her reign may be as glorious as that of her great predecessor, Queen Elizabeth
I. Let us hope we are witnessing the beginning of a
new Elizabethan Age no less renowned than the first.
We hope that Her Majesty the Queen and her Consort may live long and prosperously and may see more
peaceful days than those which fell to the lot of His
late Majesty whose loss we mourn today.

My wife and I received much consideration and kindness from other members of the Royal Family, especially
from Queen Mary. I saw her fairly often, especially when
the King and Queen were on a visit to South Africa. It
might have been thought that Queen Mary, brought up
in the traditions of Victorian England, might have re-
sented the coming to power of a Labour government, but
it was not so. She had a forward-looking mind. There
were two of our Ministers for whom she had especial regard—George Tomlinson, whom she called "My Minister," and Ernest Bevin, whom she called "My neighbour,"
as he lived in Carlton House Terrace next to Marlbor-
ough House. I felt a real sense of loss at her death.

The years since leaving office have been saddened by
the loss through death of some old friends and colleagues.
I have already written about Stafford Cripps and Ernest
Bevin. The party also suffered a great loss in the death
of Lord Addison. Achieving at a very early age his distinction as a surgeon, he entered Parliament in 1910 as a
Liberal and held high office in the Lloyd George Coalition government during and after the First World War. I
recall meeting him for the first time in 1919, when he was
Minister of Health. I was on a deputation that went to
see him on postwar housing. Lloyd George's failure to

support his housing plans led to his resignation, which was followed by his defeat at the General Election of 1922. He was only fifty-three years of age, but it looked then as if his career was ended. In reality, he was to give further and more fruitful service to his country. Although he had been a cabinet Minister, on joining the Labour party he was willing to accept the humble post of Under Secretary to the Minister of Agriculture in the second Labour government. When he became Minister he showed his capacity and left enduring marks in agriculture. His greatest service was rendered during the last fifteen years of his life, when he led the Labour party in the House of Lords, for he had been raised to the peerage at the time of King George VI's Coronation. Faced with a hostile majority, he was able, through his tact and skill, to pilot through the Upper House the great programme of the third Labour government. A singularly able administrator, he was also wise in counsel, while his personal charm endeared him to friends and political foes alike. He died full of years and honours. I was pleased that King George included him in the first Garters which he bestowed after I had relinquished the right of recommendation.

The loss of three such men as Bevin, Cripps, and Addison was a very heavy blow to the Labour party. In 1953 death deprived us of another well-loved colleague in George Tomlinson. He did not enter the House until 1938, but his original and attractive personality soon brought him to the front. He epitomized the common sense and humour of the Lancashire worker, which he joined to a deep religious faith. Bevin, who was a very shrewd man, picked him out in 1941 as the right man to help him at the Ministry of Labour. During the war he did very good work there, particularly in changing over the textile workers to munitions and in organizing the rehabilitation centres which enabled so many disabled workers to get to work again. But perhaps his best work was done as Minister of Education. The first former half-timer to occupy that position, he brought to the work great experience gained in local administration, while his humour and sympathy endeared him to all.

As soon as possible after my resignation I removed from No. 10 Downing Street. This was a considerable business because during the years of my residence there had been a substantial accumulation of goods of one kind and another, notably a number of caskets containing the Charters of the Freedom of Cities given to me by Birmingham, Leeds, Merthyr Tydfil, Dartford, Stepney, and Greenwich. These and other things now had to find their places in a small house.

Fortunately our tenants were able to move out of our new home, Cherry Cottage, Prestwood, at short notice, so that no difficulty arose on that score. We very soon settled in. As we had anticipated, our new location suited us very well. We found that we had kind and hospitable neighbours.

Our children had to find lodgings in London and became only weekend visitors. In March 1952 our youngest daughter, Alison, was married, and in 1953 she had a daughter.

After eleven years of living on the job I now had to

resume the practice of travelling to and from London every day.

In the House of Commons I reoccupied the Leader of the Opposition's Room, in which I had worked from 1931 to 1945. I was very fortunate in obtaining the services of a first-class Secretary, Mrs. Skelly, while Arthur Moyle has continued to be my Parliamentary Private Secretary.

I have now been thirty-one years in Parliament and, together with Tom Williams, I am runner-up for the position of "father" of the House.

The Parliamentary Labour party, despite the loss of its majority, was by no means depressed by its electoral setback, for our hold on the country was as strong as ever. We had by far the biggest Opposition party in my experience, and the government majority was small. One result of these small majorities has been the need for closer attendance in the House and has increased the strain on Members. Constituencies are today more exacting in their claims on Members during their weekends. I think too much so, for Members, like other people, need occasions for rest and recreation.

It is, of course, pleasant to have the backing of a large party, but numbers bring with them certain difficulties. Party meetings are crowded, and it needs considerable effort to get through the agenda in reasonable time without leaving a number of members who desired to speak disappointed. It is also harder to get cohesion, for there is a danger of sectional differences. I was again elected as Leader without opposition.

The party in the House and the country put up a vigorous opposition, while the government found it difficult to carry out the pledges they had given the electors. Two of them, however, they were resolved to implement, the reversal of Labour's policy on iron and steel and on road transport. I think this has been a regrettable departure from precedent. Hitherto, it has been the general practice in British politics not to seek to reverse the major actions of the preceding government. For instance, despite the violent objections to the Lloyd George Insurance Act by the Conservative party, it was ultimately accepted and even extended by them. There are, of course, instances to the contrary, as when the Conservatives reversed the Trade Union Act passed by the Liberal government, and the Labour party, in its turn, restored the situation; but this was a change in the law, not a change in the economic structure of the country. I think there is danger here for the stability of the country, especially when the reversal is based not on the national needs but merely on the ideological prejudices of a party.

It is not my intention to carry these autobiographical notes any further, but I would like to record one or two interesting events of the last two years.

I have been honoured by being the recipient of honorary degrees from the Universities of Glasgow and Nottingham, to add to those received from Oxford, Cambridge, London, Wales, and Reading. I was also, before I left office, made an Elder Brother of Trinity House.

In the last two years I have attended four Socialist conferences abroad—at Liége, Stockholm, Milan, and Rangoon. At Milan I addressed a big open-air meeting in

Italian, which created a new precedent for a British delegate. My visit to Rangoon had a special interest for me, in that it enabled me to visit India, Pakistan, and Burma after a lapse of twenty-four years. I found in all these countries a warm welcome and stayed with old friends, such as Ghulam Mohammed, the Governor of Pakistan, and Mr. Nehru, the Prime Minister of India. The Rangoon conference was particularly interesting as representing an endeavour to bring together the Socialist parties of Asia. I attended as a representative of the Socialist International. It was noteworthy that the official language of the conference was English, which was spoken perfectly by almost all the delegates. I think that the conference was useful in forging yet another link between East and West.

In 1952 my wife and I paid a visit to Northern and Southern Rhodesia as the guests of the Unofficial Members of the Northern Legislative Council and of the Governor General of Southern Rhodesia. I had not been in that part of Africa before and was glad to learn something of the problems from the people on the spot, for undoubtedly one of the gravest problems facing the world is the relationship between people of different colours residing in the same territory.

I had another angle on this question in a visit to Philadelphia, where a fine effort is being made to bring together people of all races and creeds in a common fellowship. I thought it particularly suitable that this initiative should be made in the City of Brotherly Love.

In the spring of 1953 I was a good deal troubled with indigestion and finally it was decided that I should have my appendix removed. This was done during the Easter Recess of the House. I well recall that when this operation was introduced, one of the earliest subjects being King Edward VII, it was considered a serious matter, but now-adays it is so easy that I was about again in less than a fortnight.

I was a member of the Coronation Committee just as I had been sixteen years previously, and in due course my wife and I attended the Coronation of Queen Elizabeth II in Westminster Abbey. I think that, except for the Duke of Norfolk, I was the only person present still holding the same office as in 1937.

Alison and Felicity witnessed the Coronation procession from seats in New Palace Yard, and, as Alison's baby was only a few months old, we brought her along and parked her in my room in the House during the ceremony, much to the interest of the custodians, who looked in from time to time to see how she was getting on.

The Coronation arrangements were a great deal better than on the previous occasion, and the enthusiasm every-where—both at home and overseas—was quite remark-able. One feature was the street parties. I went round to more than forty in my own constituency and was much impressed by the vast amount of work put in to give pleas-ure to the children.

Marshal Tito came to London on a visit in the summer and invited me to be the guest of his government. Ac-cordingly, in August I went to Yugoslavia for three weeks, where I visited Dalmatia, Slovenia, Croatia, Serbia, and Montenegro. I had never been in this country before and had a wonderful time along the beautiful Dalmatian

coast; I was especially struck by Dubrovnik. I had a most
admirable cicerone from the Yugoslav Foreign Office, who
looked after me extremely well. I ended my tour with
a visit to Marshal Tito in his lovely island of Brioni.
Apart from my interest in the scenery and fascinating
survivals from earlier civilizations, it was a great opportunity for seeing something of a country which had
emancipated itself from Soviet influence and was developing a unique economy. I was much impressed by the cali-
bre of the men, mostly young, who were running the
country. They were much more like our own trade unionists than the usual type of Communist. I have every
hope that this people will move steadily forward towards
democracy. Certainly there was none of that feeling of
constraint and fear that one gets in other totalitarian
countries.

The last important event for me in 1953 was in November, when I was presented with the Honorary Freedom of the City of London. My wife and I drove in a victoria from the Law Courts to Guildhall and were very
kindly received. Most of our family were present at the
ceremony.

In closing these chapters from my life story, I recall the
old saying, "Call no man happy until he is dead." But
having now exceeded the age of three score years and ten,
I would say that up to the present I have been a very
happy and fortunate man in having lived so long in the
greatest country in the world, in having a happy family
life, and in having been given the opportunity of serving
in a state of life to which I had never expected to be
called.

Index

Index